Inside

The Wire 347 | January 2013

D1586734

2012 Rewind by Ben Weaver

The Masthead

Issue 347 January 2013
£4 ISSN 0952-0680

The Wire
23 Jack's Place, 6 Corbet Place, London E1 6NN, UK
Tel +44 (0)20 7422 5010
Fax +44 (0)20 7422 5011
thewire.co.uk

Editor-in-Chief & Publisher
Tony Herrington tony@thewire.co.uk

Editor
Chris Bohn chris@thewire.co.uk
Deputy Editors
Frances Morgan frances@thewire.co.uk
Derek Walmsley derek@thewire.co.uk
Contributing Editors
Anne Hilde Neset anne@thewire.co.uk
Rob Young rob@thewire.co.uk

Art Direction & Design
Ben Weaver art@thewire.co.uk
Design
Patrick Ward patrick@thewire.co.uk
Design Assistant
Laura Silke

Advertising Manager
Andy Tait andy@thewire.co.uk
Licensing Manager & Advertising Sales
Shane Woolman shane@thewire.co.uk
Online Advertising Sales
Katie Gibbons katie@thewire.co.uk

Subscriptions, Circulation & Accounts
Ben House ben@thewire.co.uk
Subscriptions
Daisy Hyde daisy@thewire.co.uk

Online Editor
Jennifer Lucy Allan jennifer@thewire.co.uk
Online & Cross Platform Editor
Nathan Budzinski nathan@thewire.co.uk
Assistant Online Editor
Sophia Ignatidou sophia@thewire.co.uk
Online Development
Dorian Fraser Moore dorian@thewire.co.uk

Archivist
Edwin Pouncey edwin@thewire.co.uk

Words
Steve Barker, Mike Barnes, Dan Barrow, Clive Bell, Abi Bliss, Marcus Boon, Michael Bracewell, Britt Brown, Nick Cain, Philip Clark, Byron Coley, Julian Cowley, Alan Cummings, Sam Davies, Brian Dillon, Phil England, Kodwo Eshun, Mark Fisher, Phil Freeman, Rory Gibb, Louise Gray, Andy Hamilton, Adam Harper, Jim Haynes, Richard Henderson, Ken Hollings, Robin Howells, Hua Hsu, William Hutson, Matthew Ingram, David Keenan, Rahma Khazam, Biba Kopf, Jack Law, Tim Lawrence, Alan Licht, Dave Mandl, Marc Masters, Bill Meyer, Keith Moliné, Will Montgomery, Brian Morton, Joe Muggs, Alex Neilson, Andrew Nosnitsky, Ian Penman, Richard Pinnell, Edwin Pouncey, Nina Power, Agata Pyzik, Simon Reynolds, Nick Richardson, Bruce Russell, Peter Shapiro, Chris Sharp, Philip Sherburne, Nick Southgate, Daniel Spicer, Joseph Stannard, David Stubbs, Dave Tompkins, David Toop, Dan Warburton, Val Wilmer, Barry Witherden, Matt Wuethrich

Images
Thomas Adank, Jon Baker, Maxime Ballesteros, Frank Bauer, Emli Bendixen, Jonathan Birch, Kasia Bobula, Florian Braun, André Cepeda, Dusdin Condren, Tara Darby, Ronald Dick, Lauren Dukoff, Glen Erler, Jason Evans, Jason Fulford, Leonie Hampton, Jamie Hawkesworth, Tom Hunter, Jak Kilby, Benjamin McMahon, Tom Medwell, Jason Nocito, Fergus Padel, Savage Pencil, Gérard Rouy, Jaap Scheeren, Michael Schmelling, Bryan Schutmaat, Bryan Sheffield, Chris Verene, Eva Vermandel, Kai von Rabenau, Jake Walters, Jeremy & Claire Weiss, Val Wilmer

Welcome to 2012 Rewind, *The Wire*'s annual survey of everything of consequence that went bump in the night during the last 12 months, as seen and heard by our critics and the significant movers and shakers of the subcultural scenes making up the magazine's constituency. As our longtime readers have no doubt noticed, over the past half-decade our Rewind features have been stealthily increasing in size up to the mammoth 30-page section forming the bulk of the issue in your hands. Paradoxically, the exponential growth of Rewind is directly in proportion to the exponential decay in musical consensus among *The Wire*'s electorate. 2012 Rewind opens with a four-page spread given over to the 50 releases of the year selected by our critics. A cursory glance at the top ten places, secured by artists as wildly different as Laurel Halo, Jakob Ullmann, Bob Dylan and Ricardo Villalobos, indicates just how far our voters are divided. We also asked our voters for their top ten archive releases, and the resulting chart is equally diverse, taking in the previously unseen electronic universe of Laurie Spiegel, the organic music of Don Cherry, and a complete set of Roxy Music's studio artifices. Factor in the spread of the more genre-specific columnist charts voted for by our specialist critics, and just about every subculture desperately clinging to a tiny patch of earth has been upturned somewhere in 2012 Rewind.

But what can be learned from the far and wide spread of our critics' votes? It would appear that during the past year the artists and listeners who used to travel more openly between the myriad territories occupied by *Wire*world's rainbow coalition of subcultures have retreated to their own backyards and slammed shut the gates. When there's no money to be had, it's only natural for everyone to look out for themselves and their immediate family. This breakdown of consensus made it difficult to locate the shifts and changes leading to the fortress mentality behind the breakdown of the subcultural coalition. The Rewind essays we commissioned from Britt Brown, David Keenan and Joe Muggs each address the causes of that breakdown from very different perspectives. In Streamlined Operations, Britt elegises the death of the group as the motor force of music practice during the past 70 years. The rise of the solo operator in its wake has been facilitated by the global entertainment industry's transformation into a digital economy. The industry's fatcats weren't to know that they were signing away the complete control they once enjoyed over the manufacture and distribution of music by researching and developing the digital technology through which individuals could now make, record and disseminate their own music. The obvious downside of everyone doing it for themselves is that music often stalls once individuals have used up the small creative capital each started out with.

In Imprints Of Greatness, however, David Keenan partly argues that solitary confinement is the necessary condition of truly driven outsider artists, who have no other choice but to put out their own private press editions of their own work, either because it's too raw and unmediated or too advanced for established labels to want anything to do with it. David places a premium on the visionary purity of outsider artists unwilling or incapable of adjusting to social or industry norms. A private press release establishes an intimate one on one dialogue between the work of art and the individual holding it in ways an anonymous MP3 download of the same music could never reach.

The digital age musicians Joe Muggs writes about in his Off The Grid essay might beg to differ. His piece focuses on dance music's ever-growing psychedelic underground wing, which has been derailing the beat continuum by slowing down rhythms to a crawl and in the process opening up a new dimension for dancers and listeners to fall into. The beat continuum's hold broken, dance's restrictive genre codes no longer apply. Here's hoping the dead hand of genre hasn't been revived by the time we start working on 2013 Rewind.

Chris Bohn

Distribution

News stands

UK, Europe & Rest of World (excl USA)
COMAG Specialist Division
Tavistock Works, Tavistock Road
West Drayton, Middlesex UB7 7QX
Tel +44 (0)1895 433800
mark.foker@comag.co.uk

USA
IPD (Source Interlink Fulfillment Div)
27500 Riverview Center Blvd
Suite 400, Bonita Springs, FL 34134
Tel 239 949 4450
rsonnenberg@ucsinc.com

Bookshops

Worldwide
Central Books (Magazine Dept)
99 Wallis Road, London E9 5LN
Tel +44 (0)20 8986 4854
sasha@centralbooks.com

Independent record shops

UK & Europe
Shellshock, 23A Collingwood Road
London N15 4EL
Tel +44 (0)20 8800 8110
Fax +44 (0)20 8800 8140
info@shellshock.co.uk

USA
Forced Exposure
219 Medford St
Malden, MA 02148-7301
Fax 781 321 0321
fe@forcedexposure.com

Rest of World
Contact *The Wire* direct
Tel +44 (0)20 7422 5022
Fax +44 (0)20 7422 5011
subs@thewire.co.uk

NB *The Wire* can also supply record shops in Europe direct

Subscriptions

Print Subscription

12 issues
UK £40
Europe £56
USA/Canada US$90/£56
Rest of the World (Air) £66

Digital Subscription

12 months
Worldwide £30

See page 104 for details or go to thewire.co.uk/subscribe

The Wire is published 12 times a year by *The Wire* Magazine Ltd. Printed by Wyndeham Heron Ltd.

The Wire was founded in 1982 by Anthony Wood. Between 1984–2000 it was part of Naim Attallah's Namara Group. In December 2000 it was purchased in a management buy-out by the magazine's staff. It continues to publish as a 100 per cent independent operation.

The views expressed in *The Wire* are those of the respective contributors and are not necessarily shared by the magazine or its staff. *The Wire* assumes no responsibility for unsolicited manuscripts, photographs, illustrations or promotional items. Copyright in the UK and abroad is held by the publisher or by freelance contributors. Unauthorised reproduction of any item is forbidden.

2012

Letters

Jack Kerouac's *On The Road* scroll

Courtesy James S Irsay © Estate of Anthony G Sampatacacus/Estate of Jan Kerouac

Pussy whipped: the sequel

In response to Nick Richardson's letter (*The Wire* 346) in which he complains about my labels promo policy, Alan Licht's sleevenotes for the Harry Pussy double LP were also sent to the various promo agencies I work with, and I believe to the reviews editor of *The Wire*. If Nick Richardson was really doing his research he could have requested a PDF of the notes, as these were both quoted and mentioned in the press release. He didn't. This seems a bit lazy.

The reason download codes are used for vinyl only releases is partly financial (shipping vinyl is certainly not cheap), but it's mainly due to the desire (from labels, artists and media alike) of having reviews appear the same month as release dates. Physical copies of the CD edition (if one exists) and the vinyl (if any are left) are also sent out to selected publications like *The Wire*. Thankfully the Harry Pussy albums sold rather quickly, leaving hardly any for promo purposes. Surely the duty of a label towards the artist is selling their records and not keeping journalists stocked up on product (usually to sell, I hasten to add), or am I missing something?

Editions Mego download codes include properly tagged 320 kbps MP3s as well as a hi-res front cover and PDF of the press release (or the 'shitty gloss' as Richardson puts it). That's more than the 'half baked' product that Apple sells on iTunes.

I find Richardson's questioning of my duties towards my artists (who are fully behind me on this matter) highly offensive and totally out of order, as I spend a lot of time, energy and money on presentation, promotion and advertising (including in *The Wire*).
Peter Rehberg (Editions Mego) Vienna, Austria

Scroll with the punches

In his review of the manuscript scroll of Jack Kerouac's *On The Road* at the British Library (On Site, *The Wire* 346), Daniel Spicer notes: "There's an arresting physicality to it, scored by kinetic crossings out and corrections that show how Kerouac's spontaneous bop prosody was subject to more revision than he admitted." This gives a false impression, as the scroll has always been known as a first draft of *On The Road*, and differs significantly from the text of the novel published in 1957 – six years and three conventional edits after the scroll's creation. Kerouac did like to talk up the scroll, and elide the long and extensive process of revision undertaken with his editors at Viking, but aside from the occasional "embarrassing dope-smoking uncle", to borrow Spicer's phrase, no one's taken that story seriously for decades. If it's the one the British Library are telling, then, contrary to the assertion made in the review, they're not taking the counterculture seriously after all.
Chris Power via email

Build 'em up to knock 'em down

Though not an architect myself I appreciate that it is an artistic school with its own well-defined problems, approaches, saints and heretics. With this in mind I wonder how Agata Pyzik is qualified to dismiss "the majority of exhibitors" as producing "clumsy, pseudo-socially engaged shows" in her review of the Architecture Biennale in Venice (On Site, *The Wire* 345)? Then, of course, the stand out piece of the show was a sound piece and Pyzik does appear to be primarily a music writer. The review struck me as odd and at odds with the tradition *The Wire* has of unpacking the contents of any piece of art reviewed to examine what worked and what didn't, as well as being casually insulting to the rest of the participants.
Tim Odonn via email

Corrections
Issue 346
In the Bite on Howard Jacques and Alisdair McGregor, due to a subbing error it was stated that CADS was an acronym for Community Audio Distribution Service. It actuall stands for Creative Arts Development Sheffield. In Soundcheck, the label and title of Victor Gama's *Naloga* on PangeiArt were listed incorrectly. Also in Soundcheck, the review of The Bug's "Ganja Baby"/"Diss Mi Army" 7" stated that the sleeve was designed by Savage Pencil. The design is actually by Kiki Hitomi.

Write to: Letters, *The Wire*, 23 Jack's Place, 6 Corbet Place, London E1 6NN, UK, fax: +44 (0)20 7422 5011, letters@thewire.co.uk. Letters may be edited for space or clarity

Blondes
B L O N D E S
CD, Digital

Sensations' Fix
M U S I C   I S   P A I N T I N G
I N   T H E   A I R
Dbl LP, Dbl CD, Digital

Julia Holter
E K S T A S I S
Dbl LP, CD, Digital

Holly Herndon
M O V E M E N T
LP, CD, Digital

Sun Araw & M. Geddes Gengras
Meet The Congos
I C O N   G I V E   T H A N K   /
I C O N   E Y E
LP + DVD, CD + DVD, Digital

Maxmillion Dunbar
W O O
12", CD

2013 Alluded
Maxmillion Dunbar HOUSE OF WOO Dbl LP, CD, Digital
Bobby Callender THE WAY (FIRST BOOK OF
EXPERIENCES) Enlightened Edition Dbl LP, CD, Digital

Bitstream

News from under the radar

GZA

INA-GRM is releasing a box set of recordings of acousmatic composer **François Bayle**, spread across 15 CDs and covering 50 years. Bayle, whose notable achievements include his Acousmonium orchestra of 80 loudspeakers, said that his aim was for the listener to feel the motion and vibration of energy in the universe. He joined the Group de Recherches Musicales (GRM) in Paris in the early 1960s and became its director in 1975, and also founded the Institut National de L'Audiovisuel with Ivo Malec and Jean-Claude Eloy. inagrm.com

In the wake of Hurricane Sandy, New Jersey radio station **WFMU** was forced to cancel its annual record fair, leaving the station in its most perilous financial state ever. Electrical storms left equipment damaged and knocked the station's online stream off air (with station manager Ken Freedman playlisting an extended mix of John Cage's *4'33"* in the downtime). WFMU are appealing for donations, and have the usual swag bag of goods available in exchange for your dollar. wfmu.org

Pianist and improvisor **Steve Beresford** has been awarded a Paul Hamlyn Foundation award for composers, meaning he'll receive £50,000 (upped from £45,000 in previous years) across the next three years. The money can be spent by the award's recipients however they choose, from paying bills to funding new work and buying instruments or materials. Recipients of this year's visual arts awards are Ed Atkins, Pavel Büchler, Andy Holden, Elizabeth Price and Lis Rhodes. phf.org.uk

Yoko Ono has been named as the curator of the 2013 Meltdown festival at London's Southbank Centre, in the same year as her 80th birthday. Meltdown takes place 14–23 June 2013. No acts have yet been confirmed. meltdown.southbankcentre.co.uk

Tickets sold out in record time for the forthcoming multi-night **Kraftwerk** retrospective, taking place in their hometown of Düsseldorf this month. The group play one album per night (à la the New York MoMA show), running through

Autobahn, *Radio-Activity*, *Trans-Europe Express*, *The Man Machine*, *Computer World*, *Techno Pop*, *The Mix* and *Tour De France* (in that order). The shows will, of course, feature the usual lavish visuals, plus other tracks from the Kraftwerk back catalogue. It all take place at Düsseldorf Kunstsammlung Nordrhein-Westfalen (Grabbe Hall), 11–13 & 16–20 January. kraftwerk.com

American sound artist **Bill Fontana** has been awarded a residency based at CERN, the home of the Large Hadron Collider in Switzerland. The residency will be split between CERN in Geneva and the Ars Electronica Futurelab in Linz. Fontana visited the Large Hadron Collider in December to make some test recordings and will continue the residency through 2013. arts.web.cern.ch

The full length follow up to **Matmos**'s *Ganzfield* EP will be released on 18 February, titled *The Marriage Of Two Minds*. The vinyl version of the album includes the transcripts from Matmos's telepathy experiments which formed the basis for the project, and also features a white noise locked groove and eye coverings so the listener can recreate the experiments for themselves. Guests on the record include Dan Deacon, Dirty Projectors' Angel Deradoorian, Jason Willett of Half Japanese, among others. Matmos play XOYO in London on 19 March 2013. vague-terrain.com

Matthew Herbert is releasing a box set of rare and unreleased material in March, which comes after an expanded reissue of his 2001 album *Bodily Functions*. The original release is bundled with a disc of remixes from the likes of DJ Koze, Plaid, Richard Devine, Matmos, Jamie Lidell, Mr Oizo, Perry Farrell and others. Three will also be released as a series of 12"s. accidentalrecords.com

Dean Blunt & Inga Copeland (aka Hype Williams) have started their own imprint called World Music Group. Scant details are available, as is to be expected with the pair, but a brief missive states: "Most future recordings/works will be issued or licensed through this channel."

Arthur magazine returned to the fray last month. The free bi-monthly magazine was put into hibernation in 2009, and has now returned with a cover charge of $5 in a broadsheet newspaper format. Editor Jay Babcock is still at the helm, and the mag is now published in association with Floating World Comics of Portland, Oregon. Yasmin Khan art directs, and Thurston Moore, Byron Coley, Neil Hamburger, Nance Klehm, Dave Reeves and many others will be contributing. arthurmag.com

The Wu-Tang's **GZA** is moving into the realm of education, starting up a pilot project with Columbia University professor Christopher Emdin in ten New York City public schools. The project aims to use hiphop to teach science to high school kids.

The **Instant Composers Pool** are taking up residency at the Vortex jazz club in Dalston, East London, as part of Evan Parker's Might I Suggest festival. The residency will mark the release of the *Instant Composers Pool* box, a 50 CD set also containing three DVDs, which comes in a box hand painted by Han Bennink. London Vortex, 29 January–2 February. icporchestra.com

Artist **Dinos Chapman** is releasing his first record of electronic music. *Luftbobler* is described as "schlampige musik", which translates roughly to "sloppy music" (or as one reader pointed out on Twitter, "slutty music"). Chapman has been playing with sound for the last ten years, and made this 13 track record in his basement in East London. *Luftbobler* is released on 25 February via The Vinyl Factory on vinyl, CD and digital. A limited number will include a hand coloured etching with the artwork. There will also be a companion exhibition. thevinylfactory.com

A bootleg cassette of an **Anthony Braxton** solo concert from 1972 has been unearthed. It was sourced from a recording made on two tiny microphones taped to the arms of a pair of large sunglasses. The concert took place at Carnegie Recital Hall, New York, on 10 June when Braxton was 27. The tape, which contains around 40 minutes of material, has been converted to digital and is in the

process of being mastered, possibly for release by Braxton's Tri-Centric Foundation. tricentricfoundation.org

A book documenting the **hardcore punk scene** of the 1980s has been published by David Markey and Jordan Schwartz on Bazillion Points. It collects the pair's photos of the scene from the 1980s, contains reprints of their *We Got Power* fanzine which ran between 1981–1983, and includes essays by the authors plus Keith Morris, Chuck Dukowski, Dez Cadena, Henry Rollins, Louiche Mayorga, Mike Watt and others. bazillionpoints.com

Brion Gysin's stroboscopic flicker box the Dreamachine has been put into mass production and is available to buy in the UK for the first time, in an edition of 500. Gysin's device was intended to emit light in alpha waves to provoke hallucinations in the user, and satisfied customers in the past include William Burroughs, David Bowie, Iggy Pop and Genesis P-Orridge. This first commercial edition is built according to Gysin's design and made from stainless steel. brianjonesjoujoukafestival.blogspot.ca

Chris Cutler has curated a series of podcasts at Radio Web MACBA, titled *Probes*. The series attempts to trace the effect on music of the collapse of common practice tonality and the invention of sound recording. Cutler looks at the role of the composer, microtonal divisions based on equal temperament, field recordings from environments in a state of flux, the Latvian music scene and more. rwm.macba.cat

London's Fabric is hosting four events across the next 12 months to mark the tenth anniversary of **Ricardo Villalobos** making his debut at the club. Villalobos DJed at the first night on 24 November, and more details on forthcoming events are incoming.

As in previous years, *The Wire*'s Top 50 releases of the year from our 2012 Rewind feature will be the subject of a series of shows on Freies Radio Kassel's *Borderline: Musik für Grenzgänger* show. The show will be available on 105.8FM in Northesse,

Ted Curson

Germany, and will be available to stream online as it is broadcast, every Thursday, 6–7pm (UTC), 20 December–17 January. borderline-extra.de

New York based Peruvian sound artist **Maria Chavez** has published a book of essays and illustrations via Printed Matter, titled *Of Technique: Chance Procedures On Turntable*. The book is intended to work as a how-to manual documenting the past ten years of her abstract turntable practice, and its illustrations can be torn out to use as guidelines for creating different sounds and learning new techniques. mariachavez.org

Curating organisation **Jotta** is teaming up with SoundFjord to run two parallel pages on their respective websites with discussions and interviews focused on sound art and other artistic practice. The pages will focus on young and mid-career artists. The first interviewee was Felicity Ford, who is followed by Mark Peter Wright. jotta.com, soundfjord.org

Ralf Wehowksy's P16.D4 collective has released a box set titled *Passagen*, containing six CDs, a DVD and a 40 page booklet. It covers the period 1982–1991, and contains *Nichts Niemand Nirgends Nie*, the group's collaboration with Merzbow, plus a number of unreleased recordings. monotyperecords.com

John Napier (aka Wee Wee) of Ethyl Meatplow has died. Napier's former bandmate Carla Bozulich wrote in a Facebook post: "Like with so many of our friends it was drugs that got John." She went on to say: "John was the most dynamic performer I've ever known. Sick, scary and loving. The cat that knew the best books and records and shortwave channels. He would pull things out of nowhere. I shiver to think what I would have missed and maybe someday I'll make a list!" As well as Ethyl Meatplow, Napier also played in Incest Cattle, Neon Veins and Here Eat This, among others, and ran a label called Basura! which released a handful of titles in the 1990s. After Ethyl Meatplow disbanded he went back to school and became a social worker.

Jazz trumpeter **Ted Curson** has died of heart failure aged 77. He played on more than 500 records as a sideman, and was leader on 18. Encouraged by Miles Davis, he moved to New York in 1956. There he played with Red Garland, Vera Auer and Cecil Taylor before joining Charles Mingus's group for two years, playing on *Pre-Bird* and *Charles Mingus Presents Charles Mingus*, among others. He left the group to play freelance and lead a quartet with saxophonist Bill Barron. Curson contributed to the soundtrack for Pier Paolo Pasolini's *Teorema* although he was not credited, and stuck out a long legal wrangle in order to receive payment. In 1983 Curson took up a ten year contract to play at the Blue Note six times a week. He spent a lot of time in Europe and became heavily involved in running the Pori Jazz Festival in Finland. As a result he was awarded the key to the city in 1988.

American composer **Elliott Carter** has died, age 103. Carter received the Pulitzer Prize twice, for his *String Quartets No 2* and *No 3*, in 1960 and 1973 respectively. Encouraged to take up a career in classical music by Charles Ives, he composed throughout his lifetime, finishing his final piece of music in August. As such, he had been described as the "Methuselah of American Composers". He steadfastly refused to work to deadlines, and composed music which some trained musicians found incredibly difficult to grasp. Nonetheless he received frequent commissions, and by the 1980s his works were performed on a regular basis. □

Jak Kilby

Trip Or Squeek

By Savage Pencil

S⌂FTWARE 2012

TIM HECKER | DANIEL LOPATIN
INSTRUMENTAL TOURIST
DBL LP / CD / Digital

ONEOHTRIX POINT NEVER
RIFTS
5xLP Box / 3xCD / Digital

MEGAFORTRESS
MEGAFORTRESS
12" EP / Digital

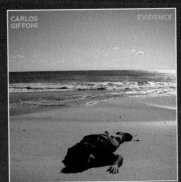

CARLOS GIFFONI
EVIDENCE
12" EP / Digital

SLAVA
SOFT CONTROL
12" EP / Digital

NAPOLIAN
REJOICE
12" EP / Digital

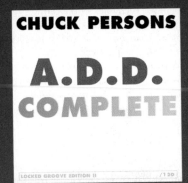

CHUCK PERSONS
A.D.D. COMPLETE
Locked Groove Editions I–IV 7" + 7" Box

BLANCK MASS
WHITE MATH / POLYMORPH
12" EP / Digital

ONEOHTRIX POINT NEVER
DOG IN THE FOG
Digital EP

TROPA MACACA
ECTOPLASMA
LP / Digital

2013: AUTRE NE VEUT — ANXIETY, SLAVA, CO LA, PETE SWANSON, HUERCO S
SOFTWARELABEL.NET

Dirty Danger

Rapid

A new collection of white labels reveals the instrumental prowess at the heart of **Ruff Sqwad**'s sound

CREW CUTS

Romance, subtlety and sentimentality aren't qualities typically ascribed to Grime, a genre renowned for its visceral and cathartic nature. But between 2003–07, East London crew Ruff Sqwad and their core producers Rapid and Dirty Danger created some of the most expressive and emotionally nuanced electronic music to emerge from the UK's post-rave diaspora. They worked with contrasts: brittle beats and bravado were paired with lush synthetic melodies and samples snatched from The Beatles and cheesy soft rock; lyrics told of love gained and lost, violence, sex and friendship. The title shared by their two studio albums – *Guns 'N' Roses Vol 1* and *Vol 2* – captured these ambiguities.

That their music was so accomplished is all the more startling given that the crew were still teenagers at the time. "We didn't know what we were doing," admits Rapid. "It was just for the fun of it. It wasn't business, it wasn't thinking 'I've got to make money'." When Rapid and Dirty Danger formed Ruff Sqwad in 2001 – alongside Slix, Mad Max (later replaced by Fuda Guy), Shifty Rydos and a pre-fame Tinchy Stryder – Grime was still in its embryonic stages and built around a DIY network of white label releases and pirate radio. For Ruff Sqwad, radio was crucial.

It provided more than just a means of exposure, although weekly sessions on Deja Vu and later Rinse FM, alongside other major Grime crews like Roll Deep and Meridian, brought them to wider attention. It was also an incentive to be creative, driving them to work on brand new material for subsequent shows. "I knew that when Monday came, we had to have something fresh and new for the listeners," says Danger. "If not," adds Rapid, "you felt like it was a waste."

The speed at which they were produced may account for the extraordinary energy of Ruff Sqwad's instrumentals from the middle of the last decade, 22 of which are gathered on a new compilation entitled *White Label Classics*. Even at their most stripped-back, they possess an uncanny psychological charge. A recording of a 2004 Deja Vu session features the DJ looping Rapid's woozy "Pied Piper" for over eight minutes as MCs jostle on and off the beat. Despite all the chat and shout-outs, the track itself is the dominant presence, cutting through the surrounding interference.

"We didn't need a vocal on them because the instrumentals were so powerful," says Danger. "I remember I had a song called "Monster", and every time I played it on radio I'd say, 'Make sure you listen to the melodies!' I wanted people to listen to what

I was doing." Both Rapid and Danger refer to the instrumentals as songs, and when pressed, cite the range of music they were listening to at the time: UK Garage, US R&B, Ghanaian music, soft rock. That doesn't quite account for the remarkably self-contained nature of the music on *White Label Classics*, however, such as the cocktail of orchestral grandeur and arrogant swagger that defines "Lethal Injection", or the way the peerless "Functions On The Low", by Ruff Sqwad associate XTC, feels painfully short despite consisting of a loop on repeat for five minutes.

One of Grime's defining characteristics is its ephemerality: unless recorded, many thrilling moments were immediately lost to the pirate radio airwaves. A similar problem cropped up while compiling *White Label Classics* – it proved impossible to track down several of the crew's legendary lost beats. They were so prolific that it simply hadn't occurred to them to make sure they kept backup copies of everything. However, admits Danger with a smile, "there could be a volume two, because we've got so many more. We used to make them like hot cakes." □ *White Label Classics* is out now on No Hats No Hoods. nohatsnohoods. bigcartel.com
Rory Gibb

Benjamin McMahon

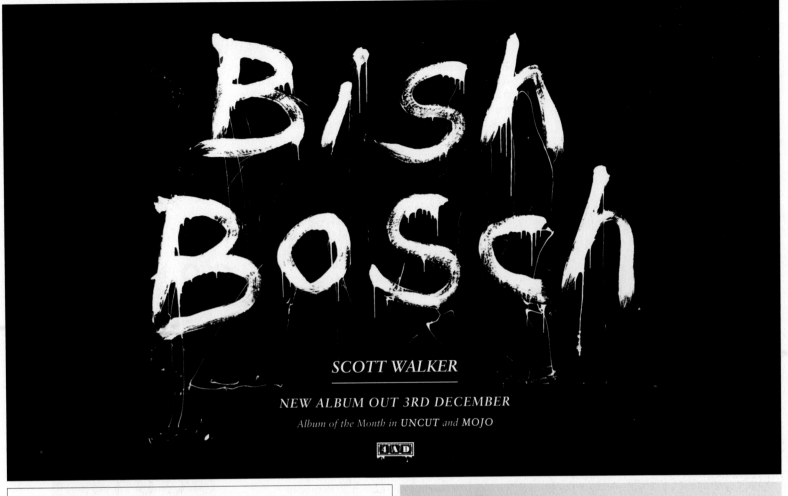

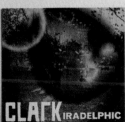

Ilan Volkov

As chief conductor of The Iceland Symphony Orchestra and principal guest conductor of The BBC Scottish Symphony Orchestra, Ilan Volkov is a pretty big deal in the mainstream classical world. Yet, as an improvising musician and founder and curator of the Tectonics festival, he's also deeply immersed in more adventurous modes.

"For classical players, it's often quite difficult to think that what they can create by themselves is as interesting as a composer's stamp of approval," he says. "That world is very used to this idea. And for some people it's much better to perform someone else's work, and they find their creativity in that. But I find that there's a lot of room to manoeuvre in between the styles."

Volkov's position enables him to bring experimentation into a sometimes conservative classical context. At the 2012 BBC Proms, he programmed an evening of Cage chance operations with an epic line-up of players including Keith Rowe, John Tilbury, Dylan Nyoukis, The Bohman Brothers and many more. Volkov himself caressed and plucked amplified cacti in the evening's finale, *Branches*. This month, Volkov and The BBC SSO will bring the rarely performed orchestral work of genre-vaulting iconoclast John Zorn to a Glasgow concert hall to mark the composer's 60th birthday.

"He's kind of been ignored in the classical scene, even though he's been writing classical pieces for a long time," says Volkov. "The orchestral pieces are very rarely played, but he has been concentrating more and more in the last 15 years on concert repertoire for orchestra, on chamber music. A lot of those pieces are very extreme, lots of contrast, lots of fragments from different material. It's very virtuosic, quite hard to do. You need to spend a lot of time rehearsing it. That's probably one of the reasons it doesn't get performed so often."

The conductor worked alongside Zorn to programme the evening, which includes the requiem *Aporias*, performed by a children's choir, the extravagant *La*

Machine De L'Etre for solo soprano and orchestra, and the world premiere of *Suppôts Et Supplications*.

"It's really exciting to get a performance of a totally new piece commissioned by the BBC," says Volkov of this latter work. "It's a major 20 minute piece dedicated to Artaud. I just wanted to have pieces that are contrasting. It's really a kaleidoscope of things. You can't programme Zorn in the context of anything else. He's really doing his own thing with the classical music that he's writing. So I think that's also one of the difficulties for people to understand what he's doing."

Although the two share a passion for both improvisation and formal composition, Volkov sees Zorn's approach as compartmentalised: "The Improv and jazz worlds that he's from influence his thoughts, but he's not trying to mix them, they're quite separate in his mind. A lot of it is to do with rituals and magic and the Jewish things that he's interested in, which are, of course, thrown into the orchestral pieces, but there's no improvisation."

Volkov's next major project will be the 2013 Tectonics festival, which in its second year will run in both Reykjavik and Glasgow. The programme will feature performances and works from Hildur Guðnadóttir, Iancu Dumitrescu, Fritz Welch, Stephen O'Malley and Hanna Tuulikki, among others.

"In Glasgow, the focus will be on Alvin Lucier. He's going to be performing some of his own electronic pieces," says Volkov. "There's a lot of potential to expand the types of people playing. I'm really keen to involve amateur choirs and kids. We will have non-classical musicians writing for orchestra, and we'll mix different players from different things together. The audience and the players are much more open to it now. There are so many possibilities there." □ John Zorn: A Portrait takes place at Glasgow City Halls on 12 January. Tectonics takes place in Reykjavik between 18–20 April, and in Glasgow in May. bbc.co.uk/orchestras/bbcsso
Matt Evans

CONDUCTING

Ilan Volkov shakes up classical conventions with a concert of John Zorn's orchestral works

ENERGIES

Sticking to the manuscript: John Zorn

UN
SOUND
DE
SIGN

James Cargill with the late Trish Keenan

How **Broadcast** created the music for *Berberian Sound Studio*

The concept of the imaginary soundtrack has become something of a cliche in electronic music. But Broadcast's music for *The Equestrian Vortex*, the fictional giallo movie at the centre of Peter Strickland's film *Berberian Sound Studio*, is some way different. Aside from its title sequence – realised with lurid glee in black and blood red hues by past Broadcast collaborator Julian House of Ghost Box – the film itself remains unseen, yet it is central to the plot of *Berberian Sound Studio* itself, providing a diegetic soundtrack for the wider story of British sound engineer Gilderoy, who is invited to an Italian post-production facility to work on the sound design of *The Equestrian Vortex*, and is drawn into a claustrophobic world of dubbed screams, sexual power struggles and vegetable based Foley violence.

The *Berberian Sound Studio* soundtrack is the first Broadcast release since the death of Trish Keenan in January 2011. Keenan and partner James Cargill had started working on the music at the invitation of Strickland but the project was still unfinished at the time of Keenan's sudden death from pneumonia at the age of 42. Cargill completed the soundtrack partly by weaving Keenan's wordless vocals into the predominantly instrumental themes and cues. "Most of the themes on the album were Trish's," he explains. "Not long after she died, I found a folder on her computer with things that she'd sung into a Dictaphone. I arranged some of them for different instruments, but they seemed to work really well."

Cargill faced the challenge of completing a soundtrack that would be convincing as the score to a mid-70s horror film of questionable quality, yet also mirror the homesick Gilderoy's yearning for the pastoral surroundings of his Surrey home, and his psychological disintegration as he has to soundtrack increasingly gruesome scenes of torture. "Rather than bombastic Goblin-like horror, a slower, emptier-sounding music seemed to connect better with Gilderoy, as well as making sense with what *The Equestrian Vortex* might be," he says. "With that, the emotional content became more powerful than the idea of it being a pastiche."

The plot of *The Equestrian Vortex* appears to involve the spirits of witches murdered by the Catholic Inquisition wreaking revenge upon the students of

IL VORTICE EQUESTRE

MCMLXXVI

Quazzo DDG Film ROMA

Julian House's titles for The Equestrian Vortex

a riding school, and Cargill took full advantage of the opportunity to notch up the sinister atmosphere with the sounds of harpsichord and church organ, the latter inspired by Nicola Piovani's use of it in his theme for Luigi Bazzoni's 1975 giallo, *Le Orme*. As well as more obvious influences such as Ennio Morricone's scores for Dario Argento, Cargill also cites Luboš Fišer, who soundtracked 1970 Czech New Wave film *Valerie And Her Week Of Wonders*, and Zdeněk Liška, who composed for Jan Švankmajer. "Those soundtracks had such a strong influence upon me when I was younger and trying to work out music. I think they still flow through me when I put my hands down on a keyboard," he says.

As a freestanding album, *Berberian Sound Studio* follows a similarly disorientating path of subconscious logic as Broadcast's 2009 collaboration with The Focus Group, *Investigate Witch Cults Of The Radio Age*. Themes recur, then dissolve, intercut with snippets of Italian dialogue, the gibbering of an actor imitating "a dangerously aroused goblin" and the actresses' lovingly recorded screams. Many of the tracks are alternative versions of themes written during production, sequenced to evoke a fuller picture of *The Equestrian Vortex*. "I think Peter would quite like to actually make *The Equestrian Vortex* one day, although I don't know if he ever will," Cargill says. Did the film take shape as more than just a nebulous set of cues? "It became a bit dreamlike, because you just had these fragments, these scenes of the girls walking through the corridors, and a series of events that didn't really have a narrative structure. It was like a de Chirico painting, these shadowy scenes."

Cargill has already been asked by Strickland to collaborate on the director's next, as yet unmade film. He is also facing the understandably daunting task of doing justice to Keenan's legacy by using material created before she died as the basis of another Broadcast record: "Trish left many great songs and vocal recordings that will eventually make up the next Broadcast album," he says. "I can't say how long it will take me to finish, but it's something we started together, so I can at least complete it in her vision." □ *Berberian Sound Studio* is out this month on Warp. warp.net
Abi Bliss

Eva Vermandel (Broadcast)

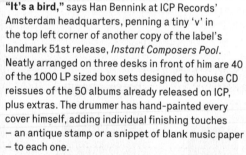

FIRST THOUGHT

Han Bennink

"It's a bird," says Han Bennink at ICP Records' Amsterdam headquarters, penning a tiny 'v' in the top left corner of another copy of the label's landmark 51st release, *Instant Composers Pool*. Neatly arranged on three desks in front of him are 40 of the 1000 LP sized box sets designed to house CD reissues of the 50 albums already released on ICP, plus extras. The drummer has hand-painted every cover himself, adding individual finishing touches – an antique stamp or a snippet of blank music paper – to each one.

"This is how it went 45 years ago," he says, referring to his cover art for ICP's very first release, *New Acoustic Swing Duo*, featuring Bennink and his ICP associate, the multi-reedist Willem Breuker, who died in 2010. For its first pressing Bennink decorated each of 500 blank sleeves with different artwork, using anything from band aids to ink stains.

ICP is both a Dutch-based improvised music collective and a record label. Co-founded in 1967 by Bennink and Misha Mengelberg, its launch signalled the new thing in European jazz, predating its German and British counterparts, FMP and Incus respectively. Starting out as a loose international collective, it soon developed into the more established ICP Orchestra, going onto collaborate with other improvisors including Dave Douglas, Peter Brötzmann and Sonic Youth.

"We've never liked the term free jazz," says Bennink, now 70. Mengelberg, aged 77, coined the phrase instant composing to better describe their mode of dadaist Improv swing. The Russian-born pianist and composer claims he was thinking of instant coffee when he came up with the description, supposedly unaware it had already appeared in the sleevenotes of a Jimmy Giuffre album. Later on he

minted the adjective spontanoid in relation to ICP's music. Rather than being strictly spontaneous, he and Bennink's Improv played around with musical phrases pulled from Mengelberg's compositions, old European songs and dances. Some titles hint at their working strategies, such as "Valse Trouvée" or "Intermezzo Between Nothing". Where British and German improvisors often chose to ignore existing forms, they set out to subvert them. In the same spirit Mengelberg also incorporated found text in his songs and poetry. "It's similar to what I'm doing in my visual art," says Bennink. "We've always liked using found objects. It all comes from art, from dada."

Bennink's habit of playing outside the drum kit, hitting everything in reach including his own body, is an extension of his art methods. "It's anything but theatre," he says. "It all depends on the audience, the acoustics, the furniture, the characteristics of the venue."

Before he and Mengelberg founded ICP, Bennink was celebrated as a tempo swing drummer in the 1950s and 60s, accompanying modern jazz artists such as Eric Dolphy on the classic album *Last Date*, with Mengelberg on piano. However, the unruly sound of Bennink's early drumming and shouting carried over into ICP. On *New Acoustic Swing Duo*, his playing resembled raw Art Blakey recordings. "When I was a kid I heard his drum solos on the American army station through my crystal radio," he says. "Can you imagine the sound?"

Although Bennink gradually departed from this role when ICP started, he has never regretted his step. □ The *Instant Composers Pool* box set is out now. The ICP Orchestra featuring Evan Parker play at London The Vortex, 28 January–2 February. icporchestra.com
Marinus de Ruiter

BEST

THOUGHT

Because a drone is basically an endlessly repeated or sustained set of tones, it lends itself to being produced by machines as much as by human bodies, ill suited as the latter are to long duration. The prototype of such machines was the sruti box, originally a bellows-operated harmonium-like instrument that simulates the sound of a tambura, used by Indian classical musicians for practice. This mutated in recent decades into portable but fairly hefty analogue slabs of hardware that electronically produce a drone. More recently, an iPhone/iPad app called SrutiBox has appeared, which digitally simulates the box, offering a variety of preset tuning systems as well as the means to create your own tunings and scales. It also comes with an endorsement from Pauline Oliveros.

Probably the most famous hardware drone box is the Beijing based group FM3's Buddha Machine, which offers a variety of infinitely repeating sonic loops, some of them drones, programmed into a transistor radio-shaped box that was originally designed for Chinese Buddhists as an automatic mantra reciting machine. FM3's fourth generation Machine comes out this month; and an iPhone/iPad app version allowing you to simultaneously operate six loops is available.

Indeed a variety of drone apps are available today. There's Drone FX, on which you can create highly cinematic drone sequences using a series of buttons and sliders that have a pretty steep learning curve. There's DJ /Rupture's Sufi Plug Ins, currently working with Ableton Live (but soon other music software), which features synthesizers tuned to North African and maqam (ie Persian/Iranian) scales, various drone producing functions, and Berber script. A hardware version is forthcoming too. And there's the remarkable Droneo (created by the maker of SrutiBox), which allows you to explore and create scales and tune the pitches of a drone in a pleasingly intuitive, but mathematically precise way. Droneo also features a beautiful spiralling visual representation of Harry Partch's 43 tone Just Intonation scale, which you can explore in a tactile way within a six octave range.

Aside from their use in performance and composition, these apps make it possible to experiment with particular drones as sustainable parts of an environment or ecosystem, much as musicians like La Monte Young, or more recently Catherine Christer Hennix, have done. But while the minimalist generation required complex, expensive analogue hardware systems and an esoteric technical knowledge of musical scales, Sruti Box and Droneo in particular open up the world of tuning systems to anyone with a little basic maths, exploratory fingers and the money for an iPad. □
Marcus Boon

Daniëlle van Ark

Global Ear

The earthquake that devastated

Christchurch

in 2011 left the city's musicians without venues and equipment, but for some, seismic shock has become sonic inspiration. By **Jo Burzynska**

Silencio Ensemble's *Chambers*

It's 12:51 pm on Tuesday 22 February 2011 in the New Zealand city of Christchurch. Suddenly the familiar soundscape is ruptured by a loud rumbling. Buildings vibrate with the rhythm of seismic waves set off by an earthquake measuring 6.3 on the Richter Scale just a few kilometres under its streets. Bricks and masonry crash to the ground, structures collapse in a series of infrasonic booms, the hillsides reverberate as boulders break loose, while dissolving soil under swathes of the city sends liquefaction gurgling to the surface.

In his workshop in the city centre, composer Chris Reddington was working with large steel tubular bells when the tremor struck. "They were swinging 180 degrees during the shaking, making an enormous bell-like clatter," he recalls. "So right from the major schism I would say I had a fairly musical experience… although it didn't become musical for me until much later."

As the dust settled on a disaster that had levelled large areas of the city, members of its experimental music scene were faced with destroyed equipment, studios, performance spaces and, in some cases, homes. Substantial aftershocks resonated at regular intervals through a city now populated by sufferers of post-traumatic stress, and most artists were forced to channel their energies into securing basic necessities rather than creative output.

"Like a lot of people, we had no water, power or sewerage for about a month, so temporarily relocated," remembers the improvising guitarist Greg Malcolm, who later left Christchurch semi-permanently. "The transient nature post-quake often made it difficult to find a work space, so I mainly just played for my own enjoyment and stress release rather than working on new material."

Many musicians speak of a creative dry period after the earthquake, disconnected and demotivated by the trauma and associated fatigue. A number found this unplanned hiatus offered an opportunity for reflection. For some, this unstable period proved revelatory, reminiscent of Walter Benjamin's Destructive Character, who "sees nothing permanent.

But for this very reason he sees ways everywhere".

This was the case for Adam Willetts, who had become frustrated by the way he'd been working compositionally. "I felt more strongly than ever that my music needed to be as unstable and dynamic as the physical, social and political environment I live in: I desperately needed to get back to an improvised way of working," he notes. He cast aside his earthquake-damaged sequencer and started building a mega-modular synthesizer: "This was the best decision and turning point in my practice ever. I'm finally making music that relates to the way I now understand the world around me in this strange post-apocalyptic wasteland, where nothing stops changing."

Christchurch was already a city with a small but rich history of improvised music. However, in this time of seismic flux, embracing the spontaneous and uncertain in music has appeared particularly relevant. With nearly all the city's venues reduced to rubble, live spaces were similarly extemporised. The portaloos ubiquitous in a city with a shattered sewer system became the site of sound installations. Garages, a wine cellar, a coffee roastery, a space originally conceived as an open-air disco on a quake-cleared block, and musician's own homes became the places for performance.

"The best thing about the quakes is the 'return to zero' aspect of venues and spaces for performance," suggests drone musician Peter Wright, one of a number of musicians for whom the current situation has offered greater freedom and affirmed the self-sustainability of the scene, although many spaces are yet to resurface. "Having to go DIY has been incredibly positive. And venues that are here now are more open to experimentation than before."

"We got quite acquainted with the sound of earthquakes," comments The Dead C's Bruce Russell. "I don't know if I felt or heard some earthquakes first, as there's a point with subsonic activity when hearing and feeling are the same thing: it's like your whole body is an ear. You feel the earthquake come, then a few seconds later it enters the sense of audition,

which is something I'd never experienced before, but happened repeatedly."

From being drained by this period of prolonged seismic activity, artists increasingly found themselves able to tap into its energy, some creating works as a direct response. Reuben Derrick, whose work is largely based on environmental recordings, captured the sonic tumbleweed of the ghost suburbs: areas devoid of inhabitants and due for demolition built on land deemed too unstable for future settlements. John Cousins created his multichannel narrative piece, *EVENT: 3468575*, from the account of a survivor of the collapsed CTV building. Seismic events also spurred Cousins to create a website where his work could be safeguarded and accessed online: before, the only place it could be heard was in his 24-channel acousmonium, Studio 174. Working under the name Stanier Black-Five, I have used my own recordings of the large aftershocks made straight after the main February earthquake in *Body Waves*, a series of live low frequency performances in collaboration with the Australian sound artist Malcolm Riddoch.

"In the wake of recent tremors, musical composition takes on new meanings regarding sound and vibration and how we might creatively use it," observes Chris Reddington, who, with his group Silencio Ensemble, recently performed a piece exploring the acoustics of a vacant lot, using the road cones that line the city's warped roadways as amplifiers. Reddington is currently working on an earthquake memorial sound sculpture, *Song Song*, to coincide with the two year anniversary of the big shake next month. It's a walk-in enclosure made of two large steel plates that can be vibrated by plucking strings on the inside walls. This creates two monochords that form a musical bridge in which visitors will be able to listen and reflect.

Paradoxically, many of Christchurch's sonic artists now consider this an exciting rather than intimidating place to be. "Somebody asked if I was going to leave," says Russell. "At no point did that occur to me. There's so much to do here and opportunities that we never would have had if it wasn't for the earthquake." □

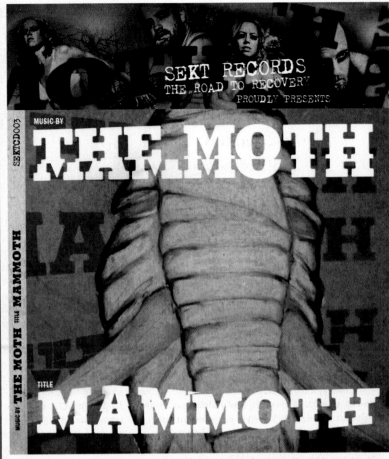

Invisible Jukebox

Each month we play a musician a series of records which they are asked to identify and comment on — with no prior knowledge of what they are about to hear. This month it's the turn of

Bryan Ferry

Tested by **Michael Bracewell**. Photography by **Frank Bauer**

Bryan Ferry was born in Washington, County Durham and studied Fine Art at the University of Newcastle. On graduation he was awarded a scholarship by the Royal College of Art and moved to London in 1969. There, he met Andy Mackay and began to put together Roxy Music while also writing the group's first album. The other core members of their early line-up would be Paul Thompson, Phil Manzanera, Brian Eno and Graham Simpson. On its release in 1972, *Roxy Music* was an immediate success, significantly garnering both critical acclaim from the pundits of the rock press and a vast teen audience. Appearing on *Top Of The Pops* in 1972, performing their first single "Virginia Plain", the group's extravagantly styled image and dazzling musical originality created an overnight sensation, making Roxy Music new stars within the pop and rock scenes of the early 1970s.

Roxy Music and its audaciously glamorous artwork (conceived by Ferry, who would do the same for all of Roxy Music's releases) were instantly recognised as a pop cultural manifesto, within which Ferry had created a collage of musical and sartorial styles, merging American glamour and European intellectualism into a new hyper-romantic yet street-cool sensibility.

Roxy Music would go on to record eight studio albums, and one live album, 1976's *Viva!*, before disbanding in 1983 (the group would reform for a highly successful reunion tour in 2001).

Ferry's career as a solo artist began as early as 1973, when he released *These Foolish Things*, a selection of his interpretations of songs by Bob Dylan, The Rolling Stones and others. *Another Time Another Place* followed in 1974, its historic cover shot (by Eric Boman) of Ferry dressed in black tie and white tuxedo doing much to seal his identity as the embodiment of the worlds of high society, high fashion and high romance which were invoked by his songs, whose moods would shift ambiguously between hedonism and fatalism.

His latest album, *The Jazz Age*, recreates a number of those songs, from both his solo albums and Roxy Music's back catalogue, as instrumentals played in the jazz idioms of the 1920s.

The Jukebox took place over two sessions, in West Sussex and West London.

Can
"Father Cannot Yell"
From Monster Movie (Spoon/Mute) 1969

It sounds like a young band, which period I don't know, but it could be any time after 67…

You're very close with the date.

I don't know whether it's a young band from now imitating that sound or being inspired by that sound… They've obviously listened to The Velvet Underground. It doesn't sound as though they had much money for the recording, which again makes them sound like a young and exploratory band… I don't know. I haven't heard it before. It goes on for a while!

Do you like it?

I think I would prefer hearing it live, rather than on a record. Partly because when I play records I'm not looking to be stimulated in that way. So I imagine if I was in a club, checking places out and checking people out, then I would find it quite… uplifting. Even though it's fairly atonal in parts. It's not what I would call sentimental.

It's Can.

Can!

When you were putting Roxy Music together, were Can one of the colours on your palette, so to speak?

Not really, no. But the first-hand source of that track was The Velvet Underground, I would have thought — and anything else that was vaguely experimental and coming out of America. My only connection with Can, really, came about through Simon Puxley who was my longtime friend and collaborator and sometime producer. He also produced some tracks for Can, later on. But that's the best thing I've ever heard by them — not wishing to be derogatory about them, at all. If we [Roxy Music] were in Cologne, or somewhere like that, one or two of them would come backstage — one, Holger [Czukay] I think, was a friend of Andy Mackay.

But [Can guitarist Michael Karoli's] sister and girlfriend were both featured, heavily, on the [1974] *Country Life* album cover. I was in Portugal, furiously typing up and writing lyrics for the completed tracks — things such as "The Thrill Of It All". I had taken along two very important figures in my artwork team: Eric Boman — photographer, make-up artist, hairdresser, stylist and sometime video performer in my case; and of course the great Antony Price, the fashion designer.

So the two of them were with me out there in this house I had taken in what was then a charming fishing village. One night we took a break to go out into a bar and we bumped into these two girls who turned out to be very connected to Can. The next day we did the *Country Life* cover shot with them — which turned out

to be one of the key images in Roxy Music's history.

Jelly Roll Morton's Red Hot Peppers
"Smoke-House Blues"
From Jelly Roll Morton Vol 1 (JSP) 1926

[Listens intently] I don't think I can place it at all — I don't think I've ever heard it… It sounds very primitive. It doesn't sound like Louis Armstrong's Hot Five, but maybe it is — the trumpet isn't so featured, though. It's got a double bass, which is interesting, considering it sounds like such an early thing. Sounds very New Orleans — very, very laidback. Because a lot of the Hot Five things are more uptempo, more lively. It's not Kid Ory's band is it?

It's Jelly Roll Morton's band, and the trombonist is Kid Ory.

Ah! Jelly Roll Morton is on my 'to read' list, so to speak — it's a bit like Proust, you know: I'm keeping it for my old age.

The Jazz Age seems to recreate this kind of sound at a deeply felt and authentic level.

It's funny how it all came about. For a long time I had wanted to do an instrumental album — I wanted to have a record that showcased me as a writer, taking away the singing part. I had considered various ideas, from bebop to orchestral arrangements in an avant garde style, but I still hadn't figured it out. I had been listening to a lot of earlier music over the years, to a lot of Charlie Parker, for example — and then working my way backwards. So for several years I would listen to Coleman Hawkins, as he is a bridge between 'old' music and modern jazz — he has it all, it seems. If I had to go to a desert island with just one person it might well be Coleman Hawkins, who I would take to serenade me through the lonely evenings…

So I bought a lot of boxed sets and realised how much I loved this earlier music — the two towering giants appear to be Duke Ellington and Louis Armstrong. Armstrong's melodic playing is incredible, and he really started 20th century modern music — Ellington refined it. It was then that I decided that I wanted to do an album of my songs in a jazz idiom and in that period style; not aping one particular band, but anything from the period, as if it was a compilation of my songs done by different bands from that time. So you could get some of the Cotton Club jungle rhythms of Duke Ellington, and also the New Orleans Armstrong style. It turned out that my melodies, things I have written over the years, sound really good in that style. I am over the moon with how it's turned out.

If someone had told me that you could successfully rerecord "Virginia Plain" and "The Bogus Man" in that style…

A lot of it is due to the inventiveness and skill of the musicians. These guys, whom I have worked with

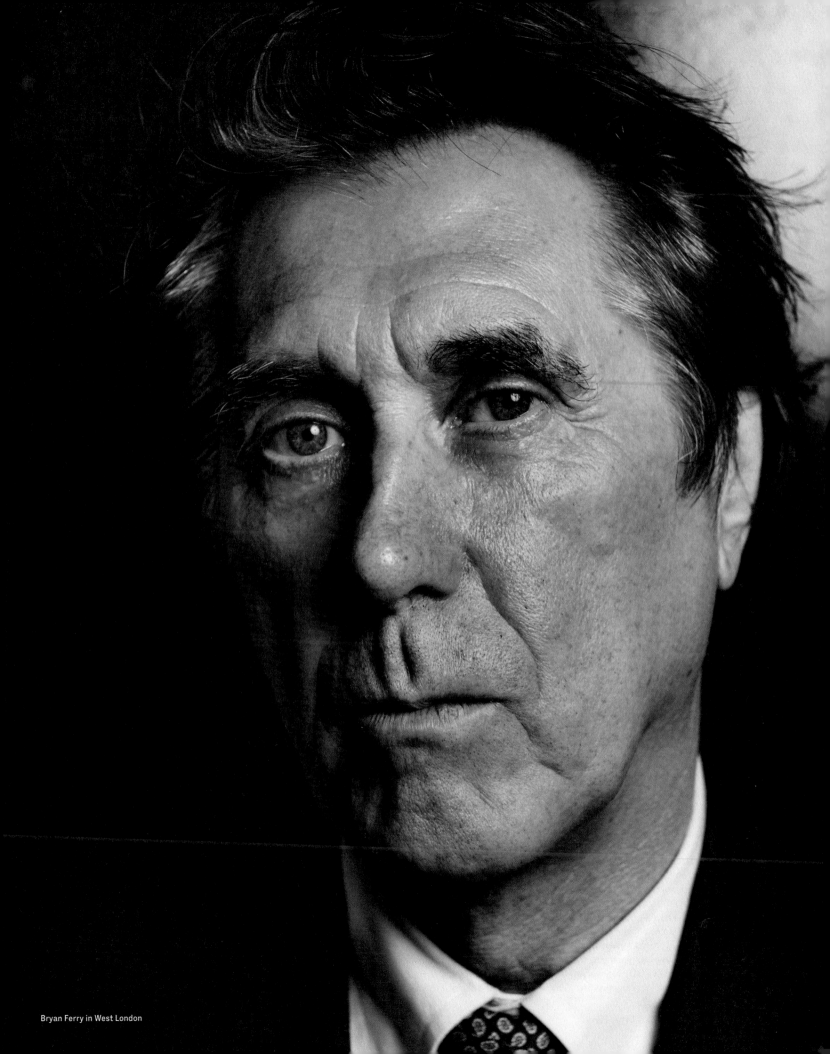

Bryan Ferry in West London

before, can play very convincingly in the style of the 1920s and 1930s – those two decades… What is the date of the track we just heard?
1926.
It sounded almost slightly earlier.
Did you find it difficult to select the tracks for *The Jazz Age*?
No. We wanted a balance of songs that had been played with Roxy, and songs from my solo albums. Some are well known, others not so well known.

Lou Reed/John Cale/Sterling Morrison
"Prominent Men (demo)"
From The Velvet Underground *Peel Slowly And See* (Polydor) 1995, rec 1965
If you'd said this was some unknown, early Dylan track, then I'd have to say I'd never heard it before. But it seems to be someone very influenced by Dylan… The harmonica playing, the form of the song… It doesn't sound like his voice though… The guitar appears to be out of tune as well… It's a total imitation, it seems, of Dylan. I don't know much about Woody Guthrie – it's not him is it? It sounds like another young voice.
It is a young voice, but one which swiftly became historic.
Damn… I know I'm going to kick myself. Whoever it is must have studied Dylan closely to play harmonica like that… This is a trick one, isn't it?
A curve, perhaps. Imagine a viola playing on it…
You're not saying it's Lou Reed?
It's a Velvet Underground demo from 1965.
Really… That's amazing – it's very good.
Would you go along with the notion that Roxy Music were the UK Velvet Underground?
Well, we were more influenced by them than most people were, so in that sense, yes. We loved the sound of their records – we liked the wildness, the wild guitar playing; the lyrics were intelligent sounding but not overly so – there was a street cool about how they sounded, and the rawness was something that appealed. So yes – we were big fans! Although we didn't want to just sound like them…
I guess that Roxy and The Velvets were both very interested in and inspired by visual arts and culture. Also there is a similarity perhaps between the artistic dynamic of Cale and Reed and, early on, yourself and Eno, with the physicality of Paul Thompson's drumming mirroring that of Mo Tucker.
There are lots of similarities there. But the fact that we had a bigger palette to draw upon was a big help – in terms of not simply sounding like The Velvets. We had the oboe, we had saxophone and we had synthesizers that could change any sound… And in one sense that was what made us sound more interesting than other people. You never usually heard an oboe in that context, or sounds being distorted in the manner that Eno treated them. So the world was our oyster, soundwise.

Whether my songs, which were the framework of the music, had anything to do with Lou Reed… I suppose we had the same sort of interests, but I was in London and he was in New York, and a bit before me… I'd say he had the vantage of living in a cooler climate, in the sense of Warhol and the Factory. We were out on a limb – but we had a European thing going as well, and my particular sources of inspiration were very wide, which gave us an edge over a lot of people. So I was

into Broadway but also into blues; into jazz but also Jimi Hendrix and stuff like that.
And visually?
Well, they had Warhol's light shows, whereas we developed the costume side of things – probably because it was the cheapest way! We didn't have a film person or anything like that. I suppose Pink Floyd had had a very interesting light show thing going – but I guess we wanted something different.

Prince And The Revolution
"I Wonder U"
From *Parade* (Paisley Park/Warner Bros) 1986
I like this. I thought it was maybe Wendy & Lisa or something, a kind of alternative funk thing… Very cool sounding. I like the soft vocal – girls' voices whispering. It sounds a bit like Prince.
Bang on.
I'm sure Wendy & Lisa would be in it… I love Prince.
What is it about him you admire so much?
[Laughs] The fact that he can do things like that! I feel a kinship with that music as soon as I hear it – like it's from my tribe. The life in it, the rhythm in it – it speaks volumes; and it's skilful and full of feeling… I love it. Some people's perception of me, I think, would place me as the opposite of Prince; but I am sure we would like a lot of the same music. I very rarely meet people whom I idolise in a fan kind of way, but I did meet him and we talked as much as we could – we could have talked for days, actually – about certain musical things.

I could talk for hours about Prince! Not only does he sound incredible and inventive, and covers a lot of musical ground, on stage he's an electrifying performer – he's in a different league to most people who are around. He can play his guitar, dance, jump on the piano, do anything… A Little Richard thing – but at the same time he's aware of Elvis. He's a maverick – he's his own man, in his own category, which I would quite like to be as well.

Chic
"Happy Man"
From *C'est Chic* (Atlantic) 1978
Sounds like Nile [Rodgers]. Don't know the track yet, but those chords… [Laughs] I've never heard this track. It's extraordinary: Nile is never very loud in the mix, but you just feel him – it's his thing, this amazing rhythm that is so infectious, and has created some of the best dance records ever.
Are Chic the black Roxy?
It just feels fantastic – it's that amazing combination of two principal parts: Bernard Edwards's bass and Nile's rhythm guitar playing. Nile has always said that he saw Roxy and knew that he wanted to do a black version of that. He tells the story slightly differently each time! But basically he's in London and sees us on *Top Of The Pops* doing "Love Is The Drug" [in 1975], and I'm wearing an eye-patch and have the girl backing singers… He says: I've got the idea for the group! And calls them Chic.

As soon as I heard them I just thought they were amazing. We never had the feel that they had. I was very lucky with my solo records to be able to pick and choose the wish-list of players, and I met Nile Rodgers through Bob Clearmountain, who was Chic's engineer… He mixed "Dance Away", which was a big hit, and had some of the Chic sound. I later found that

Chic, 1978

Nile knew quite a lot of the guys who were playing on *Boys And Girls* [Ferry's 1985 solo album] – he went to school with [bass player] Marcus Miller… These were the top guys in New York, and I so wanted to have the top guys in New York on my record! Since then, Nile has played on nearly all of my solo albums, including most recently *Olympia* [2010].
The Chic sound conjures up a particular picture of New York in the 80s. Did you ever go to Studio 54?
Yes, and I got in. Famously, Nile and Bernard didn't get in, when they had just started out, and so they went away and wrote this huge hit, "Le Freak", about being turned away… I don't know who I was with, probably Fred Hughes [Andy Warhol's business manager] and Barbara Allen, who was on the cover of my record *The Bride Stripped Bare* [1978] – she was very much on the inside track of everything that happened in New York. Her ex-husband owned Andy Warhol's *Interview* magazine, for example. There was a period when I hung out a lot with her and Fred Hughes and Bob Colacello [*Interview*'s first editor]. But I was always just a visitor really. It was great to hear those records in a club like that – with young Greek gods in hot pants serving drinks on rollerskates, that kind of thing. Crazy.

Sam Cooke
"Change Is Gonna Come"
From *The Gospel According To Sam Cooke* (RCA Victor) 1964
The late great Sam Cooke. I first heard this song done by Otis Redding, which is also very beautiful. Sam Cooke had an amazing voice, obviously; but to me the arrangement is always a little bit square, which is a shame. He wrote this, didn't he? He was a huge influence on lots of singers everywhere – but a tragic end [in December 1964, Cooke was fatally shot in Los Angeles, in circumstances that remain disputed]. I have always loved black American music – soul, blues and all the great singers that inspired me.
You covered "Wonderful World" on *Another Time Another Place*, a song that again was covered by both Cooke and Otis Redding.
Exactly. Very soulful voices, very expressive – both amazing…

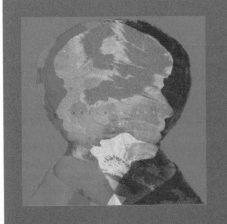

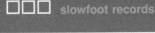

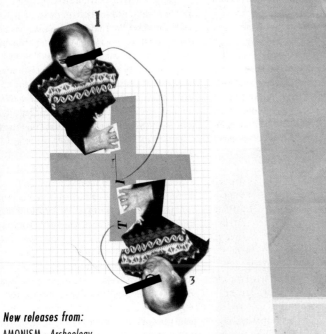
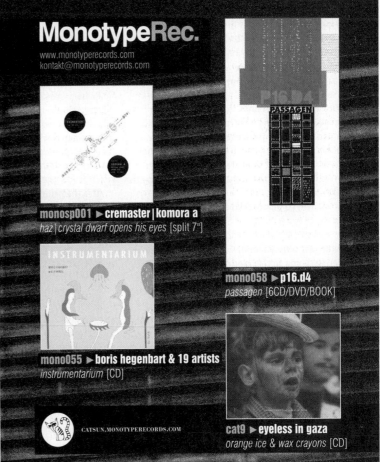

At what point did you realise you could sing?
I would say on the second Roxy Music album, *For Your Pleasure* [1973]. Because on the first album I was experimenting – like the Lou Reed song you played earlier, I was still searching for my voice; whereas on the second album I was beginning to find my voice – and I guess that gave me the confidence to do the first solo album, where I was the singer, arranger and co-producer, not the writer. But I do like other people's voices, which is why on my own albums I always try to put other voices on as well – it's as if you're thinking you're not worthy or something. It's a shame that as you get older, your voice starts changing; and then you have to try to adapt to what you can and can't do. For instance, somebody sent me a dance mix the other day of [Roxy Music's] "More Than This" [1982], using the original vocal; and it's way above what I could sing now, in terms of register. I wish I'd done more albums while my voice was younger; but then again there's perhaps more expression now.

Bob Dylan
"Tempest"
From *Tempest* (Columbia) 2012
[Immediately] It's the new record by Bob Dylan. Very good – somebody played that track to me the other day. This is the kind of music that Dylan must have heard when he was about ten years old, at barn dances in Minnesota or wherever – like Country swing. He does it incredibly well and it sounds very authentic – like he's come home, interestingly enough. Not that he should do music like this all the time, but it's something that sits very well with him, I think. I suppose that I've gone back to one of my roots, as well, which is early jazz…

Trad jazz was very popular in England in the 1950s, and that's how they started to play the original versions of it on the radio. Lonnie Donegan had a huge hit [in 1956] with "Rock Island Line" – because often trad jazz bands would slim down and become a skiffle group, which happened with Chris Barber's band, in which Donegan played banjo. So he had this hit with Leadbelly's "Rock Island Line" and then people started to hear Leadbelly's original version. And that's really how people in England got into blues music, through the popularisation of it by white bands at first. Once you got past that, you heard the better versions by the black artists.

So this is how you discovered someone like King Oliver?
Exactly – you would start making your own discoveries and doing your own research. So from 1955 onwards I've been listening to this kind of music; and this record I've made has been a joy. Recreating a period sound is a really interesting thing to do. Whether this means I have come full circle remains to be seen. I have new work on the go as well, which will hopefully see daylight next year. Exploring music from other periods has been a very interesting part of my career for me; and not only different periods, but also different genres and different songwriters.

I get the impression that Dylan doesn't have the same editorial fears that I may have – I imagine he lets things go much more easily. He would probably write 100 verses for a song like that, whereas I would refine it down.
It was interesting how well your voice and musical

approach responded to Dylan's work on your *Dylanesque* album [2007].
I had a fear of writing myself out, you know, or running out of fresh ideas. And so it's been a useful thing for me to do, in terms of giving myself a breather as a writer, to record interpretations of other people's songs as well. But with Dylan, more than any other writer, I suppose, I felt very comfortable working with his material. He is such a good lyricist.
Your interpretations of songs by other people seem always to become self-portraits – an example being the version of "A Hard Rain's A-Gonna Fall" on *These Foolish Things*.
I certainly found something of myself in it. It was my first foray into that world, and in some ways the most successful. Unless you can find something of yourself in a song, there seems little point in doing it.

King Crimson
"Larks' Tongues In Aspic Part II"
From *Larks' Tongues In Aspic* (Island) 1973
I haven't really got a clue who it is – the nearest I can think of is King Crimson…
It *is* King Crimson.
That was a pretty good guess, then – just because of the time signatures… But it didn't sound like [Robert] Fripp, that's the interesting thing. Which period is it?
1973, from *Larks' Tongues In Aspic*.
I knew the first album, *In The Court Of The Crimson King* – it was a great record. And I probably wouldn't have had my career in music if it hadn't been for Robert Fripp. Because that was how I met EG Management, who took Roxy Music on, and it all happened through Robert Fripp. I was working with [bass player] Graham Simpson, before I met Andy Mackay, and I was writing the first batch of Roxy songs. I wasn't sure if it was going to work, I didn't have a band, but I used to read the music papers and there was an ad for King Crimson, who were looking for a singer who could play bass. I couldn't play bass, but I went along to the audition anyway – just around the corner [from here] in Fulham [West London]. It was in a basement, and sitting there were Pete Sinfield and Robert Fripp. I did the audition, and I guess they did like me, but they really wanted someone who could play bass as well. So I said no problem, and told them that I was writing my own songs, and trying to put my own band together.

King Crimson, 1973

They suggested I should take my music to EG – which I did about a year later. So I certainly recognise the feel of their music.
Early Roxy tracks also contain a lot of tempo changes. Did you see any affiliation with early Roxy and this kind of prog sensibility?
They do have tempo changes, but are not usually in such a strange signature as that King Crimson track. But I did see a connection between Roxy and prog, very much so – Crimson and Pink Floyd were some of the best things about British music at that time. But in my case, as well as being into that kind of stuff, I was also into the blues, jazz, Broadway, Kurt Weill… My head was swimming with lots of different, contrasting types of music.
How comfortable are you with the notion that Roxy Music were the first postmodern group?
Well, it's better than being called a glam rock band. The great feature of the first Roxy album is that it was an exercise in collaging different styles of music. And if there's a criticism of some of my later work, I suppose it would be that it didn't attempt as much of that. I think that as I got older, I wanted a song to be more of a 'set' thing, rather than jumping around so much.

Brian Eno
"What Actually Happened"
From *Nerve Net* (All Saints) 1992
I think it's really good! Some very good sounds on it… Is this a trick question? It's not by Brian Eno is it?
It is.
That's an amazing guess! I wanted to say, I wish this was by Brian Eno, because I didn't think it was him but I thought it was the sort of record that he should be making. God, I wish he'd done that with me. I was also going to say, halfway through, Brian Eno would like this. I immediately thought of him – how fascinating.
Would you like to work more with Eno?
It's probably hard for both of us to think too much about that kind of thing, because we have both spent so much time and irritation fending off people who say, 'Why aren't you working together?' But we are very complementary talents, and it's true that we work well together. It's a shame that we didn't work together more away from the spotlight. Because now if we do something there is too much attention… But that's one of the best things of his that I've heard.

Frank Sinatra
"Guess I'll Hang My Tears Out To Dry"
From *Sings For Only The Lonely* (Capitol) 1958
Frank Sinatra – one of my favourite people. That song could have been written for me. This is all about the lyrics and the voice – very sentimental. I like the whole thing about Sinatra – I like that whole period: the clothes they wore, the girls they dated, and all that pre-Elvis, pre-Beatles, pre-rock 'n' roll era. And the Nelson Riddle arrangements – beautiful orchestrations, although that one's a little slow for my taste.
Is it too simple to say that one of the things that has been central to your career is the hybridisation…
… of all these things we've just played? [Laughs] I like the exploration into different musical territories; and if you keep darting around you can go back and revisit things – which gives a fresher outlook. So I think that it has worked for me. □

The prolific output and troubled life of the spiritualist and artist

Madge Gill

made for enduring art, which now finds echoes in the music of David Tibet and James Blackshaw's Myrninerest group. But her reputation as an archetypal Outsider artist remains problematic, says **Frances Morgan**

Madge Gill working on a roll of calico at home in East London

The archive of Newham Heritage Services, as described by Rosamond Murdoch of the Nunnery Gallery in Bow, East London, is one of those caches of local history that London's boroughs like to hide in plain sight. A four-storey building in nearby Plaistow, it houses the contents of the now closed Passmore Edwards museum and more than 1000 works by local artist Madge Gill, currently the subject of a retrospective at the Nunnery.

Yet this archive doesn't hold Gill's complete works. On her death in 1961 aged 79, her son Laurie donated these works to the Borough of Newham; other pieces found their way to galleries such as Jean Dubuffet's Collection de l'Art Brut in Lausanne, Switzerland, as well as into private collections, including that of Current 93 musician and artist David Tibet. Gill's prolific output, consisting mostly of pen and ink works ranging from postcard miniatures to calico scrolls many feet long, as well as the compulsive, repetitive style of her self-taught drawing, and her interest in spiritualism and mysticism, ranges her with the other Outsider artists collected by Dubuffet, as does the story of her troubled life.

If one defining characteristic of Outsider artists is the attention given to their personal history relative to the work they produce, Gill certainly fits the bill. Around her often disturbing, dreamlike imagery hangs a biography of illegitimacy, childhood trauma, forced emigration, illness and grief in the East End of London, itself a place ripe for mythologising. Her great spate of work began in 1919 after the deaths of a son and a daughter, and mute, wide-eyed faces haunt her

best known drawings. Whether memorials of her lost children or manifestations of Myrninerest, the spirit guide through which she said her art was channelled and for whom it was made, they hint at an immense sadness within vortices of confusion.

"It's either a term of abuse or love, and it's completely inaccurate," says David Tibet, who has also collected work by Louis Wain, another London artists frequently labelled as Outsider art. "Outsider now just tends to mean an artist that we think is weird. Why isn't van Gogh an Outsider artist? He seems to check some of the boxes! Now, it seems to cover the art of people who are mentally or emotionally unstable or challenged; at one point it was just seen as the art of the mentally ill. But then it seemed to take in people who are untaught, and Louis Wain was obviously not a self-taught, naive artist."

Tibet's most recent musical project, a duo with James Blackshaw, is named after Gill's avatar, Myrninerest, and her distinctive handwriting appears on the music's artwork. Blackshaw's cyclical guitar patterns and simple harmonium form a web around Tibet's lyrics, which pour compulsively through Myrninerest's debut album *"Johnn," Uttered Babylon*. At first overwhelming, the narrative's dense inner logic is suggested by incantatory repetition, both musical and verbal.

"I do use repetitive melodies, or references to particular phrases that are meaningful to me, but I was doing that before," Tibet reflects. "Perhaps that's why I was attracted to Madge Gill – I didn't *take* that from Gill, it's just always been the sort of music and art that

I love that is continually self-referential and internally referential. Gill's always referring back to her own work – it's both hermetic and hermetically sealed."

The Jhonn of the album title is of course Coil's Jhonn Balance, Tibet's close friend, who died in 2004. The music was performed for the first time at 2012's Meltdown with films of Balance projected onstage. I wonder if the Myrninerest project is an act of memory for Tibet, akin to some interpretations of Gill's work as being born from grief. But grief is not a simple emotion, and art's relation to it is similarly complex: "I hoped it might have been an exorcism, or [that] I could remember him with less pain and less longing, but that didn't really work," says Tibet. "It brought him back to me even more, if that makes sense."

Outsider art is a term that has come to feel increasingly prescriptive as the role socioeconomics, gender and race play in determining whether someone is seen to be possessed by genius, or just plain possessed, is more widely understood. Outsider aesthetics filter into more established art, both in style and methodology: Deanna Petherbridge, in a book accompanying the Nunnery show, notes that the obsessive process of artists such as Gill is encouraged in today's art teaching. And those perceived as Outsiders are themselves increasingly aware of and vocal about the way in which they're described: in *The Wire* 340, R Stevie Moore defined himself against "Wesley Willis or Daniel Johnson, or these people that are touched in the head and have a certain gift."

Such contradictions abound around Madge Gill, too. Her work is found in the Bethlem Royal Hospital

Madge Gill *Untitled*

Paul Johnson *Neptune... Neptune... Neptune* (2012)

museum, yet she was never institutionalised. A keen craftswoman, skilled abstract artist and gallerygoer, in the 1930s and 40s she was a regular exhibitor at the Whitechapel Gallery's open shows for local amateurs: not exactly a recluse. It is this Madge Gill that Rosamond Murdoch, and the artists with whom she has worked on the Nunnery's three-part retrospective, want to bring to the fore. Since last summer, Murdoch and artists Sarah Carne, Jack Hutchinson and Paul Johnson have presented three exhibitions combining Gill's work with their own material.

"The residency was originally for an artist to co-curate Madge Gill's work alongside their own," says Murdoch. Instead of choosing from their existing works, though, she says, "all three artists chose to create new work over a six-week period. It was a surprising response from all of them."

The current and final show is sparse: around ten of Gill's postcards sit alongside collage and sculpture by Paul Johnson, who deliberately chose to go small-scale after finding a small album of postcard works in the Newham archive. "All the other works seemed to fade away," he says. "I was suddenly just looking at this book. It's a sea of images that you can't instantly relate to her work. There was no black and white in there, no small faces coming out of geometry... it looked like something very different."

Johnson's vivid collages echo the colours of Gill's postcards; meanwhile, pieces like his *Poor Man's Rainbow* portray mysterious female characters that have been a feature of Johnson's work for some time. Previous collages, he says, have played with the idea

of auras; *Guide* (2007) shows a woman decorated with and surrounded by vaguely occult shapes, imaginary forces made real.

Johnson's close relationship with – and critique of – the idea of Outsider art arguably shaped his contribution to the Gill retrospective. Showing the work of self-taught Idaho artist James Castle as part of a group exhibition in 2003, he chose to leave out biographical details such as Castle's profound deafness, "just to see what would happen and how people would interact. And from that point onwards I thought, does the [artist's] disadvantage have to be so heavy that that's what comes first?"

Rosamond Murdoch sees Gill's biography, as one that's about far more than disadvantage, suggesting that her work liberated as much as consumed her.

"Her production must have been so prolific that it interfered with 'seemly' behaviour," Murdoch muses. "She must have been scribbling away at points when people would have expected her to be out shopping or visiting or cleaning.

"You look at someone and you think, why did you step outside the norm? Was it through psychological damage that happened to you as a child, or being ostracised from your family? The temptation is to make all sorts of assumptions. But I think her response to it is a celebration, which is making art, like making music – a way of processing, of creating out of something that could have been quite destructive." □ Madge Gill & Paul Johnson is at London's Nunnery until 31 January. Myrninerest's releases are out now on Coptic Cat. nunnerygallery.org, myrninerest.com

Over the next 30 pages, we present *The Wire*'s review of the last 12 months in underground sound and music. From the releases of the year to the reflections and analyses of a host of artists and critics, here is your guide to the audio culture highs and lows of 2012

2012 REWIND

Releases of the year 32

We asked our contributors to nominate their Top 10 CDs, vinyl and downloads of the year, then we counted up the votes. Here are the results

Critics' reflections 36

Wire writers offer their personal pros and cons from the last 12 months of underground music activity and beyond

Columnists' charts 42

Our specialist critics select the music that rocked their corner of the subculture, from Avant Rock to Size Matters

Streamlined operations 44

Britt Brown on the decline of the group

Imprints of greatness 46

David Keenan on the rise of the private press

Off the grid 48

Joe Muggs on the dequantization of dance music

Archive releases of the year 50

This year we again invited our contributors to vote for their Top 10 reissues, anthologies and unreleased historic recordings from the last 12 months. Here is the second crucial poll of 2012

Artists' reflections 54

A cast of 2012's most active movers and shakers shine the spotlight on their cultural year

Views from the office 58

Wire staff riff on some of 2012's most significant trends in live music, online life and more

Releases of the year

1–10

1

Laurel Halo
Quarantine
Hyperdub

The follow-up to last year's *Hour Logic* saw the Brooklyn based electronic musician explore darker, more disorienting sonic territory than its Acid-bright predecessor, with increasingly waterlogged synth textures, analogue and digital noise fragments, and refracted, disintegrating rhythms. But Halo's confidence with melody and her deftly written and direct, often harshly vulnerable vocal lines raised *Quarantine* above the vague techno-dystopian mood that permeated much of 2012's electronic music. Not content with merely creating atmosphere, Halo placed herself at the centre of this drowned world, a skilful avatar of the near future. We said: "A general wrongness fills and warps [the tracks], as if the very air that carries these sounds was toxic to breathe… 'Songs' is both too enclosing and too sloppy a term – these are smears of technological colour that spill across the canvas, just abstract enough to be perturbing." (June/340)

2

Sun Araw & M Geddes Gengras meet The Congos
Icon Give Thank
Rvng Intl

Sun Araw's Cameron Stallones and his friend M Geddes Gengras took a trans-Caribbean jaunt and found a veteran reggae collective alive and well in a St Catherine Parish compound (documented on the accompanying film *Icon Eye*). The collaboration was a meeting of sublimely stoned minds: a blissed out psychedelic dub encounter with a burning core of Rastafari righteousness, recorded in a studio cloudier than when Lee Perry set fire to his Black Ark. We said: "Gushes of white noise, long-chain percussion loops and guitar squall – albeit at a Caribbean tempo – predominate… Cedric Myton's honeyed tenor remains an instrument of glory and power and his group's harmonies still cohere with ragged majesty." (March/337)

3

Actress
RIP
Honest Jon's

The title of London producer Darren Cunningham's third album was not a death knell but an invitation to a twilight interzone between rest and wakefulness. *RIP* is a suite of oblique dubstep tangents, zen melodic sketches and tonal laments, all painstakingly forged through manual sound processing way off the grid of commercial electronic software, and all obliquely wrapped around the narrative of Milton's *Paradise Lost*. We said: "He plays games on the margin of what works on a dancefloor… Deliberately crossing these lines adds another layer to dance music's tension-release formula, making it more perverse and more gratifying at the same time." (April/338)

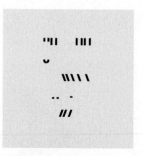

4

Jakob Ullmann
Fremde Zeit – Addendum
Edition RZ

Three discs of some of the quietest, most intense works in all of contemporary composition. The four longform pieces here used graphic scores and empowered performers to create lengthy, almost static performances which, when heard closely, became teeming ecosystems of sonic activity, incorporating the noise of the instrumentalists themselves and huge recording spaces. The East German composer's music is intended to be played just above the threshold of ambient noise, forcing the listener to hear more closely, and hear more. We said: "It's enticing and yet somehow unobtainable, always a few feet ahead, just out of reach, always causing the ear to be strained… All of the pieces are beautifully still on the surface, but this tranquillity betrays a wealth of detail." (April/338)

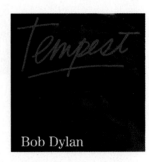

5

Jason Lescalleet
Songs About Nothing
Erstwhile

6

CC Hennix & The Chora(s)san Time-Court Mirage
Live At The Grimm Museum Volume 1
Important

7

Bob Dylan
Tempest
Sony/Columbia

After numerous collaborations, *Songs About Nothing* was US tape tweaker Lescalleet's first solo album proper in six years. The result was a tantalising MC Escher puzzle of bastardised remixes, electroacoustic sketches, urban field recordings and oblique riffs on Big Black's hardcore classic *Songs About Fucking*. Its two discs, one of spiky fragments and the other a single multilayered track, presented radically different sides of the same coin, united by subtle motifs and thematic echoes. We said: "A fragmented, self-reflexive and quizzically conceptual collection of collages and cut-ups… convincing evidence of Lescalleet's gradual emergence as one of the US Noise underground's more distinctive voices." (October/344)

This rarefied wave of sound, made by Swedish-American composer Catherine Christer Hennix with a group including Amelia Cuni, Robin Hayward, Hilary Jeffery and Michael Northam, was constituted from an alchemical brew of high mathematics, quantum physics, dhrupad modes and Just Intonation blues. The rising and falling audio mist provided one of the year's most hallucinatory sonic experiences. We said: "… Like something deeply earthed, something uncoiling around your spine from the ground up… It's a stunningly beautiful piece of music, with just enough undertow hints of remembered pain as well as blissful pleasure". (June/340)

In another lifetime a Dylan song would get you running for shelter from the storm, but on *Tempest* his words fell right in step with his regular touring group's take on roadhouse blues, Country swing and atavistic boogie modes. As ever, it was the voice that kept pulling you back in – weary and worn out, but also dirty, low down and sly enough to keep you guessing where these songs were coming from and where they were going. We said: "*Tempest* reveals not only phantoms of Dylan's previous work but also many key preoccupations… a sense of dues paid as a continual creative replenishment, rather than a swansong." (November/345)

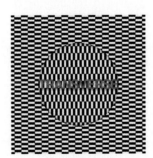

8

Julia Holter
Ekstasis
Rvng Intl

9

Carter Tutti Void
Transverse
Mute

10

Ricardo Villalobos
Dependent And Happy
Perlon

The Californian composer's background is steeped in music theory, classical literature and philosophy – heavyweight influences that made the airy, dreamlike pop miniatures on her second album seem all the more fresh. The title of *Ekstasis* was inspired by Ancient Greek poetry, as was its predecessor *Tragedy*, yet Holter deals not in academic detachment but lo-fi intimacy, realised on bedroom electronics, twinkling keyboards, cello and heartfelt vocal harmonies. We said: "Don't expect ecstasy in a traditionally climactic mode… *Ekstasis* might be full of… undermining moments, but it's free of the knowing kitsch that characterises so much contemporary production." (April/338)

The introduction of a third party into the hermetic duo of Chris & Cosey was first mooted in 2011, when Carter appeared live with London trio Factory Floor and that group's guitarist and vocalist Nik Void then collaborated with the post-Throbbing Gristle duo – an experience Tutti described in *The Wire* 332 as "a joy". This live set, recorded at London's Roundhouse, was a buzzing circuit of energy and synergy, Void and Tutti deconstructing their respective electric guitars in a percussive semaphore of scratch and squeal amid Carter's darkly grooving analogue pulses. We said: "Sonically enthralling… the welcome rarity of a female-dominated electronic noise collaboration can hardly be understated." (April/338)

Ricardo Villalobos's first studio album in nearly a decade, released across no less than five LPs in its vinyl edition, trumpeted his domestic bliss in its title, but family life seemed to have spurred the Minimal Techno producer into ever deeper experiments in sound. A perpetual central pulse was the only fixed reference point as around it sounds morphed like plasticine, voices chattered and swooped, and live percussion drifted through the mix. We said: "This is magic in the truest sense, where sleight of hand makes the inconsequential sublime and vice versa, with its maker's apparent idleness hiding music of ferocious potency." (December/346)

Releases of
the year
11–50

11

Scott Walker
Bish Bosch
4AD

12

Josephine Foster
Blood Rushing
Fire

13

Fushitsusha
Mabushii Itazura Na Inori
Heartfast

14

Keiji Haino/Jim O'Rourke/Oren Ambarchi
Imikuzushi
Black Truffle/Medama

19

Wandelweiser Und So Weiter
Various
Another Timbre

20

Morton Feldman
Crippled Symmetry: At June In Buffalo
Frozen Reeds

21

Richard Skelton
Verse Of Birds
Corbel Stone Press

22

The Bohman Brothers
Back On The Streets
Peripheral Conserve

27

Killer Mike
RAP Music
Williams Street

28

Shackleton
The Drawbar Organ/Music For The Quiet Hour
Woe To The Septic Heart

29

Rhodri Davies
Wound Response
alt.vinyl

30

Ariel Pink's Haunted Graffiti
Mature Themes
4AD

35

Lee Gamble
Diversions 1994–1996
Pan

36

Heatsick
Deviation
Pan

37

Duane Pitre
Feel Free
Important

38

Raime
Quarter Turns Over A Living Line
Blackest Ever Black

43

DJ Rashad
Teklife Vol 1: Welcome To The Chi
Lit City Trax

44

Charles Gayle Trio
Streets
Northern Spy

45

Frank Ocean
Channel Orange
Island/Def Jam

46

Pye Corner Audio
Sleep Games
Ghost Box

15

Death Grips
The Money Store
Epic

16

Emptyset
Medium
Subtext

17

Dean Blunt & Inga Copeland
Black Is Beautiful
Hyperdub

18

Andy Stott
Luxury Problems
Modern Love

23

Kendrick Lamar
good kid, m.A.A.d. city
Top Dawg Entertainment/
Aftermath/Interscope

24

**Michael Pisaro & Toshiya
Tsunoda**
Crosshatches
Ertswhile

25

Bass Clef
Reeling Skullways
Punch Drunk

26

Aaron Dilloway
Modern Jester
Hanson

31

Wadada Leo Smith
Ten Freedom Summers
Cuneiform

32

Thomas Köner
Novaya Zemlya
Touch

33

Annea Lockwood
In Our Name
New World

34

Earth
*Angels Of Darkness, Demons
Of Light II*
Southern Lord

39

Swans
The Seer
Young God

40

**Mark Ernestus presents
Jeri-Jeri with
Mbene Diatta Seck**
Mbeuguel Dafa Nekh
Ndagga

41

Cooly G
Playin' Me
Hyperdub

42

Traxman
Da Mind Of Traxman
Planet Mu

47

Peter Cusack
Sounds From Dangerous Places
ReR Megacorp/Berliner
Künstlerprogramm Des DAAD

48

Pelt
Effigy
MIE Music

49

DVA
Pretty Ugly
Hyperdub

50

**Peter Brötzmann/Masahiko
Satoh/Takeo Moriyama**
Yatagarasu
Not Two

Critics' reflections

Jennifer Lucy Allan

Pros: A tax rebate to spend on records. An incredible 65 track dancehall mix found in a hire car. Getting a shout-out from Joe Bussard (albeit as Jemberser, a particularly baffling misreading of my name). Evensong mass in St Paul's Cathedral. Trying out Sacred Harp singing in a Hampstead Heath Baptist church basement. My first trip to Glastonbury. Going deep reading about and listening to foghorns. Unexpected opera in a pub at 2am. Taking my little sister to see *Watch The Throne* and her knowing all the words. Michael Pisaro and Toshiya Tsunoda's *Crosshatches* while watching YouTube videos of dust storms. London stepping up to reverse the disaster that was Bloc. Eating oysters at Off The Page in Whitstable. Music channels in foreign hotel rooms (especially the soothing CGI of Thai Buddhism TV in an apartment in Krakow). Heatwave Soundcloud mixes. Dallas police radio (hat-tip Derek Walmsley). Excessive rotations of 2NE1's "I Am The Best", Sean Paul, a 12 minute extended Tom Moulton mix of "Don't Leave Me This Way", night after night sat on a stoop listening to Beefheart's *Shiny Beast*. Also: Åke Hodell, Alice Coltrane's devotional cassettes, The Necessaries, old Sähkö 12"s, Ike Yard, Funkinevil, and more recently Erkki Kurenniemi. Getting lost in the digital tunnel network of Laurie Spiegel's handbuilt HTML website. Lots of live music that I felt as much as heard. Highlights: William Basinski, Factory Floor in London's Tate Tanks, two hours of Fushitsusha at Unsound, Krakow, extended sets by CC Hennix, Grouper and Hieroglyphic Being, The Congos harmonising live.

Cons: Paying rent in London; a death.

Mike Barnes

This year's much discussed topic has been the lack of recognisable movements or scenes in music – the sort that journalists love to name. How do you even try to define the zeitgeist now? Only a few years ago it was possible to identify successions of waves, but now it's all constantly choppy waters, riptides, vortices and the odd obscure rockpool to poke about in. I can't decide whether this is a pro or a con.

A major journalistic con is the decline of print publishing, the uncertainty as to what will replace it and then figuring out how that can generate revenue. If the future is digital, many publications seem to be walking into it most uncertainly. Personally speaking, the biggest con was the physically and mentally exhausting task of clearing out my parents' house in Hampshire, the family home for more than three decades, virtually singlehandedly.

Pros are pretty much the same as they were in 2011 and probably will be in 2013: a book deal looks imminent; the long-running musical project is near completion; still playing with the fuzz organ ensemble Pimmel. My top personal pro was finding an old friend on Facebook who I thought had committed suicide about 25 years ago – a huge but pleasant shock. In second place was meeting Scott Walker and getting him to autograph my vinyl copy of *The Drift* with a silver pen, albeit in a barely decipherable scrawl. The beacon of fandom burns brightly.

Dan Barrow

A weird year. I survived the first anniversary of moving to London and received my Masters degree, but all this seems rather peripheral to the unencompassable turmoil of culture in the long wake of the crisis: too vast, too wracked by contradiction, by the hunger for new forms of cultural struggle, for even the most clued up culture columnists to grasp. Or at least to think usefully or interestingly about, much less to understand it in relation to lived experience – in my case, the usual postgraduate comedy of heightened aspirations and dwindling prospects, of high theory, heavy drinking, fleeting conversation and dragging unemployment. (File under both Pro and Con.) The more frustrating half of the puzzle is that culture looks largely the same as it did at the end of 2011 – some very good albums aside.

There were a whole bunch of melancholy positives. Handily, in a year when I was writing obsessively about Chris Marker, non-fiction film seemed to undergo a renaissance, with the likes of *Nostalgia For The Light*, *All Divided Selves*, *The Nine Muses*, *Patience (After Sebald)* and Ben Rivers's quiet, rapturous *Two Years At Sea*. (Pity Marker had to die in the middle of my dissertation.) *Tabu* won the prize for Best Soundtrack Use of The Ronettes, and Steve McQueen's *Shame* the prize for Best Ass Shots. There was Marker's *Silent Movie* at Louise Blouin Foundation and Ed Atkins's *Us Talk Dead Love* at the Chisenhale. Summer nights of "sounds and sweet airs": Roly Porter and Bill Kouligas in Peckham, Charalambides, Astral Social Club and AMM (John Tilbury banging the piano lid) at Cafe Oto, the John Cage centenary Prom, Bass Clef at the Bishopsgate Institute. Readings by Carol Watts, Allen Fisher, Sean Bonney, Keston Sutherland and Fabian Macpherson. Here's hoping 2013 brings more of it all: more smarts and strength and mutability and severity and kindness; because boy do we need it.

Robert Barry

Highs: New films from Béla Tarr, Rian Johnson, David Cronenberg, Athena Rachel Tsangari and Michael Haneke; Haneke's production of *Don Giovanni* at Opéra de Paris and Heiner Goebbels's 'spectacle musicale' *When The Mountain Changed Its Clothing* with the Vocal Theater Carmina Slovenica; exhibitions by Sanja Ivekovic at MUDAM in Luxembourg, Cécile Bart at MAMCO, Geneva, and Laurent Grasso at Jeu de Paume in Paris; new books by Jonathan Sterne, Owen Hatherley and Douglas Murphy; concerts by Terry Riley (with Gyan Riley and Tracy Silverman) in Arles and by Pierre Henry in Paris; Raster-Noton anniversary concerts in Paris and L'Audible Festival in Bagnolet. But mostly a year of old things – visiting public libraries and revival cinemas to fill some gaps in my familiarity with the films of Lubitsch, Browning, Lang and Lupino – plus, the slow improvement in my French language skills.

Lows: An execrable remake of *Total Recall* by Len Wiseman and a disappointing new release from Terence Davies; so many projects I'm working on myself and still haven't finished; dealing with impossible bureaucrats in two countries; the horror and misery of finding out Marine Le Pen had won nearly 20 per cent of the vote in the French presidential elections.

Andy Battaglia

Another year of too many people duped by doom and too few ready to reconcile. Good music and fruitful sounds, though, in all the cross-cultural forms they deigned to take. Pros: The further consecration of psychoacoustics via Florian Hecker, Ben Vida et al. Fertile ground for new song forms tilled by Laurel Halo. Hype Williams's mercilessly signal-scrambling show. Philip Glass working like mad in New York

City (especially *Music In Twelve Parts* in full at Park Avenue Armory). Shackleton casting out Ray Manzarek-like synth lines live. The human foibles at play in the 1870s–1940s primary source anthology *Music, Sound, And Technology In America* (so much better than the hamfisted title).

Cons: The confounding continued inexistence of a digital music interface more spatial and layered than iTunes. Creeping acquiescence of the term EDM. Movies, en masse, still not yet wise enough to go music-less like Hitchcock's *The Birds*. Fleetingness of any/all kinds, all the more...

Clive Bell

Dexter Fletcher's London gangster flick *Wild Bill* deployed "The Watershed" by Mark Hollis at a crucial moment of high emotion, sending me back to Hollis and Talk Talk. *Position Among The Stars* is a stunning documentary that vividly sets you down in the slums of Jakarta. Improvisation: Dimitra Lazaridou-Chatzigoga's zither is a fresh voice, vinegary and vital. In June Tom Chant played eloquently on Walter Benjamin's old tenor sax alongside Angharad Davies, John Edwards and Benedict Drew at Soundfjord's V22 space. Other memorable concerts: Joe McPhee and Chris Corsano at Cafe Oto, and Oren Ambarchi twice, engaging with Charlemagne Palestine and John Tilbury. Likewise Josephine Foster twice, once jamming with Michael Hurley. Cafe Oto has me on a short leash at the moment; on a rare occasion when I dragged myself away – to a Club Integral event in Kennington – I marvelled at Lepke B's hilarious highwire act, nothing but a DJ's CD deck between him and the void.

Dashed expectations: the follow-up to her fabulous *Hour Logic*, Laurel Halo's *Quarantine* is a joyless experience, and someone forgot the drums. Hallo? Meanwhile, I'm reading John Dower's *Embracing Defeat*, a fascinating and detailed look at the US occupation of Japan. In 1946, militaristic songs were suddenly replaced by upbeat ditties like the theme of Tadaichi Hirakawa's let's-learn-English radio show: *"Come, come, everybody/How do you do, and how are you? Won't you have some candy/One and two and three, four, five."*

Britt Brown

For all the Mayan hype, 2012 was pretty underwhelming. It felt like a year too distracted by its own expectations of itself to really commit to something. Culturally, the steady encroachment of Cyberdyne Systems-style digital assimilation progressed by leaps and bounds (it's revealing that America was stirred to more of a frenzy by the iPhone 5 than the presidential election). YouTube views and Facebook neuroses continued to climb while local shows hit new lows in terms of attendance and the youth public's overall giving-a-shit-ness. Face to face contact is fast becoming the new California ghost town. In contrast, Britain and the rest of Europe's niche music worlds seem more questing and engaged than ever (inasmuch as a three week tour affords you a legitimate perspective on what a city is actually like). Late nights in Berlin, Bristol, Madrid, Glasgow, Lisbon and Amsterdam were all rich with vibrant and exhilarated artists, producers, promoters, strangers. Enthused CD-R/flash drive traders gifted us hours of hazy, unironic, innervision explorations of various electronic modes and moods (Acid, House, unclassifiable, and beyond). Staying stoked is half the battle, and then some: protect yr passion.

Out with the apocalypse, and in with the post-apocalypse. That's what we've all been waiting for anyway.

Nathan Budzinski
Pros: SoundFjord's performance series during the V22 Summer Club provided the greatest listening experience of my year: during Stephen Cornford, Patrick Farmer, Dominic Lash and Lee Patterson's two and a half hour performance that wandered through the dynamics of a vast, empty factory space in South London, I realised that I'd never again be able to listen to most MP3s through earbud headphones without feeling a bit disappointed. London gallery Cell Project Space's CyCLORAMA series captured the current video installation zeitgeist well, especially installments by Laura Buckley, Benedict Drew and Mark Aerial Waller. A retrospective at Oslo's OCA of the work of film maker Peter Watkins was also a highlight. Some consistently rich online offerings from the file sharing wiki Monoskop, with their regular updates of texts on digital culture and Eastern European sound arts proving as engaging as they are questionable in terms of copyright. Online arts magazine *Triple Canopy* published top quality (and original) articles, the standout being Alix Rule & David Levine's "International Art English", a history of the rise of art press-release jargon. Peter Strickland's film *Berberian Sound Studio*, a take on Italian giallo and the unfurling psychosis of synced sound, fulfilled a sonic/cinematic desire that's been dormant since seeing Coppola's *The Conversation*. Following the theme of (mostly) pleasurable hallucination through over-attention, a rainy summer week in Scotland rummaging through Stirling University's John Grierson archive revealed some treasures about the documentary film maker and theorist.

Cons: Empire, illness, distance, semicolons, apps that don't work.

Nick Cain
12 things from 2012, in alphabetical order: Edition Filmmuseum's *Die "Oberhausener"* and James Benning collections; a Hollis Frampton *Odyssey*; archival Godard (and related): *Ici Et Ailleurs/Numero Deux* on DVD, *Introduction To A True History Of Cinema And Television*, *Three Popular Films By Jean-Pierre Gorin*; Lars Iyer *Dogma*; Patrick Keiller *The Robinson Institute* at Tate Britain; just about everything published by NYRB Classics, but especially: Robert Walser *Berlin Stories*; Thomas Browne *Religio Medici*; Pauline Oliveros *Reverberations*; Luther Price screening at LUX/ICA Biennial of Moving Images, London; David Rosenboom *Roundup*; Paul Sharits *Shutter Interface*, JJ Murphy *Print Generation* and CC Hennix & The Chora(s)san Time Court Mirage at Sonic Acts XIV; slow cinema, past and present: *The Theo Angelopoulos Collection Volumes 1–3*, *Aurora*, *Once Upon A Time In Anatolia*, *The Turin Horse* (and László Krasznahorkai's *Satantango* finally in English translation); Aldo Tambellini *Cathodic Works 1966–1976*.

Daniela Cascella
Pros: Mostly a year of reading. I've been surprised by these blogs: Salomé Voegelin's *SoundWords* pushes the boundaries of listening and writing; the constant sense of discovery and wonder in Steve Roden's *Airform Archives*; Cheryl Tipp's revealing series of posts on wildlife sound recordings for *The Field Reporter*. Printed matter: *Her Not All Her*, where Elfriede Jelinek inhabits the space of Robert Walser; the wit and subtle disquiet in Enrique Vila-Matas's *Dublinesque*; the wealth of documents uncovered and connected by Luciano Chessa in his book *Luigi Russolo*; the mutual and paradoxical longing for sound and text in Craig Dworkin's *Handbook Of Protocols For Literary Listening*. A study in darkness: TV series *The Bridge*. A study in 21st century sublime: *Prometheus* on the IMAX screen.

Live: David Toop challenging media and memory at the Ephemeral Sustainability conference in Bergen; Lee Patterson/Patrick Farmer/Stephen Cornford sounding the V22 Biscuit Factory; Valerio Tricoli's haunted tape loops and terminal voice at Cafe Oto and in my brain; Pauline Oliveros speaking and performing a lifetime of listening at Her Noise. Shows: Signe Lidén's mesmerizing installation *Under* at LAK. Copenhagen. Edvard Munch and his ghosts in London and Oslo.

It was exciting to see my first book in English, *En Abîme*, published by Zero Books. I was surprised to find a voice and a space to explore while reading in front of audiences.

Cons: to encounter categories such as sound art, music and archive as self-confined notions. To see my homeland Italy drifting; but the UK, where I now live, is not much better off.

Philip Clark
Pros: I loved the Olympic Games, not for the tedious bullshit of the sport or opening ceremony but because minds were focused on the irreversible damage being done to London by Seb Coe suits everywhere. At Cafe Oto, Iain Sinclair and Anna Minton gave a passionate account of London disappearing behind gated communities and chain coffee blandness. Otherwise this year has been viewed through the prism of witnessing my heroic mother recover from serious illness; music and reading slotted in around the worry and travel up north to see her. Duke Ellington's *Second Sacred Concert* has been the consoling soundtrack to this difficult time. Seeing The Vienna Philharmonic play Webern under Simon Rattle completely changed my view of the composer; going to John Cage's old New York apartment and recording sounds around his neighbourhood was, I found, the best way to come to an appreciation of his music.

Cons: Did I mention the Olympic Games? Meanwhile the New Music scandal of 2012 was composer Colin Matthews's attempt to fix it so that all public funding filtered through the UK's Sound And Music organisation went to composers engaged in 'manuscript paper' composition. Improvisors, sound artists, et al are not welcome here. Lowdown, self-serving behaviour. RIP a string of great people: Lol Coxhill, David S Ware, Borah Bergmann, Elliott Carter, Hans Werner Henze, Clive Dunn.

Mark Fisher
In *The Wire* this time last year, I expressed high hopes for 2012. It turned out to be largely a disaster. In the UK, neither the Queen's Diamond Jubilee nor the Olympics provoked any serious discontent: much of mainstream culture was like 1977 without The Sex Pistols, a massive carnival of reaction. For me personally, the year has been shadowed by health problems, so that the precariousness of my work situation was reinforced by a sense of the precariousness of the body. Work and health stress meant that I tuned out for much of 2012, but fortunately I tuned back in for a remarkable series of albums. These were records one could live inside, records that disclosed a world: Pye Corner Audio's subtly unsettling *Sleep Games* – Ghost Box asked me to work up some concepts for its sleeve: a gratifyingly easy task, since the album was both one of the label's strongest releases to date, and a real break from everything else GB have put out; Raime's *Quarter Turn Over A Living Line*, in which they discovered a previously unexplored space between Swans/Sunn O)))/Ben Frost doomcore and post-dance music; eMMplex's *Izod Days*, wherein Baron Mordant finally gave full rein to his Stanley Unwin-meets-Raymond Roussel nonsense; Ricardo Villalobos's *Dependent And Happy*, more deliciously queasy time dilation and melting angles from the master of digital psychedelia; and Vindicatrix's *Mengamuk*, a masterpiece of controlled derangement, the high angst of art pop meeting 21st century body music. In my piece for *The Wire*'s 2011 Rewind issue, I invoked David Peace. The Jimmy Savile scandal showed that reality and Peace's novels are converging ever closer. Along with the Hillsborough enquiry, the Savile scandal shows that the crisis of legitimacy that erupted in 2011 (but which was contained throughout much of 2012) is exploding again, with David Cameron in the role of janitor for the ruling class, running around trying to clear up the excrement and excesses of past cover-ups, conspiracies and abuses. 2013 sounds like an impossible date, the year after the end of history, but perhaps it will be the year when the 21st century finally starts.

Phil Freeman
I think my personal tastes got more conservative in 2012. The jazz I liked best was more melodic and swinging; the Metal I liked had choruses and comprehensible vocals; work intended primarily to shock or provoke inspired only scorn and ridicule. A lot of artists who meant a great deal to me died, including guitarist Pete Cosey, author Harry Crews, Stax Records bassist Donald 'Duck' Dunn, Deep Purple organist Jon Lord and of course saxophonist David S Ware. Not only did I love David's work, I also knew him personally.

Maybe I was hit by too much music for any of it to have a serious impact. Even albums that amazed me on the first few listens were shunted aside by the avalanche of things that needed to be heard. And when too many crap albums arrived in a row, I sought shelter in 1970s hard rock or 60s hard bop – auditory comfort food, unchallenging and guaranteed to please. I suspect this worrisome development may be an inescapable consequence of nearly two decades spent as a critic – call it heard it all disease. But I'm confident that I'll overcome it; I'm forever optimistic that the next thing I hear will be great and get me jabbering enthusiastically on Twitter and Facebook – and *The Wire* editors' inboxes . So onward to 2013!

Louise Gray
Pros and cons: I was thrilled that artist/composer Hanne Darboven finally got her first UK solo show (even if she died in 2009), and all credit to Camden Arts Centre for delivering it. Darboven is feted chiefly for her visual work, much of which has a lesser known musical corollary, and CAC honoured this in full. Music (from Jocelyn Pook) and action in Akram Khan's solo show *DESH* at Sadler's Wells was overwhelmingly beautiful; working with Linder Sterling after commissioning her *Stringed Figure (Octobass For The 21st Century)* for Latitude Contemporary Art in the summer was riotously inspiring; Southbank Centre's inventive Conlon Nancarrow season was excellent; Matthew Akers's Marina Abramovic documentary, *The Artist Is Present*, was stunning. Her Noise's Feminisms And The Sonic season at Tate Modern – complete with Pauline Oliveros – stimulated more circuits than I can count and, in pursuit of a new project, it's been great starting a conversation with Oliveros and other composers. Just sorry to have missed Victor Gama's Instrumentos presentation at the Royal Opera House, and the 25th anniversary of Shoom, where, all those years ago, I spent many dissolute hours...

Adam Harper
This year felt particularly prolific for musical experiences, with the drying wells of some of my preferred areas forcing me into new territories and contexts. My main change of habitat (first aural, then literal) was to America, where lively art pop networks and fresh dance and hiphop sounds are putting the continued archive fever of much UK electronic music to shame. Particularly heartening was the glittering (if often sarcastic) return of hi-fi, exiling all that tragic, crumbling nostalgia back to yesteryear: the New Weird finally trumping the Old Weird. Burrowing ever deeper into the web-friendly US underground, I had a summer romance with Bandcamp, where thousands of musicians are streaming and selling their work direct to listeners, leaving me confident about the current and future state of music (at least until it sells out to become the new Facebook). Meanwhile my research took me deep into the Library of Congress, where I pored over 1980s cassette culture magazines and listened to an incredible live bootleg of Daniel Johnston circa 1990. But it was an unforgettable year for live music: folk and wistful pop in the nooks and crannies of Tallinn, Cage's *Freeman Etudes* and a collaborative sound space in Darmstadt, Boredoms, Earth and Jeff Mangum at All Tomorrow's Parties, How To Dress Well in Washington DC, and wandering through newfangled audio-visual exploration environments like Proteus and Exo. The high point was fulfilling a very old ambition to see Philip Glass's opera *Einstein On The Beach*, which finally reached London and had me transfixed for five short hours.

Jim Haynes
Small Cruel Party. The pseudonym of former Seattle-ite Key Ransome neatly sums up a stubborn trend in the human condition. His sound constructions, frenetically built during a six or seven year period around the millennial turn, conjure an intense minimalism through aggregate textures and tones that refused to blink in their thousand yard stare. 2012 witnessed a major retrospective of Small Cruel Party's work, thanks to Harbinger Sound; and it's one that will stay on the stereo for years to come. Other major contenders for my limited amounts of time included Thomas Köner's jawdroppingly glacial *Novaya Zemlya*, the sombre impressionism of Je Suis Le Petit Chevalier's *Age Of Wonder*, Death And Vanilla's bubblegum retro-futurism, and the fifth opus from KTL. The witching sounds of Demdike Stare and Aluk Todolo provided a fascinating connection between the divergent specialists of the dark arts. The San Francisco Bay Area played host to far too many great performances to attend, but the performers that struck me included Relay For Death, Ashley Belouin & Ben Bracken, Machine Shop, Ensemble

Economique and Sudden Infant. On a personal note, 2012 found me happily relocating to the suburbs, with San Francisco pricing out everyone except for Twitter and Facebook executives; and I spent a month with seven other immensely talented people at the Djerassi Artists Residency Program after far too much time neglecting my own art. I know I'll be sifting through the psychological and psychic artefacts of this experience for quite a while, but the immediate outcome is an effluence of new material amounting to two, possibly three albums and a completed short film. I'm sorry.

Richard Henderson
Pro: Neil Young reunited with Crazy Horse and made *Psychedelic Pill*.

Con: Neil Young reunited with Crazy Horse and made *Americana*.

Hua Hsu
Pros/Cons: I moved into a smaller apartment last winter so I spent much of the past year revisiting my record collection, contemplating a possession-free existence, deciding on the opposite, selling off chaff and reacquiring all the bits I've lost along the way ("Dress Code (Remix)"). The new music that stood out really stood out: Andy Stott, Burial, half of Frak's *Muzika Electronic*, Fort Romeau and SFX Acid's jack moves, the return of El-P, Killer Mike and The Coup, transcendent moments/verses from Trimbal, 2Chainz, Gunplay, A$AP Rocky. The lo-fi Smith & Mighty reissue. Action Bronson and Riff Raff's "Bird On A Wire"; BJ The Chicago Kid & Kendrick's "His Pain"; the casual time travel of Frank Ocean's "Pyramids"; every Jamie xx mix I could find; Kendrick Lamar's world. Elsewhere: *Get A Life* DVDs (without laugh track), Jay-Z's precedent, David Axelrod LPs in a hurricane, *Room 237* (still never seen *The Shining*, though). A vibraphonist playing The Chi-Lites as she walked down the aisle, "All My Friends" blaring as we neared midnight.

Cons: RIP Adam Yauch, among others. Election year and another reminder that certain among us believe more in Super PACS than climate change. The second 'once every hundred years' storm in two years. As time passes, that which we once held sacred begins to seem more utopian and foolish than ever, whether it's politics or websites run by hardcore rap fanatics. But what's troubling me is the desire to leave that spirit as bygone, to keep fantasy safely in the past, to never judge. And then a student born in the mid-1990s sneers to the rest of class, "I listen to dubstep – but not the really commercial dubstep you probably know", and order is restored.

Sophia Ignatidou
Pros: *The Wire*'s Off The Page afterparties (whatever happened in Whitstable stays in Whitstable). Unsound's organising team who made us feel so at home, plus Holly Herndon and Mala In Cuba's amazing live sets. Squarepusher's *Ufabulum* show at Sonar, evoking early Warp Records memories. *The Wire* Salon with Robert Wyatt reminded me how much music can mean to people, creators and audience alike. I also enjoyed (albeit belatedly) Simon Reynolds's *Bring The Noise*, where I came across some of the funniest, most poignant and challenging pieces of music journalism. I was relieved to see international media (*The Guardian*, *New York Times*, BBC) holding the Greek corrupt elite, which ultimately is to blame for the crisis Europe is facing, to account.

Cons: Talking to or reading journalists and writers disillusioned by the scarcity of ingenuity in most contemporary electronic music and realising I can't really blame them. GEMA's legislative plans to squeeze the German club scene and subsequently the artists that base their existence on those venues. Bloc as the worst festival experience of recent years. A growing sense of silent despair for all the Greeks who fell victim to their political system's collapse, and exasperation for all the those who contributed to or didn't do anything to stop it.

Matt Ingram
Pros: Critical Beats Panel, Los Angeles in March; DJing for Ike Yard; Woebot live at the Barbican. R Stevie Moore, Chairlift and Metronomy at Field Day, IX Tab/Hacker Farm/ Kemper Norton in Somerset, Werner Herzog speaking at Curzon Soho, Bradley Wiggins Tour De France, trampoline at the Olympics, The Muppets, Samsara, 70s soul, old Detroit Techno, The Kinks, Anthony Powell *A Dance To The Music Of Time*, Lawrence James *The Rise And Fall Of The British Empire*.

Cons: Car drivers' irrational anger towards cyclists. Abusive labour relations.

David Keenan
Pros: 2012 was dominated by New Zealand, both musically, with an avalanche of archival releases, and personally, when I finally visited both islands in October. Too many highlights to list from our stay but a night spinning rare NZ sides with Bruce Russell and Kate McRae, breakfast with Michael Morley and family, a night at The Flying Fox, seeing amazing shows from Omit, Greg Malcolm & Chris O'Connor, Rosy Parlane, Antony Milton, Eye, Roy Montgomery and Heather Leigh's earth-quaking duo with Robbie Yeats from The Dead C, wild camping in the depths of the wilderness, sampling so many great new NZ microbrews (Parrot Dog and Garage Project were the pick of the bunch) and so much great food, reading and talking at the Russian Frost Farmers art space in Wellington, seeing the amazing work that NZ's Audio Foundation are doing, all contributed to making it the trip of a lifetime. Back home the soundtrack was heavy on the NZ reissues, especially the Pin Group retrospective on Flying Nun, which might be my single most played release of the year, alongside Bruce Russell's expertly compiled *Time To Go* compilation, Brian Crook's *Bathysphere*, Gate's *The Dew Line*, the Bill Direen EPs on Unwucht and the Max Block LP on Siltbreeze. Also very happy to see the reissue of A To Austr's masterful *Musics From Holyground* LP, long a desert island dream, as well as heavy psych reissues from Doug Jerebine, Wicked Lady, Misty Hush Revival, Mad River and Crystalline. Too many great releases from the revitalised Australian underground to even list. Very productive year for writing, with two novels finally completed, *The Comfort Of Women* and *The Tomb Of The Song*, the first already with a publisher, and partway through a third, *Adieu To All Judges And Juries*. Also very excited to finally get started on the music book I'm co-writing with John Olson, *Life Is A Rip-Off*, due late 2013. Read a ton this year, particular standouts: finally tackled William H Gass's monumental *The Tunnel*, fell completely under the spell of Elliot R Wolfson, especially *A Dream Interpreted Within A Dream*, returned to longterm romances with Lester Bangs (finally found copies of all those live Van Morrison concerts he talked about), Rilke, Cendrars, Melville and Lowry, loved Phil Baker's Austin Osman Spare biography (and his talk to tie in with the excellent Spare exhibition at the Hidden Noise in Glasgow), Steve Moore's *Somnium*, Peter Cole's *The Dream Of The Poem* collection, Timothy Snyder's *Bloodlands*, Joseph Roth's *The Radetzky March*, Walker Hamilton's *All The Little Animals*, Kluge & Richter's *December*, Breton's *Arcanum 17* plus novels by Vila-Matas (especially *Bartleby & Co*), Molina, Aira, Chejfec. The return of Fushitsusha felt fairly triumphant, can't stop spinning the Harry Pussy and Shadow Ring collections, loved Dylan's *Tempest* – has his voice ever sounded better? Penultimate Press's collection of works by Jacques Brodier may well be my last minute album of the year. Richard Youngs's live shows continue to provide some of the most gripping, challenging and uncomfortable gig going experiences. A memorable night with Heather Leigh and Keiji Haino at Cafe Oto. Lon Milo Duquette's talk and solo performance in Glasgow *was* the dharma. But truly 2012 was the year that life outstripped art and the most memorable and affecting experiences went beyond art's remit; the odd conflict of feelings while watching the exactingly controlled demolition of the first of the Red Road Flats in Glasgow; an incredible night of Mixed Martial Arts at the city's QMU presented by The Edge gym; the thrill and challenge of sparring every week; the occult Barbie-isation of Valeria Lukyanova; RAF Leuchars's Diamond Jubilee Airshow; turning up on the wrong night for a Neoist event in Glasgow in the company of Mark Pilkington and Rose Kallal and having the most profound 'Neoist' experience of all due to our heightened expectations; all these things made art seem somehow less than life. But spending a few days in the company of Peter Brötzmann in Wuppertal and my subsequent experiences in New Zealand did much to restore my faith.

Cons: The passing of David S Ware and Lina Romay.

Rahma Khazam
Cons: Sound art exhibitions that reiterate the sonic status quo, a prime culprit being Sound Art. Sound As A Medium Of Art at ZKM Karlsruhe. This mammoth nine month exhibition claims to present for the first time the development of sound art in the 21st century, but in practice does little more than lump together the usual 20th century suspects, from Bernhard Leitner to Maryanne Amacher and La Monte Young. Important as their contribution is, the development of sound has gone beyond the point where it's enough to merely go back over familiar ground, without acknowledging the new territories being explored by today's generation of sound artists. No less disturbing is the playful, hands on approach to sound running through many of the works — sound art can have a critical and analytical content to it, but these aspects were sidelined.

Pros: Sound related exhibitions that do investigate more thought-provoking orientations, among them Sounds Like Silence at Dortmunder U. This show analyses the continuing resonance of John Cage's *4'33"* through the work of Manon de Boer, Pierre Huyghe, Jens Brand and others, exploring our desire for silence and how much of it we can actually cope with.

A final pro, in a very different vein: the new version of Gavin Bryars's *The Sinking Of The Titanic* — masterfully performed in Paris by The Gavin Bryars Ensemble and Philip Jeck to the accompaniment of Bill Morrison and Laurie Olinder's mesmerizing images. 100 years after the shipwreck of the spendthrift luxury liner — a symbol, if ever there was one, of man's desire to subdue and humiliate nature — and 40 years after the premiere of the original version, Bryars's piece remains as haunting and relevant as ever.

Stewart Lee
TV: *Morse Year Zero* in ITV's Endeavour. BBC's *Sherlock Holmes*, *Call The Midwife*, *Hollow Crown*, *She Wolves*, *Vikings* and *Upstairs Downstairs*. E4's *Cardinal Burns*, C4's Grayson Perry's *All In The Best Possible Taste*, Sky's *Touch Of Cloth*. Books: David Rees's *How To Sharpen Pencils* (book of the century so far), Penguin's new edition of Arthur Machen's *White People*, Keith Lowe's *Savage Continent*, *You Are Nothing*, a deliberately unreliable history of obscure 90s comedy by Robert Wringham, Julian Cope's *Copendium*, Sean Howe's *Marvel Comics The Untold Story*. Film: *Troll Hunter*, *The Artist*, *Avengers Assemble*, *Looper*, and Andrew Kötting's comically and calmly meditative *Swandown*, which I was in for five minutes. Gigs: Giant Sand's Howe Gelb and pop's KT Tunstall together and unannounced in a Stoke Newington cafe, Han Bennink solo at Bishopsgate Festival, Jane Bom Bane's harmonium and bespoke hats mash-up on the Edinburgh Free Fringe, Kunt & The Gang's scatological Depeche Mode grooves, The Caesareans acoustic at a birthday party, Fushitsusha transcending time and space at St John's Church Hackney, Patti Smith shaming everyone in Bethnal Green. Theatre/comedy: Dublin Gate's *Watt* at the Edinburgh International Festival, Teatr Biuro Podróży's satirical stiltwalking sci-fi space rock opera *Planet Lem*, Jeff Achtem's Beefheartian kids' puppet show *Swamp Juice*. Bad thing: Paddy Power desecrating the Uffington White Horse. Good thing: Obama, relatively speaking.

Dave Mandl
Being a parent continues to make it hard for me to get out to gigs, but I did manage to see some great ones this year, including the Touch.30 festival and SEM Ensemble, both at Issue Project Room, Shelley Hirsch and Simon Ho at Roulette, Hallock Hill in a tiny restaurant in Brooklyn (a live WFMU broadcast), and, during a trip to my spiritual home of London, Thomas Ankersmit and Helm at Cafe Oto. Also in London I was honoured to do a radio show at Resonance FM with my pals Clive Graham (Paradigm Discs) and Lepke Buchwalter. Among the embarrassingly few films I saw in 2012, two of the best were Antonioni's visually breathtaking *Red Desert*, and *The Good, The Bad And The Ugly*, which I never tire of, on Film Forum's big screen. By far the best kids' film I saw was the wonderful French animated feature *A Cat In Paris*. I was able to devote large chunks of time to one of my great creative passions: exploring and photographing far-flung, derelict industrial neighbourhoods in my native Brooklyn. Quitting my gruelling day job meant finally being able to write more or less full time. Towards the end of the year, Hurricane Sandy devastated entire neighbourhoods in NYC, but also triggered a massive self-organised recovery effort that was as heartening as Sandy was destructive.

Marc Masters
I'll remember 2012 mostly for new perspectives on drone based music. Motion Sickness Of Time Travel, High Aura'd, Tidal, Derek Rogers, Duane Pitre, Rambutan, Mike Shiflet, Nicholas Szczepanik, Kyle Bobby Dunn, Jazzfinger, Derek Rogers, Jason Urick and many more

pointed towards new ways of making and thinking about drone, and labels like Type, Spectrum Spools, Hooker Vision, Avant Archive, Desire Path, Hands In The Dark, Under The Spire, Students Of Decay and Tape Drift helped gather it all into an unspoken movement. Especially impressive is Ohio distributor Experimedia, a tireless champion of all these artists and, I hope, a symbol of people buying, selling and creating forward-thinking drone into the future. On the other end of history, 2012 was a great year for archival releases – Can, John Fahey, Pauline Oliveros, Zs – but the best nostalgia trip was Deathbomb Arc's three disc retrospective of San Francisco group Rrope, a missing link of 1990s weirdo indie rock whose brand of catchy dissonance and sly humour seems rather scarce today.

Peter Meanwell
Highlights: Hearing the immensity of Stockhausen's musical vision unfold under the direction of Graham Vick in a Birmingham industrial estate. Suffering information overload at dOCUMENTA (13) only to have it all blown away by the fear and exploration of a magical five minutes in the dark courtesy of Tino Sehgal. Spending a fascinating morning with Christian Wolff, only to discover that the one way to really understand Cage is to perform him, and getting that chance at Cafe Oto with the Langham Research Centre. Hearing Patti Smith recollect life with Robert Mapplethorpe in the drizzle at End Of The Road Festival. Musical friends in Mali coming to no harm. Amalia Pica at Chisenhale. Eavesdropping on people along the River Thames. Having my ears nearly blown off by Jin Sangtae and a car horn at Lowrise in Seoul, and then recovering eating pork and kimchi with Otomo Yoshihide and Ryu Hankil. Losing myself in the Maryanne Amacher *City-Links* recordings at DAAD, Berlin. Finally finishing the breakfast book. Remembering meeting Elliott Carter. Wandering through House Esters and Lange in Krefeld and feeling deeply envious of the Bauhaus. Playing old time tunes with Tom Paley in my local. Camping the night inside Objectif Exhibitions, Antwerp.

Bill Meyer
Here in the USA, this has been a year when the nauseating trends that elevate ignorance and selfishness as virtues, and codify brute repression at home and abroad, have ramped up. How does an administration that vigorously defends indefinite detention without due process get away with being perceived as the progressive option? Pros: The music of Christoph Heemann, Vanessa Rossetto, and Michael Pisaro & Toshiya Tsunoda, which reconciles performed and collected sounds in a way that posits self-aware harmony with the world at large; Canary Records' collections of 78s from the Anatolian Diaspora, the source of some marvellous music made by people surviving and creating while living under extremely heavy manners; and Neil Young and Crazy Horse ride again. Cons: The passings of David S Ware, John Tchicai, Ted Curson and too many others; Ansar Dine's effort to ban music in Mali; and no-nothing-ism everywhere.

Frances Morgan
When I started at *The Wire* in February I was looking forward to working with the magazine's writers, many of whom I'd read and admired for years. They haven't disappointed – and, when I broke my right hand six weeks into the job, made a frustrating time easier with kind emails and phone calls, and good copy. Overseas festivals were memorable for the sounds on the peripheries as well as the main stages – hearing rare 1960s and 70s works from Stockholm's EMS at Perspectives in Västerås, Sweden, and getting caught up in the pots and pans soundscape of a student protest in Montreal, where I was interviewing Keith Fullerton Whitman and A Guy Called Gerald for Mutek. Live highlights included Roscoe Mitchell with John Edwards and the sadly missed Tony Marsh at Cafe Oto; a performance of Pauline Oliveros's *To Valerie Solanas And Marilyn Monroe In Recognition Of Their Desperation* at Her Noise at the Tate Modern; Black Twig Pickers at a bluegrass pub in Leyton; Pelt at Newcastle's Tusk Festival; Mark Fell's snd reconfiguring a dancefloor; Robin Fox's lasers; and Rob Lowe aka Lichens' celestial modular synth jams. But gig of the year was a chance encounter in St Bavo's Cathedral in Ghent, where I happened to arrive in the middle of an organ festival. As a Bach cantata thundered around the medieval building, I noticed flutterings in my peripheral vision. Although there are theories (as instrument builder Sam Underwood would inform me at Supersonic festival) about church organs' infrasonics prompting divine visions, in this case the cathedral had a very real bat population, whose low-flying antics grew bolder in almost inverse relation to the solemn music. A few weeks previously I'd been very excited to interview computer music pioneer Laurie Spiegel for a feature around the reissue of her *Expanding Universe* and thoughts of human/machine interaction, animals and Baroque counterpoint were much in my mind, so it was an evening of happy and unexpected synchronicity.

Brian Morton
Best musical moment of the year was Tony Bevan blowing bass saxophone in our old byre, to an audience of bemused but impressed locals. Theo Bleckmann was another B who got an A for going 'Bush'. In the cause of thematic consistency, tried to make a switch from E flat to B flat but it felt all wrong; too much iron round the neck. Apart from that, the year was a clusterfuck of hospital visits, earth moving, too much work and not enough 'work', obits and no-shows. Can't get any further west or more remote now. Mobile signals and British/Scottish politics blah don't reach out here.

Joe Muggs
Pros: I've been working hands on with music – DJing, label managing, scouting – far more this year and it's been a joy, primarily for two reasons. 1) Despite the supposed decline of the recorded music industry, I see creative musicians falling in love with the recording and manipulation of sound as never before, eager to get involved with all the opportunities of the digital and physical worlds (and indeed to dissolve and re-order the boundaries between the two) in order to keep musical production a viable activity and important part of life, and to build and maintain stable subcultural communities. 2) The constant neurosis about genre, which is an occupational hazard for commentators and analysts, melts away when you pay more attention to the practical, social, financial, technological, logistical, chemical nuts and bolts of culture. It is, as they say, what it is. I have also enjoyed experiencing the indestructibility of Grime, participating in the Dimensions festival in Croatia, bringing togeether a cross-generational dance underground, and spending a lot more time with young children, experiencing culture through their eyes and ears.

Cons: Well, the world is pretty screwed, isn't it? Being seemingly powerless to save the NHS, BBC and the idea of public services in general. Rape culture omnipresent as banter or apologias for heroes, even as we look back in horror at the abuses of the last century like they were unconnected. The street reportage/prurient suffering porn dichotomy of hiphop reaching crisis point, as Chicago turns into a bloodbath while producing astounding music. Flood, war, famine, pestilence, Florence And The Machine.

Alex Neilson
2012 has been the Scottish Year of the Albatross for me, having finally limped over the finishing line of my twenties. But, as a recent UK tour with Josephine Foster's group indicated, there is much cause for optimism with venues like Cafe Oto, Manchester's Islington Mill and Bristol's Cube Cinema going from strength to strength while maintaining a commitment to experimental film/music and beyond. Elsewhere, the recently opened Glad Cafe in the less fashionable Southside of Glasgow has helped revitalise the city's music scene by hosting regular outré events with acommunity minded ethic (and artisan beer).

Personal highlights have included Lucy Stein's painting exhibition Orgasms In Hell in Amsterdam. The Pre-Raphaelite: Victorian Avant-Garde exhibition at Tate Britain. Graham Sutherland at MOMA in eternal Oxford, and reading about a gaggle of other Romantic Moderns like Samuel Palmer, DH Lawrence, Paul Nash, Peter Lanyon, Philip Larkin and Eric Gill. A consecutive year at Padstow's whacked-out May Day celebrations following the red 'oss around town. Hooking up with Jandek and Richard Youngs for a gig at St Margaret's Church in Manchester. Also, happening across a stack of naive paintings of rural Yorkshire, signed by SS, in Todmorden fleamarket.

Anne Hilde Neset
The Wire's Off The Page – the music festival for talking and thinking about music rather than listening to it – kicked off the year with a raft of great conversations, illuminating talks and late night parties in Whitstable. Also in the spring followed a sold-out symposium at the Tate Modern based around the Her Noise Archive. The archive was started by myself and Lina Dzuverovic back in 2001 while we were researching the show Her Noise (2005) and is still very much alive, housed by the London College of Communication (in a glass room next to the Stanley Kubrick Archive) where students make work responding to the archive every year. This year it was also shown at Oslo Museum of Contemporary Art's I Wish I Was A Song exhibition. Two concerts organised at the spectacularly resonant Vigeland Mausoleum in Oslo: Rhodri Davies playing Eliane Radigue's *OCCAM I* and Diamanda Galás's a cappella performance in the same space produced Arabesque overtones still ringing in my ears months afterwards. I was also lucky enough to work closely with Galás as her work was orchestrated by Norwegian composer Jon Øivind Næss for the Norwegian Broadcasting Orchestra during the Ultima Contemporary Music Festival, which produced a stunning combination of voice, piano and orchestra and even a choir of howling Finnish wolves (recorded, I hasten to add). Delving into John Cage's vast body of work in preparation for presenting Late Junction's Cage centenary celebration, I was reminded of the sheer beauty present in so much of it, a point which often gets overshadowed by its conceptual underpinnings. The *50 Modern Classics* podcasts – also by BBC Radio 3 – has been keeping my tram journeys up and down the hills of Oslo idea-rich and inspiring.

Richard Pinnell
Pros: Another year of great music, and nothing like 2011's great year. Jürg Frey's clarinet playing. The silence on the Isle of Skye. Who needs music? Ilan Volkov's Cage Prom for the BBC: an impossible success. Stewart Lee, as usual. Soundfjord's residency in the incredible space at the old Peek Freans biscuit factory in Bermondsey. Patrick Farmer's first book. Hearing John Tilbury play live several times – each time better than the last. Recording Radu Malfatti and a fly in an Oxfordshire countryside church. The increasingly wonderful swearing on *The Thick Of It*. More excellent concerts in Oxford. It's not just about London.

Cons: CD sales at an all time low. CD sleeve design following suit. Jeremy Hunt/Michael Gove/Boris Johnson (insert scumbag of your choice here). John Cage overload. Not being able to temporarily emigrate during the great British summer of nationalistic idiocy. Some idiot damaging a Rothko in the Tate. Not enough time to listen to everything. No Instal festival in Scotland, No i and e Festival in Ireland. An Olympic Games in London.

Edwin Pouncey
Pros: Getting my *Battle Of The Eyes* painting collaboration project (battleoftheeyes.com) with fellow artist Chris Long on the road was this year's personal highlight. Our three week residency at Norwich Castle during this year's Norfolk and Norwich Festival of Arts allowed us to show 18 large paintings, together with film work and live performance. The adventure continues with the release of our new short film, *What We Do*, featuring a soundtrack from drcarlsonalbion and the reading of a Sun Ra poem by veteran UK actor Dudley Sutton. Equally exciting was the publication of my *Trip Or Squeek* book by Strange Attractor Press. Thanks to *The Wire* for running the strip for the past ten years.

Films of the year: *Killing Them Softly*, *The Dark Knight Rises*, *Cosmopolis*, *Crossfire Hurricane*, *The Bruce Lacey Experience*, *The Artist Is Present*, *Berberian Sound Studio*.

Concerts of the year: Earth at Union Chapel, Sun Ra Arkestra at Barbican, Conlon Nancarrow at Purcell Room, Camille O'Sullivan at London Wonderground, Kimmo Pohjonen Accordion Wrestling at York Hall, Londinium's Flights Of Angels at Saint George's, Bloomsbury, Buffy Sainte-Marie at Antony's Meltdown, Mike Nesmith at Queen Elizabeth Hall.

Books of the year: Ed Sanders *Fug You*, Bob Gluck *You'll Know When You Get There: Herbie Hancock And The Mwandishi Band*, Jason Weiss *Always In Trouble: An Oral History Of ESP-Disk'*, Andrew Chumbley *The Leaper Between*.

Cons: The closing of record shops in Central London due to hostile and inflationary rent rises forcing small traders out, the most recent victim being Intoxica! Records in Portobello Road. This, and Music And Video Exchange's addled decision to close down the rare record department at its flagship Notting Hill Gate branch and merge it with regular low end shop stock, means there are barely any collectors' record shops left standing in the area.

Another disappointment was Jeremy Grimshaw's flawed biography of La Monte Young, which should have been the last word on this important figure in 20th century music. Instead, Young denounced the published book on his website – partly due to the author's laboured theory that a kind of cosmic Mormonism motored his musical oeuvre.

Nina Power

I spent much of 2012 thinking about the mechanised voice – the automated female voice in train stations and supermarket checkout machines – that reassures and cajoles in equal measure, and how the techno-feminist future got screwed up and securitised, along with everything else. Although I once again spent lots of time in court listening to other kinds of ritualised voices, I tried – on pain of being accused of being a miserable git once again – to enjoy the following: Laurel Halo, Angel Haze (thanks Petra), Frank Ocean (thanks Amanda), the new Godspeed! record (thanks Godspeed!), the Afronoise of La Bruha Desi La, a summer immersion in the peasant communism of Pier Paolo Pasolini, the films of John Akomfrah, Harun Farocki and Hito Steyerl, the dress designs of Stepanova and women's liberation music from the 1970s. In other voice-related excitement, starting a radio show on Resonance FM – *The Hour Of Power* – was fantastic. My students at both Roehampton and the RCA are excellent as usual, and demonstrate once again why cuts to arts and humanities, and education in general, are a mark of how profoundly vicious, petty and chiselling the current government are. Cons this year included the realisation that friendships can just evaporate if people let it happen, and that I achieved neither of my two overarching life goals, namely being published in *Private Eye*'s Pseuds Corner and/or winning their crossword competition.

Agata Pyzik

So it's already over? Been and gone? Culturally I remember nothing. It felt like the world was only taking a run-up to something really scary or amazing: the overthrow of capitalism or foundation of the New World Order. 2012 seems like a traumatic acting out of 1989, not only because I spent most of my time excavating fragments of dead countries and ideologies for my book on Cold War 'dreamlands'. Nations, including my homeland Eastern Europe, are trying to wake up from the nightmare of history, and go to the streets after decades of consumerism-driven lethargy. The Cold War strangely continues, especially when Russian anarcho-punks Pussy Riot are taken under Westerners' wings.

Why, then, is culture so apathetic, unable to keep up? This year's Unsound festival felt like one big Ostalgia fest, with Andy Votel mixing a hit from my childhood, "Mr Blot". The grand finale took place in Krakow's spooky Forum Hotel, with its splendid late Soviet-era carpets and golden futurist chandeliers all now in decay, once again proving that hauntology really works only in places charged by history. Hauntology seems the most influential and intellectually compelling aesthetic today, with hordes of artists creating moribund soundscapes, but with so little to say or stand for. Nostalgia for the mid-2000s is a fact. Meanwhile, as Tory Britain spent money on the Jubilee Year and Olympics, it revealed itself as a country worse than David Peace's novels. Increasingly boring cultural production was at

total odds with what was happening; only now do we see the degree to which the Thatcher generation, much more affected by the crisis than their older colleagues, is alienated from its place. Big-ups to: SYRIZA, Jodi Dean's *The Communist Horizon*, Yugomodernism & Red Vienna, Slovenian Marxists, Polish Radio Experimental Studio, Roxy Music, Bruno Jasieński, Zero Books, DEFA films from GDR, Rollin, Zulawski, Fassbinder, *The Nine Muses*, Skolimowski, socialist music show at Łódź MOMA. Whenever I couldn't take it, watching *Six Feet Under* with my boyfriend.

Simon Reynolds

I've always been more about records, not so much about live. So perhaps it's a sign of the times, or a sign of something, that the music experiences that affected me most this year weren't artefacts but performances. When the prevailing modes of distribution and consumption have the effect of at once reifying and insubstantialising music into units of decontextualised data, there's much to recommend being forcibly reminded that actual living beings made the sounds you're hearing. So the moments that linger in the memory mostly involve the presence of the performers (and, of equal analogue-flashback importance, an audience). The imposing ludicrousness of Mayhem at by:Larm in Oslo, and of Laibach at Incubate in Tilburg. Also at Incubate: the frangible exhilaration and frayed nerves of Maria & The Mirrors; Chris & Cosey, thick and wet and absolutely stunning; Raime's rhythmic stealth and lustrous monochrome; the charisma of Carla Bozulich; Buzzcocks blasting down memory lane, even with Diggle's daft guitar heroics; getting coerced into conga-ing to the Schlager-tastic De Deurzakkers. Ariel Pink's peculiar hissy fit of a show at the Fonda Theatre, Los Angeles. Totally nowtro: Skrillex's digi-maximalist audio-video barrage at Hard Summer; Kode9 slaying a Berlin club crowd and showing that post-step eclecticism needn't be tepid and diffuse. Totally retro: Go-Gos at Hollywood Bowl; Nightingales in St Gallen (bizarrely sounding closer to Family and Groundhogs than a shambling-band nostalgia act). Some records did manage to sneak through the numb info-overload anomie and make an impression: Ariel's *Mature Themes*, especially the gorgeous last three tunes, and "Steviepink Javascript" off his R Stevie Moore colaboration *Ku Klux Glam*; Death Grips; the brave move of Woebot's *Hallo*; Maria Minerva; Mark van Hoen's *Revenant Diary*, particularly the astonishing "Holy Me"; the Sun Araw/Congos communion; Hyperdub women Cooly G and Laurel Halo.

Nick Richardson

The best two musical experiences happened over the same weekend. The first was listening to a pickled old farmer from la Creuse, France, singing regional songs over pastis in a tiny rural bar on Bastille day. The second was cycling out with a crate of beer to an enormous wind turbine at midnight and listening to my friend duet with it on his sax. How could any mere gig compare? Skyforger, in York, towering over the crowd in velvet capes and tunics and playing thrilling, thugged out Pagan Metal, came close; as did the reanimated Fushitsusha, who blistered the paint and raised the roof at St John in Hackney. It was also pretty great to see the Bactrian camel save the world by shitting planets at the Birmingham Opera Company's premiere of Stockhausen's *Mittwoch*. I liked

being published in a real book – *Black Metal: Beyond The Darkness* – and all the weird opportunities that came out of it, including being allowed to talk to a candlelit Cafe Oto at *The Wire* salon, and getting interviewed by Irish radio and a Spanish horror zine. Really though, the best thing about this year has been getting the group I play drums in, Taman Shud, up and running. It's been heartening to discover that people don't hate us, and I've acquired a new and profound respect for the hundreds of great groups that gig tirelessly and unpretentiously, week in week out, purely for the love.

Bruce Russell

The best thing about 2012 is that politics (real, in your face, how life actually is politics) once more became the subtext of artistic production in my city. Disasters make cities, in the same way that revolutions do. Paris has not been destroyed by nature in the recorded past, though it has been destroyed by revolutions, and is therefore accorded primacy among great conurbations. Dublin has its Easter Rising, and Barcelona its 1936. Lisbon, Santiago, New Orleans, LA, Christchurch, NZ, and Lower Manhattan, NYC, have all been destroyed by nature – and such a catastrophe will make a city as surely as any myth of proletarian defiance and cries of "A las barricadas!" The way such cities are made is through an alliance between artists, musicians, architects and other culture workers on the one hand, and a populace awakened to their real situation through a disruptive shock that shatters the entente cordiale which normally papers over the social cracks. Detroit has a creative community second to none, even as the city disintegrates totally. Sustained and widespread demolition smells like high voltage electricity and cordite, and believe me, there is nothing more bracing than smelling the air in such a city. I think the predictions for this city are favourable, given how stuffed up everything is. Everyone's back is to the wall and all bets are off. I've been to the best gigs in a decade in a yacht club, an improvised coffee roastery and a double garage behind an ex-car yard. Street art is abounding, and made by everyone as a commentary on a daily reality whose degradation defies logic. Even students self-publish samizdat publications about urban design and rock 'n' roll that defy the pink robots of Control and the Spectacle to do battle with Yoshimi and her comic book allies. Everyone is on anti-anxiety medication. Things have never been worse objectively, or more exciting subjectively: bliss it is in this dawn to be alive. Lower Manhattan is in for a treat once the dice stop spinning, and everyone accepts it is now the Yankee Lower Ninth Ward – welcome to our nightmare, do join us on our barricades of sewage.

Sukhdev Sandu

2012 has mostly been endless hazewanderings through New York's Chinatown, drifting in and out of its singular soundscape: elderly opera singers at Columbus Park, erhu players performing to infants on Doyers Street, rising choruses of street vendor patter meshing with Brooklyn bound trains and blaring car horns. It's a vexatious, restorative antidote to the flattened acoustic environments of Bloomberg's city. Post-Hurricane Sandy, during noctambulations through eerie, blacked out Lower Manhattan, the lanes around East Broadway buzzed with Christina Kubisch-style generator hum as local traders hawked Double D batteries, dumplings and torches. It was, at

a time of city-wide anguish, a reassuring show of local personality and subaltern recovery, presaging (I like to think) America's rejection a few days later of Mitt Romney's noxious brew of ethno-parochial crony capitalism.

Publishing-wise, I was delighted with offerings from imprints such as Unit Editions, Zero (especially Neil Kulkarni's *Eastern Spring*), The New Press and Strange Attractor; journals such as *News China*, *Bidoun*, *The Caravan*, *Lucky Peach*, *Monocle*, *Cinemascope*, *Little Joe*, *LRB* and the revived *Chickfactor*. Record labels Blackest Ever Black, Pre-Cert Home Entertainment and Second Language were on top form. Shows I enjoyed included Michael Rakowitz's *The Breakup* at Lombard Freid Projects, Chris Watson's *The Bee Symphony* at Our Lady of Lebanon Cathedral, Triple Canopy's three day public reading of Gertrude Stein's *The Making Of American*, Caroline Bergvall's sound poetry at Space, Pittsburgh, Chris Marker retrospectives at Horse Hospital, London, and Light Industry, Brooklyn (the former curated by Chris Drake and Gareth Evans). Another year not exactly brimming with Big Themes, but full of poignant pleasures.

Nick Southgate

The longer you listen to music, the more you listen to music, the more you need the thrills that make it new again – and the harder they are to find. 2012 gave me two epiphanies. In the frozen basement of the Betsy Trotwood pub in Farringdon, Two Wings feathered my joyless heart with the soaring span of an angel's glowing embrace to make rock sweet and vital again. Meanwhile Pat Thomas's digging into Black Power gave us the muscled and articulate *Listen Whitey!* compilation that reminded me of the righteous anger that heals in the devil's music. Julian Cope's *Copendium* held nothing new for a devoted reader of his album of the month column, but reminded me of the worth of great critical writing and made me resolve to try harder next year.

But the archives delivered many weighty blows to my love of music. Maybe I'm weak. Maybe I'm wrong. But my musical brain struggles to move in units of six CDs and endless alternate takes. Perhaps that's why I responded to the poles apart immediacy of Two Wings and *Listen Whitey!*. They made me long for releases that didn't feel like scholarly acts or exercises in comparative studies. Perversely, contemporary artists are frequently both wildly prolific and obscure in their releases that I long for a box set to make sense of it all. And just as I get nostalgic for a simpler and more innocent world of single-album-tour and an appearance on *Top Of The Pops*, that memory is tarnished forever as well.

Daniel Spicer

Pros: Many fine adventures were had with my Bolide brothers this year: summer UK tour in a van with the mighty Temperatures; fiddle music and Exquisite Corpse in a Sunday night pub in Cork; intense fun at Supernormal festival woodland jam, liquid golden afternoon sun slanting through the trees; Gafferfest in Lyons, bunking at Ground Zero, squat castle and centre of much French underground activity; and big yucks Cage Rattling at King's Place, monkeying about with found materials. Back home, enjoyed late nights with new friends in Brighton's Marxist poetry cadre, and was happy to perform a cut-up piece at the Brighton Poetry Festival. Found weeping in my kitchen on a Sunday afternoon, listening to Ginsberg sing "Father Death Blues" on the newly unearthed 1979 recording on Sloow Tapes. 2012's most visionary experience had no witnesses: stumbling alone around the Misery And Splendour Of The Flesh exhibition at Museo d'Arrte in Ravenna, Italy, in the grip of wretched red wine hangover, with every painting – from Caravaggio to Bacon – screaming diamond personal cosmic relevance. Couple of standout gigs: Taco Bells at Brighton's Cowley Club – raw, righteous free jazz with punters literally whooping for joy; and the bittersweet experience of seeing Roscoe Mitchell blow everyone away at Cafe Oto, without realising it was one of the late Tony Marsh's very last gigs. Bookwise, Philip K Dick remains reliably mindbending, Cormac McCarthy one of the only writers who can keep me up all night in page-turning, anxious ecstasy. Oh yeah, and I finally got Bob Dylan.

Cons: The commercial, PR-driven UK jazz scene is about as far from the idea of jazz as you can get. Puh-lease!

Joseph Stannard
Pros: The past 12 months have dealt musical riches in abundance, but for me the biggest revelation arrived early with Van Halen's *A Different Kind Of Truth*, their first album since 1984 to feature David Lee Roth. Explosive and ageless, it sounded less like a return to form than a manifestation of the eternal NOW hinted at by John Scanlan in his deliriously brilliant 2012 analysis of the group, *Exuberant California, Zen Rock 'N' Roll*. The other great rock album in a year dominated by electronic excellence was the debut of Jennifer Herrema's new outfit, Black Bananas, which served as a reminder that rock 'n' roll can still flex and stretch like Silly Putty when warmed by the right hands. In terms of live music, Emptyset, Roly Porter, Sparks and El-P all resolutely failed to bore me.

It was almost as good a year for cinema, particularly its uncanny division: Peter Strickland's *Berberian Sound Studio* was a disorientating culture-clash nightmare with a striking central performance from Toby Jones and a beautiful soundtrack by Broadcast; *V/H/S* dragged the portmanteau horror film kicking and screaming into the 21st century whilst paying tribute to obsolete analogue technology; Ti West's *The Innkeepers* maintained an eerie stillness via mumblecore reticence and masterfully sustained tension; and Pascal Laugier's *The Tall Man* cleverly subverted the expectations of its audience, myself included. On YouTube, atmospheric DIY web series *Marble Hornets* expanded the mythos of 21st century folk devil Slender Man (aka The Operator) to unsettling effect.

Cons: I encountered so much viral hype regarding certain releases that I ended up heartily sick of them before I'd heard a single note. I groaned at the timidity of reviewers who seemed unable to deliver an honest assessment of music they clearly didn't think was very good. The swing towards Industrial revivalism left me unimpressed, not to mention uneasy about its whitewash effect on Techno. The misguided belief that hauntology is a musical subcategory rather than a spectral subcurrent led to some risible attempts to board the phantom bandwagon. Dear old Auntie Beeb missed the point too, cynically rebooting the long dormant Radiophonic Workshop as an online show pony with no discernible function. The corporate impulse to ransack history drove DC Comics to commission a series of beautifully crafted yet morally indefensible prequels to Alan Moore's *Watchmen*, while another Moore creation, working class occultist John Constantine of the sadly cancelled *Hellblazer* series, was remodelled in safer, more saleable form. In other (bad) news, May saw the deaths of Donna Summer and Robin Gibb, intern(et) culture continued to exploit the willing and marginalise the skilled, the ConDems hammered the final nail in the coffin of the NHS and the mainstream left wing media (oxymoron alert) continued to be dominated by middle class privilege.

Zakia Uddin
This year has been about digital radio for me, from extended magazine shows and essay programmes, to the live-streamed Los Angeles police scanners layered with minimal compositions on *You Are Listening To*. Finding great stuff among all the links is half the joy – it's an addictive, versatile form. Also, good radio shows escape the quick turnover of internet culture – it takes time to produce a decent programme – while also being very much part of the moment you're in when you're listening to them air. Saying that, I was mildly obsessed with Daniel Jones and Peter Gregson's six month project *The Listening Machine*, where the prosody of tweets was turned into musical notation (it's a logical extension of the incredibly moving *Listening Post* installation by Mark Hansen and Ben Rubin). The former was inspired by the 1930s Mass Observation Project – I like how it gave social networking another dimension through sound. Musically, I've been drawn to albums which take up space and demand slow listening such as Jam City's *Classical Curves*, Holly Herndon's *Movement* and Vessel's *The Order Of Noise*. I loved *Teen Mom* star Farrah Abraham's Autotuned oddity *My Teenage Dream Ended* as well – and loved seeing what it revealed about critics' preconceptions about creative control and who can make experimental music.

Salomé Voegelin
My cultural life was full of wonderful sonic events in 2012. Among the highlights was the Her Noise conference at Tate Modern, particularly the talk by Pauline Oliveros and the subsequent performance of her seminal work *To Valerie Solanas And Marilyn Monroe In Recognition Of Their Desperation* (1970) by an all-female ensemble. Rather disturbing was the Invisible show, which ran at the Hayward Gallery from June to August. Despite not being a sonic exhibition, it had attracted my attention for the potentially sonic sensibility inherent in the absent, the silent, the barely there. The show was overly pedagogical, focused on documentation, which laid bare the starkness of the gallery rather than the work, initiating a threat to the viewer, which some of the work and the show's curatorial layout amplified. A brighter spot was the ICA's Soundworks exhibition, still available online. 100 artists had been invited to respond to Bruce Nauman's *Days*, and while some of it is predictable in its dealing with the Nauman piece, the exhibition has some wonderful sound works to offer.

The Olympic summer drove me abroad, where the ZKM in Karlsruhe's Sound Art, Sound As Medium Of Art beckoned. The ZKM is an impressive building with lots of space, but sadly this show was confined to the ground floor, cramping a lot of sound works into one space with an obvious result. The show had a slightly schizophrenic character: not enough big names to be a canoniser, but neither was it curated with the confidence to ignore some big names in favour of an interesting experience.

Derek Walmsley
Pros: For economic, ecological and ideological reasons, I took the train rather than the plane in search of new music this year. Reconnecting with grassroots scenes/sounds/fests in Nottingham, Oxfordshire, Newcastle, Lyon and beyond kept me psyched for the whole of 2012, and my wanderlust was satisfied by the dispatches of freshly zipped music from around the globe in my inbox each day. The boundaries around the album are getting ever fainter, so these were the intimate audio epiphanies that made my year: walking around London for three months with the complete studio works of Prince on my smartphone; *The Black Saint And The Sinner Lady* on vinyl touching places MP3s can't reach. In conversation, Niney The Observer breaking down the workings of a rhythm with his mouth; Keith Fullerton Whitman breaking down the workings of his remote-controlled car. Loren Connors and Suzanne Langille talking music for three hours on WKCR. Strange strains of highly evolved Techno from Powell, Vessel, Andy Stott, Suum Cuique and others. Noise Park. The multiverse of ideas spanned by *The Wire*'s Collateral Damage series. Robert Wyatt blinking back tears while "Forest" played at *The Wire* Salon. "In a world in which Snoop Dogg records a duet with Willie Nelson, science fiction no longer exists."

Cons: The uncomfortable questions posed by the rise of the the boutique deluxe box set, which rather than spreading music far and wide, trades on exclusivity, questionable historical hypotheses and an elusive sense of aura. Colour Out Of Space, the most original fun fest in the UK, getting no arts money this year. Among many sad deaths, Adam Yauch.

Dan Warburton
Reflections: After finally pulling the plug on my beloved *paristransatlantic.com* webzine in July – though the site's still there and still getting hits! – the rest of the year has been devoted more to listening to back catalogue, which includes discs received only a few months ago but only ever played a couple of times, as well as authentic quadruple vodka blasts from the past (I'd forgotten how good John Bonham was). And watching the shelves fill up with DVDs as the bank account empties accordingly. Musical pleasure has come from diverse and surprising sources, from old road-warrior heroes Scott Walker and Donald Fagen (each checking in with strong new work in 2012, though *Bish Bosch* and *Sunken Condos* couldn't be more different) to new voices – check out Swiss accordionist Jonas Kocher, y'all. Most touching, as one approaches the half century and the past fills up with failure (though as another silver surfer sez, it's better to regret something you have done than something you haven't), is the music which looks over its own shoulder, both near (Jason Lescalleet's 'reading' of Big Black, General Strike's affectionate takes on Sun Ra and The Cuff Links) and far (Keith Rowe's stunning use of Dvořák on *September*).

Barry Witherden
With greed, mendacity, fraud and intolerance still in the ascendant – I blame the badgers – even politically engaged art can seem irrelevant and self-indulgent. It's nonetheless vital for the health of personal hope and sanity, no matter how self-deluding. Parochial pros have been the increasing amount of leftfield and other specialist music on my local community radio station and the survival – indeed, the expansion, against all the trends – of the local independent record shop. Live musical highlights were The Unthanks' 'back to the club roots' tour, Nils Petter Molvær's magical gig with Trio Mediaeval, the Bang On A Can All Stars' Field Recordings concert at the Barbican (very much a curate's egg, but I'd have been sorry to miss it) and Wadada Leo Smith's residency at Cafe Oto. Cons: Just before Smith gave me an interview, we heard that John Tchicai had suffered a stroke. There were far too many obituaries this year, but the death of this man, who was responsible for probably my all-time favourite LP and the most memorable gig I ever attended, was especially sad.

Turning to my record of the year, at first I was a little ashamed that I found it so much easier to build a list of archive/reissue material than of new music, but relieved to realise this was not because, in my dotage, I have become less receptive to contemporary sounds: it's just that the reissues category can call on a century of performances that have stood the test of time. The seemingly inexhaustible supply of previously unreleased bootlegs featuring John Coltrane is especially gratifying.

Rob Young
This year has been soundtracked by cavernous spaces (Dusk + Blackdown, Emptyset, Raime, Bass Clef); balls to the wall (Julian Cope's *Copendium* compilation, Bushman's Revenge, Death Grips, Meshuggah); rep-rep-repetition: (Cave/Bitchin Bajas, Duane Pitre, Can's *Lost Tapes*), titans of song (Bill Fay, Scott Walker); abrasive drift (ECM's Gurdjieff CD, Richard Skelton, Hallock Hill, Helm, Jozef van Wissem & Jim Jarmusch); and the sprawling ambition of Terre Thaemlitz's *Soulnessless*. Before I lit out for a new life in Oslo last summer, I was honoured to write catalogue notes for Jeremy Deller's Hayward retrospective, talk on wyrd British TV at the Southbank, eulogise Peter Christopherson at Newcastle's AV Festival, and contribute to BBC Radio 3's *Fifty Modern Classics* podcasts. Ilan Volkov's superb John Cage Prom and EM's *John Cage Shock* collection were highlights of a year in which I absorbed more of the mycologist's music than ever before. Rhodri Davies playing Eliane Radigue at the Emanuel Vigeland Mausoleum, Oslo was utterly transcendent; Felix Kubin's Paralektronoia presentation offered alternative history as edutainment. Patrick Keiller's *The Robinson Institute* at Tate Britain, Camden Arts Centre's Bruce Lacey Experience, and the BFI's *Lacey Tapes* DVD presented obsessive research as art. On the flatscreen: *The Thick Of It*, *Veep*, *Forbrydelsen III*, *Borgen*, *The Hollow Crown*, *Black Mirror*, *The Devils*, *Roll Out The Barrel: The British Pub On Film*. Grayson Perry's *British Taste* series went beyond remit to analyse the state of the UK class system. *Berberian Sound Studio* pushed all the right (Bakelite) buttons, and thanks to Peter Strickland for the walk at Portmeirion. On the page: Matt Thorne's *Prince* epic opened up an unknown realm of bootlegs, aftershow tapes and alternative LPs. John Dack & Christine North's translation of Pierre Schaeffer's *In Search Of A Concrete Music* was long overdue but revelatory. As were: Dave Arthur *Bert: The Life And Times Of AL Lloyd*, Bob Gluck *You'll Know When You Get There: Herbie Hancock And The Mwandishi Band*, Geoff Dyer *Zona*, Lloyd Shepherd *The English Monster*, *Copendium*. ☐

Columnists' charts
A–Z

Dub A–Z

Dennis Bovell
Mek It Run (Pressure Sounds)
Breadwinners
Dubs Unlimited (King Spinna)
Dubkasm
Brixton Rec (Bristol Archive)
Da Grynch
Release The Hounds (Necessary Mayhem)
Keith Hudson
Rasta Communication (Deluxe Edition)
(Greensleeves)
Fred Locks
Black Star Liner In Dub
(17 North Parade/VP)
Pale Rider
Sometimes Coffee, Sometimes Tea
(Cassava Outernational)
Lee 'Scratch' Perry
Disco Devil: The Jamaican Discomixes
(Sanctuary)
Adrian Sherwood
Survival And Resistance (On-U Sound)
Wrongtom meets Deemus J
In East London (Tru Thoughts)

Compiled by Steve Barker

Critical Beats A–Z

Blacksmif
...And the Sun Rose Out (Synchronicity)
Boddika
Acid Jackson (Swamp81)
Chunky
Rugged (Swamp81)
Coki
Onboard (DMZ)
Funkystepz
Jigga (FLY)
JME
96 Fuckries (Boy Better Know)
Lorca
Love Like This (Lorca Refix) (Church)
Mr Mitch
Super Freak (Gobstopper)
Psychemagik
*Valley Of Paradise (Time & Space Machine
Remix)* (Psychemagik)
Randomer
We Laugh, We Scream (Hemlock)
Myth Rychards
Rock Rock The Spot (It's A Bass Thing)
SBTRKT
Hold On (Sisi Bakbak Remix) (Young Turks)
Shy One
Aztec Bwoy (DVA Recordings)
Silkie & Swindle
Unlimited (Butterz)
Visionist
Control This (Signal Life)

Compiled by Joe Muggs

Global A–Z

Various
Aimer Et Perdre (Tompkins Square)
Various
Dabke: Sounds Of The Syrian Houran
(Sham Palace)
Getachew Degefu
Wedding Songs (Domino Sound)
Various
*Don't Trust Your Neighbours: Early Albanian
Traditional Songs & Improvisations 1920s–
1930s* (Hinter)
Thonghuad Faited
*Diew Sor Isan: The North East Thai Violin Of
Thonghuad Faited* (EM)
Various
Golden Beirut: New Sounds From Lebanon
(Out Here)
Jeong Ga Ak Hoe
Thinking Being Irresistibly Burnt
(Akdang Eban)
Various
I'm A Romany Rai (Topic)
Various
*Korea – Jongmyo Jeryeak: Ritual Music For
The Royal Ancestors* (Ocora)
Sory Kandia Kouyaté
La Voix De La Révolution (Sterns)

Compiled by Julian Cowley

Avant Rock A–Z

Aluk Todolo
Occult Rock (Norma Evangelium Diaboli/Ajna
Offensive)
Oren Ambarchi
Raga Ooty/Nilgiri Plateau (Bo'Weavil)
Oren Ambarchi
Sagittarian Domain (Editions Mego)
Jessica Bailiff
At The Down-Turned Jagged Rim Of The Sky
(Kranky)
Crazy Spirit
Crazy Spirit (Toxic State)
Richard Dawson
Magic Bridge (Pink Triangle)
Fushitsusha
Mabushii Itazura Na Inori (Heartfast)
The Howling Hex
Wilson Semiconductors (Drag City)
The One Ensemble
Oriole (alt.vinyl/Pickled Egg)
People Of The North
Steep Formations (Jagjaguwar)
Swans
The Seer (Young God)
Alexander Tucker
Third Mouth (Thrill Jockey)
Alexander Turnquist
Like Sunburned Snowflakes (VHF)
Two Wings
Love's Spring (Tin Angel)
Richard Youngs
Amaranthine (MIE Music)

Compiled by Nick Richardson, Nick Southgate
and Joseph Stannard

Electronica A–Z

Bee Mask
We Were Eating Unripe Pears
(Spectrum Spools)
Carter Tutti Void
Transverse (Mute)
Vladislav Delay
Espoo (raster-noton)
Diamond Version
EP1 (Mute)
Fay
Din (Time No Place)
Mark Fell
Sentielle Objectif Actualité (Editions Mego)
Russell Haswell
Factual (Editions Mego)
Heatsick
Deviation (Pan)
Robert Hood
Motor: Nighttime World 3 (Music Man)
Khan Kurra
World View EP (Fluorescent)
Konx-Om-Pax
Regional Surrealism (Planet Mu)
Lukid
Lonely At The Top (Werk)
Monolake
Ghosts (Imbalance)
NHK'Koyxen
Dance Classics Vol 1 (Pan)
Andy Stott
Luxury Problems (Modern Love)

Compiled by Sam Davies and Adam Harper

Hiphop A–Z

Chief Keef
Back From The Dead (Glory Boy Entertainment)
Future
Pluto (Freebandz)
Gucci Mane
Trap Back (Brick Squad)
Gunplay
Bogota Rich: The Prequel (MMG)
Ka
Grief Pedigree (Iron Works)
King Louie
Val Venis (Epic)
Kendrick Lamar
good kid, m.A.A.d. city
(Top Dawg Entertainment/Aftermath/Interscope)
Starlito
Post Traumatic Stress (Trash Bag Gang)
Ty Dolla $ign & Joe Moses
WHOOP! (No label)
Shy Glizzy
Law (No label)

Compiled by Jack Law and Andrew Nosnitsky

Modern Composition A–Z

William Berger/Iain Burnside
Insomnia (Delphian)
John Bischoff
Audio Combine (New World)
Philip Blackburn
Ghostly Psalms (Innova)
John Cage
Etudes Australes (Wergo)
John Cage
Sonatas And Interludes (hat(now)ART)
Edison Denisov
Au Plus Haut Des Cieux (Harmonia Mundi)
Barbara Monk Feldman
The Northern Shore (Mode)
Michael Finnissy
Second & Third Quartets (NMC)
Hans Werner Henze
In Lieblicher Bläue (Wergo)
Annea Lockwood
In Our Name (New World)
Anthony Pateras
Collected Works 2002–2012 (Immediata)
Katharina Rosenberger
Texturen (hat(now)ART)
Skogen
Ist Gefallen In Den Schnee (Another Timbre)
Frances White
In The Library Of Dreams (Pogus)
Joanna Wozny
As In A Mirror, Darkly (Kairos)

Compiled by Philip Clark, Julian Cowley and Brian Morton

Size Matters A–Z

Big Nils
Bitch Gutsssssss (Abscess 7")
Body/Head
The Eyes, The Mouth (Ultra Eczema 7")
J Collin
High Peak Vibrations Vol II
(Winebox Press MC)
Sharon Gal
Melancholic (American Tapes 7")
Marineville
Face (Epic Sweep 7")
Nones
Defecating Grey (Hozac 7")
Orchid Spangiafora
Tin Windows (Orchid Spangiafora 7")
Bill Orcutt
Why Does Everybody Love Free Music But Nobody Loves Free People? (Palilalia MC)
Telescopes
Black-Eyed Dog (Trensmat 7")
Christian Wolfarth
Acoustic Solo Percussion Vol 4
(Hiddenbell 7")

Compiled by Byron Coley

Outer Limits A–Z

Stephen Cornford
Binatone Galaxy (Senufo Editions)
Angharad Davies/Tisha Mukarji/Dimitra Lazaridou-Chatzigoga
Outwash (Another Timbre)
Aaron Dilloway
Modern Jester (Hanson)
Kevin Drumm
Relief (Editions Mego)
Helm
Impossible Symmetry (Pan)
Eli Keszler
Catching Net (Pan)
Thomas Köner
Novaya Zemlya (Touch)
Jason Lescalleet
Songs About Nothing (Erstwhile)
Perispirit
Spiritual Church Movement (Digitalis)
Michael Pisaro & Toshiya Tsunoda
Crosshatches (Erstwhile)
Vanessa Rossetto
Exotic Exit (Kye)
Floris Vanhoof
Cycles Of Confusion (Kraak)
Ben Vida
esstends-esstends-esstends (Pan)
John Wall & Mark Durgan
John Wall & Mark Durgan (Entr'acte)
Nate Young
Regression Vol 3: Other Days (Rockatansky)

Compiled by Nick Cain, Jim Haynes, William Hutson and Nick Richardson

Jazz & Improv A–Z

Barrel
Gratuitous Abuse (Emanem)
Tony Bevan/Joe Morris/Tony Buck/Dominic Lash
Tony-Joe Bucklash (Foghorn)
Peter Brötzmann/Masahito Satoh/Takeo Moriyama
Yatagarasu (Not Two)
John Butcher
Bell Trove Spools (Northern Spy)
Rhodri Davies
Wound Response (alt.vinyl)
Charles Gayle Trio
Streets (Northern Spy)
Kay Grant & Alex Ward
Fast Talk (Emanem)
Alexandra Grimal Quartet
Andromeda (Ayler)
Andrew Lamb
Rhapsody In Black (NoBusiness)
Joe Morris/William Parker/Gerald Cleaver
Altitude (AUM Fidelity)
William Parker Orchestra
Essence Of Ellington (Centering)
Eddie Prévost/Sebastian Lexer/Seymour Wright
Impossibility In Its Purest Forms (Matchless)
Wadada Leo Smith
Ten Freedom Summers (Cuneiform)
Wadada Leo Smith & Louis Moholo-Moholo
Ancestors (TUM)
David S Ware & Planetary Unknown
Live At Jazzfestival Saalfelden 2011
(AUM Fidelity)

Compiled by Philip Clark and Daniel Spicer

STREAM LINED

Flying solo: Britt Brown

In 2012, underground music was dominated by solo artists rather than groups. **Britt Brown** ponders the economic and technological factors behind a subcultural phenomenon

OPER ATIONS

2012 irrefutably marked a new high point in the slow-burning ascendancy of the solo project as the preferred vehicle for musical expression. Flip through the pages of this magazine for proof – the distinct majority of the albums discussed and artists interviewed are individuals, not groups. The factors and motives responsible for this phenomenon are numerous, and interrelated, but exceedingly simple. It may be rash to sound the funeral gong for the Death of the Group just yet, but actual bands – those in which two or more people legitimately share creative control – are fast becoming an endangered species, and the coming years will only see the situation accelerate.

Let's start with the basest reason for this cultural trend: money. These days, there is less and less of it to go around, and therefore less incentive to split what little remains among unnecessary personnel. Royalties have hit historic lows, so whatever drummers and non-songwriting bassists can be cut out of the equation have been. The undying ambition of all musicians worldwide is to not have to maintain a day job, but unfortunately the population is not paying for enough music to make this dream a reality for everyone. The quickest fix is to go it alone.

To put the state of the global music economy in context, consider this: currently, less than 15 per cent of all music purchased is bought by individuals in the coveted 18–36 demographic. (This age group has the least disposable income but is the most computer-savvy, making them ideal candidates to acquire their music via illegal/unpaid means.) The ramifications of this trend have only begun to be felt, but drastic shifts in consumerism forecast shifts in cultural capital, which essentially means that youth will cease to dictate youth culture for the first time since the 1960s. With such a markedly reduced market to fight over, musicians must compete more aggressively with one another, increasing the likelihood of groups splintering into isolated, self-interested parts.

Touring, as a feasible source of income, is in even more dire straits. Collating travel expenses, hotels, meals, work visas, equipment repair or rental, plus the wages of any touring personnel (sound engineers, merch help, roadies, nannies for those with young children, etc), the costs stack up quickly. Only huge acts can command guarantees large enough to financially justify expansive entourages such as those required for a fully functioning five-piece group. Once again, time has shown us the decision most musicians have been arriving at, and it's the same one as the rest of the economic world: lay-offs and cutbacks.

Money may make the world go round (and be the root of all evil and all that), but groups have faced hard times and slim chances of success since forever, so it's not all money's fault, obviously. Another element that's helped grease the rails of this separatist slide is music technology itself. Looping pedals and samplers have been commonplace since at least the early 1980s, but it wasn't until the 2000s that they became so omnipresent. Lower prices, larger memory banks, preset digital FX and more user-friendly interfaces helped birth an infinity of bedroom noodling, but also slashed the ranks of rhythm guitarists, percussionists and other textural metronomic players. Why suffer the hassle of another human being's presence and schedule when you can just loop something and handle it all yourself?

The popularity of the personal laptop computer is another keystone in this movement. Idiot-proof programs like Ableton Live empower the individual by transforming their bedroom into a state of the art recording studio, but they also erode the need to interact or collaborate with other musicians, especially when it comes to performance. As technology has become so impenetrably intertwined with the music creation process, audiences' standards for live shows have plummeted. No one is shocked, disappointed, or even much notices when an artist emerges on stage only to press play on their laptop or iPod (or, if they're mildly archaic, their four-track) and karaoke along on a microphone. 20 years ago, pulling this kind of stunt in front of paying customers would have most likely resulted in hurled bottles, or at least a shower of boos. But in my own lifetime I've witnessed at least 50 sets of this nature, none of which were received unfavourably.

Without question one of the more significant factors in this revolution (or devolution, depending on your attitude) – though it's the one people are least interested in discussing – is the internet. Before the net achieved such absolute supremacy in contemporary society, music was still largely perceived as requiring some sort of interpersonal engagement to reach fruition. Playing alone was more of a means to an end, whether to grow adept enough to join a group of likeminded players, or amass a catalogue of compositions around which to build one's own ensemble, or create demos to share in the hope of landing a recording contract, etc.

To triumph in the pre-internet musical landscape frequently required a communal sensibility. Interbreeding ideas and sonic explorations with others on a similar wavelength (aka bandmates) helped ferment, strengthen and define core concepts. To pick a random example, if Genesis P-Orridge had launched Throbbing Gristle as a solo project in 1975 instead of banding together with Chris Carter, Cosey Fanni Tutti and Peter Christopherson, it's hard to imagine they would have made as deep an impact as they did, or be as relevant as they are today. And make no mistake: a 2012 TG, just starting out, would be one weird young man with a bass, a Line 6 loop pedal and a laptop, standing at a table. There are thousands of them.

It cannot be disputed: the internet has granted musicians (and artists in all media) unprecedented

power and freedom. Preformatted audio template websites such as Bandcamp and Soundcloud, like MySpace before them, make it appallingly simple to establish one's online identity and begin sharing your wares. Facebook allows individuals – and corporations – to build the architecture for a fanbase, and insinuate their activities into the lives of many. Such free, instantaneous connections have rendered record labels obsolete, because anyone can post their recordings onto YouTube and achieve higher visibility than 100 independent record shops combined. Every middleman in the musical culture chain has been cut out and left in the dust, except for one: the listener. Without an audience, music is like a tree falling in the forest, unheard.

What's ironic is that, while it has never been a worse time to pursue music as an occupation, it's never been a better time to be a listener. More music is being made – and uploaded and downloaded – than ever before. (In 2009, Ian Svenonius parodied the glut of registered groups on MySpace with his Felt Letters song, "600,000 Bands"; that figure is now woefully inadequate.) New artist-run, boutique record labels sprout forth every day, as do new Mediafire-linking blogs attempting to disseminate this massive deluge of audio content. A person could literally spend a lifetime clicking and skimming without ever hearing a fraction of what's out there.

Not only are we in the throes of the Age of the Solo Project, but the phenomenon is threatening to multiply at an exponential rate. These days not only does every member of most groups have their own solo project, they have several. It has become increasingly common for individuals to sustain a spectrum of parallel aesthetic identities, each with its own slight shade of variation. Of course, it being the modern age, each project necessitates a separate empire of Gmail accounts, Tumblrs, Blogspots, Instagrams, etc. (No wonder bandwidth is such a precious commodity of late.) The logic is straightforward: the more art one throws into the digital ether, the higher the likelihood that some of it will strike that elusive, zeitgeist-y chord. And, until that happens, there's no need to tour or perform live in physical space. One simply keeps jettisoning sounds into cyberspace like a Vegas veteran at a slot machine.

Of course exceptions to such generalisations do exist. Many of these, however, come with qualifiers. One arrangement that is oddly prevalent lately is the 'couples band', where the two members are in a romantic relationship. Technically this counts as a group, but the intimate nature of the relationship blurs the lines, as these are, in spirit, solo projects; in love, and in life/art, it's two striving to be one. Consider acts like MV + EE, High Places, Matmos, Moon Duo, Blues Control,and even recent Earth, to a certain extent. Another common exception is the 'hired guns' set-up. This is where one individual

dictates and directs the entire operation, but is either incapable of performing all the parts alone or simply prefers the public image of having additional musicians involved in the project, and thus pays people to take orders, or invites free agents to participate for particular undertakings. Examples are countless but some that come to mind are Evangelista, Excepter, Zola Jesus, US Girls and Ariel Pink's Haunted Graffiti. These groups are, at their core, essentially solo projects.

It should also go without saying that in certain realms of music, the Age of the Solo Project means almost nothing. Hiphop is ruled by distinct personalities, be they producers, beat makers or MCs. (Even in hiphop collectives, the individual is never subsumed by the group: think of Wu-Tang or Odd Future.) Electronic and dance music, too, have always been the domain of solitary producers. Larry Levan, like so many others (Hieroglyphic Being, Actress, Frankie Knuckles, etc) didn't need a collaborator standing next to him in the DJ booth. Jazz is another domain governed by the identities of the individual players. Ensembles are constantly mutating into fresh configurations, based on instrumentation, stylistic desires, funding or creative compatibility. Aficionados follow the discographies of beloved trumpeters or drummers regardless of the assemblage they happen to be playing with. And obviously, in true commercial pop music it is always one name, one personality, supersized on the marquee (even if behind the scenes a team of svengalis and investors are masterminding the operation).

Some will say that the rise of the solo project is purely positive. That performing in a group context only leads to compromise, and compromised art shortchanges the true vision of its creator. There is no denying that this has indeed been the case, on many, many occasions.

There is another part of me, though, that sees it differently; that sees communal creations as drawing on the best talents of everyone involved, with their indulgent tendencies whittled out by peer editing and group decision making. For my tastes, Sonic Youth are superior to Thurston solo and Kim solo and Lee solo; Spacemen 3's alchemy is timeless, whereas Sonic Boom strays too far to the esoteric and Spiritualized dips too deep into pure bombast. Recording-wise, The Dead C together trump the sum of their constituent parts; same goes for The Velvet Underground, Suicide, Sleep, Skinny Puppy, The Stooges, Neu!, Pärson Sound, Bad Brains, Boredoms, Big Black, Crass, Kraftwerk, Electrelane, Lightning Bolt and on and on. That the alternative path exists is wonderful (and clearly such solo freedoms are bearing plenty of strange fruit), but it's disconcerting to think that next generation versions of groups like these are less and less likely to arise. □

IM PRINTS OF GREAT NESS

2012 saw the growth of music's private presses. **David Keenan** hails a self-reliant publishing model with creatively stimulating risks attached

In the literary world, private press has become virtually synonymous with vanity publishing. But in music it is more often lauded as a mark of artistic seriousness, and as a conduit for otherwise unassimilable impulses from 'real people' and non-musicians.

In the face of the hijacking and cheapening of the individual artistic voice through its indiscriminate dissemination across Spotify, Pandora, YouTube, blogs, file sharing sites and the like, 2012 saw a reformulation of private press, both as a financial survival strategy, and as an intimate, unmediated channel of communication between artist and audience. Private press restores the record as an object imbued with an essence that is not endlessly replicable.

In the past 12 months there has been a discernible shift away from the prolix documentary style of endless CD-R and cassette releases, towards a refocusing on albums as big statements. When the trio of Mick Flower on Japan banjo, Chris Corsano on drums and Matt Heyner on electric bass co-released *The Count Visits* on their own Hot Cars Warp and Flower House imprints, it trumped the work-in-progress feel of endless free improvised sides with a set that felt like the apex of a particular style of aggressive avant rock. Aaron Dilloway's epic self-released double LP *Modern Jester* brought together several years' worth of obsessively twonked loops and degraded eight-track noise in what felt like a summation of his work to date.

Private press means putting something out because you believe in it. By contrast, crowdfunding sites (such as Kickstarter et al) guarantee the kind of focus group audience that most labels would kill for. Shielded from risk, crowdfunded records should be more accurately classified as public press. Back in 1978, Jandek was a completely unknown outsider artist when he started up Corwood Industries, using private press as a means of seeding the future conditions for the reception of his art. If Jandek was making his first record now, there is no way in hell anyone would be signing up to pay for its release. Even the way the records were presented refused consensus, with no credits and no artist name or title on the covers, which instead featured various images of Jandek himself or the interiors of rooms or badly photographed instruments, underlining one aesthetic of private press, which is often personal to the point of obfuscation.

The German musicians and artists Kommissar Hjuler und Mama Baer released some of the most uncompromising works of pornographic sound poetry and improvised noise of 2012 on their own Asylum Lunaticum and Der Schoene-Hjuler Memorial Fond imprints while pioneering an alternative approach to funding. Issuing CD-Rs in runs of ten to 30 copies with elaborate handmade packaging, they doubled up as calling cards for likeminded individuals interested in upgrading them to vinyl, the most spectacular instance of which was Inyrdisk's elaborate double LP edition of Mama Baer's collection of feral nursery rhymes and refusenik guitar, *Exorcismes From All My Fingers*.

Some had to wait a little longer for their moment in the sun, as when, earlier this year, De Stijl offered digital editions of all ten *Poetry Out Loud* LPs, originally privately issued by Peter and Patricia Harleman and Klyd and Linda Watkins between 1969–77. They still sound singular, extrapolating poet Charles Olson's vision of Projective Verse into live vocal improvisations with just enough repetition and effects to nudge it into the realms of primitive psychedelia.

Grouper, aka Portland's Liz Harris, has consistently chosen to release her records through her own Yellow Electric imprint, keeping control of presentation and print runs while expanding her roster in 2012 to take in releases by acknowledged inspirations like New Zealand guitarist Roy Montgomery alongside archival releases by his group Dadamah. Pat Murano of The No-Neck Blues Band, a group that is almost synonymous with the more hermetic end of private press, launched his own Kelippah label in order to facilitate the release of an ambitious series of minimal electronic LPs under his Decimus guise, all themed according to the astrological attributions of the first century Latin poet Decimus Magnus Ausonius.

Key 1990s underground groups Harry Pussy and The Shadow Ring both presented expanded double LP collections of rare and unreleased material via their own Palilalia and Kye imprints, while established underground acts like Marcia Bassett's Zaimph (on *Imagine Yourself Here...*) and Ben Chasny's Six Organs Of Admittance (*Maria Kapel*) returned to their private press roots to release music that pushed beyond their established musical identities. In the tradition of Jandek's Corwood Industries, guitarist Willie Lane, who has previously released works through Matthew Valentine and Erika Elder's Child Of Microtones label, and Norwegian multi-instrumentalist Nils Rostad both self-released limited run vinyl editions that perfectly captured the sound of lonely. But one of the undisputed jewels of the 2012 private press revolution was Damon McMahon aka Amen Dunes's self-released three track 7" EP, *Ethio Covers*, wherein he hymned his love for 1960s and 70s Ethiopian and Eritrean music in a series of translations that traded sub-Saharan heat for the oceanic appeal of *Starsailor*-era Tim Buckley.

In parallel to the new wave of private press releases, 2012 saw plenty of deep digging into the vaults in search of historical models of artistic self-sufficiency. None was more salutary than the rescuing from oblivion of A To Austr's *Musics From Holyground* by Anasitzi Records. Originally issued by the Holyground collective in Wakefield in 1970, it's widely regarded as the UK's first true private press

imprint. Even by this year's standards, it remains inviolable to time and trends, with its vision of a parallel, specifically English psychedelic tradition that draws as much on imagined vaudeville, folk and eccentric experimental strains as it does on what was actually happening at the time. Archaia's self-titled 1976 private press LP, an inspired combination of Cro-Magnon rhythms and manhandled electronics that outstripped punk's vision of primitive excess before it even got started, finally got the reissue treatment thanks to Papaaver, a new label dedicated to unearthing lost classics. Italy's Wah Wah Records issued deluxe editions of postcards from oblivion like the pre-Gong/Universal Mutant Repertory Company project Princess Flower And The Moon Rays, originally issued in a run of 100 copies in 1968, and the sole album by Spacecraft, the sci-fi/punk duo of John Livengood of Red Noise and Ivan Coaquette of MEV. Numero Group presented the first authorised reissue of Circuit Rider's self-titled late 70s/early 80s biker rock masterpiece, while Belter Records' *Bonehead Crushers* compilation series culled the cream of private pre-Metal/post-psychedelic singles from the late 60s through the early 70s, presenting an alternative canon that privileged emphatic volume over emotive volubility. But it was left to the appropriately grey area/no label reissue of Jayson Black's verging on psychotic *Basic Black* LP from the 1970s, reputedly pressed up for distribution among fellow Alcoholics Anonymous members and family and friends, to exemplify private press's lack of truck with conventional taste, presenting the musings of a self-described "revolting human being" to a soundtrack of surreal concrète assemblage.

Private press has always existed as a form of samizdat publishing, as revolutionary reformulations of consensus reality circulating via an underground railroad. In the late 1960s radical free jazz was almost completely ignored by the major labels, outside of the influence of figures like John Coltrane, so that artist-

William Parker

run private presses sprung up out of necessity, such as Sun Ra's Saturn, Amiri Baraka's Jihad, Charles Tyler's Ak-Ba, Rashied Ali's explicitly named Survival and Milford Graves and Don Pullen's Self Reliance Project, as well as European counterparts like FMP, Incus and ICP. 2012 was rich in free jazz reissues from artist-run labels, premier among which was *Father Of Origin*, the jawdropping two LP/CD/book box set from Eremite dedicated to the secret history of Juma Sultan's Aboriginal Music Society. Established in Woodstock in 1968, the AMS was led by Sultan, a member of Jimi Hendrix's pre-Band Of Gypsys group, Gypsy Sun & Rainbows, and at points in their history they included members of fellow art collectives like St Louis's Black Artists Group and Chicago's AACM. The music expands the standard free jazz set-up into an affirmation of get-down grassroots testifying that even the expertly mastered vinyl can hardly contain, especially on the side that features a gloriously bloodied pre-*Black Beings/World Galaxy* Frank Lowe on saxophone.

But it's William Parker's *Centering: Unreleased Early Recordings 1976–1987* six CD box set, on the Lithuanian NoBusiness Records, that best captures the spirit of private press and its historical and economic challenges. Presenting a series of ferociously radical live and straight-to-tape performances from the heyday of the free jazz underground, the bulk of which were originally scheduled to be released on Parker's own private Centering imprint, the set's highlight is a revelatory dance music piece from 1980 scored for Parker's partner Patricia Nicholson and played by the late David S Ware on saxophone, Parker on bass and the late Denis Charles on drums. The booklet included mock-up sleeves for the intended releases, underlining the utopian ethos of private press as a vision of the future that might never truly come to pass, but in whose dreaming, in time, was birthed the historical conditions necessary for its reception. □

Shawn Records (Grouper); Ken Weiss (Parker)

Liz Harris aka Grouper

Across 2012's dance musics, fluid tempos, slipsliding beat patterns, sonic magnification and data overload produced enthralling derangements of the senses. By **Joe Muggs**

OFF

Beneath

THE

OM Unit

Club music's relationship to regularity has always been complicated, but 2012 saw the music pushing at the constraints of its patterns and grids in radical ways. While for many the story was of a retreat to the safety of familiar forms – mid-90s House and Techno in particular dominated, with a nascent Jungle revival – in darker corners things were pulsing and warping, oozing out of the steady four-square rhythm patterns that have been dance music's foundation at least since the invention of the sequencer. This was not a new genre or style in the conventional sense, rather the convergence of some key trends in 21st century music as certain pressures – slowness, rhythmic slippage, and a more obviously physical interaction with digital production – came to a head, creating an uneasy but thrilling sense of potential.

The tendency towards slower tempos has been brewing for a long time but was everywhere this year. In 2012 the likes of Andy Stott, Demdike Stare, Raime, Holy Other, Old Apparatus, How To Dress Well, Lukid, Om Unit, Hype Williams and Downliners Sekt all dropped releases with rhythms so stretched that they became textural waves, magnifying the surface of every sound. Tracks such as these, when played on suitably sizeable speakers, are chambers into which one can enter – desolate and forbidding with Raime; voluptuous and dangerously seductive with Holy Other; *Tron*-like and glossy with Om Unit; or fantastical and bejewelled, as in the baroque complexity of this year's EPs by Old Apparatus. This was post-dubstep not in the sense of simply applying dubstep's tropes to new rhythms, but in building entirely new takes on what it could have been, from first principles.

Dubstep itself had an eye on those first principles, too. 2012 was the year that the so-called dungeon sound became prominent. This creepy-crawling update of the earliest half-step rhythms with added production finesse and heightened sonic detail saw the stock of originators like Distance, Tunnidge and Kryptic Minds, and newer talents like Mancunians Compa and Biome rising. It was a reminder that dubstep's original appeal was about bodily immersion and undulating push-pull physical dynamics rather than the rave rush and the spectacle of the drop. The increased profile of Digital Mystikz' Coki – only now, after a decade of dubstep production, becoming a full-time musician and launching his own label – was a reminder that even the harder end of dubstep doesn't have to be dependent on percussive impact: at the heart of even Coki's most violent tunes is always the sluggish undercurrent of his preposterously fractal, semi-liquified scrambled egg bass tones.

Even drum 'n' bass flirted with slowness. While one end of the scene intensified, just as commercial dubstep has done, into hyper pop music, reaching vast new global audiences in the process, the spaced-out half-tempo sound of the Autonomic label continued to develop. An album from ASC, various releases on the Space Cadets label, and most fascinatingly a terrifyingly psychedelic EP by Archer & Asanyeh on Romania's DubKraft label all turned drum 'n' bass's velocity in on itself, creating suspenseful, gravity-loosened environments in place of demented drive. House rhythms, too, proved capable of suspending time, particularly in the hands of those re-examining the sparser strains of UK Funky and how it can draw dubstep and Grime's sonorities and double-time funk into eerie, strangely static rhythms, as heard in recordings by Wen, Visionist, Beneath, Filter Dread, Shy One, DVA and Cooly G. And throughout the underground, like an underlying pulse that shapes all around it, ran samples of or references to the trap sound of US hiphop: sluggish, layered 808 kicks, separated by yawning spaces, with pitched-down vocal samples running alongside; a 21st century counterpart to the dread signals of reggae vocalists that were cut into 90s Jungle.

GRID

Cooly G

Coki

As Bristol DJ/producer Pinch put it in his Invisible Jukebox interview (*The Wire* 346), "The way we perceive tempo and the rhythms we're most affiliated with does change, based on situations you're in and the way you tune your head to the world." These new techniques allow us to tune not just the head but the whole nervous system of the listener. Where the rhythmic codes of other dance rhythms may aim for the head, hips and feet, the enveloping flows and larger spaces between the beats of slower music speak to the entire body.

When music is slowed, it seems to come in waves as much as beats or pulses, and there are parallels here with the increasing tendency of dance music to slip off the grid of the 4/4. The psychedelic hiphop of Flying Lotus and co has been elaborating on the rhythmic lurch of J Dilla and the analogue funk of Sa-Ra for some years now, but in 2012 tracks like Flying Lotus's "Pretty Boy Strut", Mark Pritchard's beats for Wiley, and the gloriously juddering melting pots of Geiom's and dÉbruit's albums proved that this was dancefloor music, not simply elaborate gentrification of the form or neo-triphop. It's no coincidence that the London club night where Kutmah, Om Unit, Kidkanevil, Blue Daisy & Offshore play these kind of decentred beats is called Tempo Clash.

Irregular rhythms have had an impact on how the music is made, too. Complex real-time jazz playing is sampled, hands dance across the pads of an MPC sampler, the passed-down skills of the scratch DJ are applied to CDJ decks, touchscreens and other Ableton controllers. This return of the B-boy drive in the scrawling of digital wildstyle lines has been obvious for a while, but in 2012 tempo meltdown and rhythmic looseness converged with this new revelling in physical music production. In dramatic contrast to the overtly cerebral abstractions of 1990s IDM, the input-output between fleshy bodies and digital transmission systems was now bigger, sloppier, stranger.

Contemporary music technology now enables us to zoom into the finest detail and view the inhuman complexity of those sonic surfaces and spaces: we are reminded how much information is being pushed through digital signal processing (DSP), and that the dancefloor experience is our interface with that vertiginous information flow. If the hyper-acceleration of Jungle illustrated the foaming wave of the digital future cresting as it rushed towards us, so this tendency speaks of it having broken and immersed us.

There are parallels here with the New Aesthetic – the mainly visual movement that coalesced in the spring of 2012 around a panel organised by British theorist James Bridle and popularised by writer Bruce Sterling. The New Aesthetic zooms in on the cracks in our everyday datasphere, the glitches in normality and the moments when the comforting shields of digital culture wobble and you see the bots' myriad eyes peering out at you. Revelling in the ruptures between what we have naively cast as two separate worlds, the physical and the digital, the New Aesthetic – and the lurching weirdings of electronic club music that warp the regularity of sequencer patterns – convey the horror and thrill of realising that what is inside the computer and what is outside are all the same system.

William Burroughs's adage that "when you cut into the present the future bleeds out" has some traction here. By defamiliarising the rhythms of common genres, we may be discovering ways through the perceived impasse of 'everything available all at once'; the sense of being overwhelmed by the sheer amount of music available from past and present. These techniques are a way of breaking the comfort and ease that readily available sound manipulation technology – in particular the omnipresent Ableton Live – engenders. The sensual surges of sound in Holy Other, the flailing iPad abuse of Gaslamp Killer or the rusted and irregular edged Grime of Filter Dread and Sd Laika can all be seen as a reaction to the predictably mixed

and mixable flows of the Ableton DJ generation. When precision and perfection become easier than making mistakes, magnifying and repeating errors suddenly seems more compelling.

Whether these experiments will go further or remain just pockets of resistance remains to be seen. Dance music by its very nature is predicated on some degree of regularity and coherence, and the global forces of EDM – the all-encompassing term used since House and dubstep gatecrashed the US music mainstream at the turn of the decade – seem to increase the pressure to create easily packaged units of DJ culture. In *The Wire* 346, Pinch also talked of wanting to emulate the freedom of tempo and metre in the Asian qawwali that he has often taken inspiration from, but bemoaned his lack of the "musical intelligence" he perceived in qawwali musicians. In this statement, there's a hint that a new understanding of rhythm is needed to cope with the possibilities of more flexible and expressive technology.

Dr Matt Yee-King, lecturer in Computer Music at London's Goldsmiths College, and researcher into technological interfaces between sound, mind and information, says, "Musicians might start to realise that the best way to escape the grid is not to use the grid", that is, to abandon sequencers entirely in favour of all-live coding and manipulation. But it is still extraordinarily rare for club musicians and DJs to break loose completely from the metronomic diktats of sequencing tools like Ableton. The grids are still in place. The slippage and melting of rhythmic and tempo constraints that have come to a head in 2012 are not yet a revolution in themselves. Could a digital Coltrane or Hendrix, or a collective sound as improvisatory and free as qawwali, emerge and actually become a part of the world's nightlife rituals? For the first time maybe since the peak of Jungle's rhythmic fury, these extreme possibilities seem tantalisingly within reach. □

Ashes57 (Cooly G)
Cooly G

Archive releases of the year

1–10

1
Laurie Spiegel
The Expanding Universe
Unseen Worlds

New York composer Spiegel realised these computer compositions on Max Mathews's GROOVE system at Bell Labs in the mid-1970s, quietly releasing her first album in 1980 on a folk label. This much expanded reissue, painstakingly remastered by Spiegel herself, included an hour's worth of other GROOVE pieces and established the title track as a key, often neglected work of American minimalism. We said: "She may have written in Fortran code… but folk rhythms and classical counterpoint were embedded in her compositions, giving them a timeless quality that balances out the time stamp of the electronic sounds she used." (November/345)

2
Can
The Lost Tapes
Mute/Spoon

Sifted from more than 50 hours of unheard live and Inner Space studio tapes, this beautifully boxed three disc set collected glorious, gravity-defying and occasionally OTT moments from the Cologne collective's 1968–75 heyday. From onstage freakouts to taut motorik funk, there was material here easily the equal of much of their official album canon. We said: "Can's 'all gates open' sound was anything but sprawling: it takes a high degree of control and self-discipline to get to where they got to… a welcome re-opening of the gates." (June/340)

3
Pauline Oliveros
Reverberations: Tape And Electronic Music 1961–1970
Important

An essential, if initially forbidding, document of Oliveros's early experiments with tape and oscillators, released in the composer's 80th year and including works from her tenures at San Francisco Tape Music Center, Toronto University and Mills College, as well as home recordings. With many of the works previously unreleased, this collection soldered some vital connections in the story of early electronic music. We said: "Through her work, it is possible to retrospectively reconfigure what the aural 20th century was, and what it could still be. If the 20th century has a sonic afterlife, there are few people better placed to tap into it than Oliveros." (June/340)

4
Don Cherry
Organic Music Society
Caprice

Recorded at the beginning of the 1970s, this richly spiced Fourth World jazz formed one of the best expressions of Cherry's pan-global multikulti philosophy. Featuring percussionists Nana Vasconcelos and Okay Temiz, plus a handful of Swedish players, *Organic Music Society* was a utopian crucible of sounds from Africa, India, Tibet, North and South America. Several tracks were recorded in a geodesic dome in Stockholm, and there were two versions of a piece by Terry Riley. We said: "Cherry fulfilled countercultural ideals more thoroughly and with more generosity than any number of posturing contemporary rock stars… the yearning of a mighty soul indeed." (October/344)

5

AR Kane
The Complete Singles Collection
One Little Indian

6

Roxy Music
The Complete Studio Recordings 1972–1982
Virgin

7

Captain Beefheart & His Magic Band
Bat Chain Puller
VAULTernative

The London duo's late 1980s releases emanated from a strange, undefined place perched between Jesus And Mary Chain-style guitar noise and the echo chambers of dub. This extensive collection of early EPs, singles and remixes revealed Rudy Tambala and Alex Ayuli's long-defunct project as an unwitting influence on contemporary hypnagogues, but also reminded us why their spectral and narcotic pop continues to hypnotise. We said: "The duo seem to scream down the years at their stunted millennial progeny – for fuck's sake, if you're going to dream, DREAM BIG!" (December/346)

Remastered from the original analogue tapes, Roxy's studio catalogue – from *Roxy Music* to *Avalon* – was remodelled for a new era, and collected for the first time in a box set. As well as the eight LPs, two bonus discs of singles, B sides and alternative mixes highlighted their singular interventions in the charts over the years. We said: "Most groups find their own voice by... imitating that of others, but, even though Roxy Music's was saturated with references to the past, there was no precedent for their sound." (August/342)

The first official release of this much bootlegged 1976 album smoothed out some rough edges via a dynamic remastering job from the original tape, disinterred at last from the Zappa archives. But the grit and weirdness of Beefheart's vision and the elastic playing of a group of Magic Band members old and new remained undiminished, with hallucinatory biker lore, raging blues stomps and laconic monologues populating an album whose mythic status was now trumped by a vibrant reality. We said: "Loud, beautiful and totally seductive, *Bat Chain Puller* is a very shiny, sexy beast indeed." (April/338)

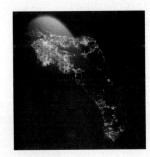

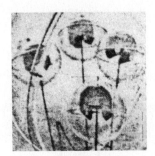

8

Personal Space: Electronic Soul 1974–1984
Various
Numero Group

9

Eliane Radigue
Feedback Works 1969–1970
Alga Marghen

10

Philadelphia International Classics:
The Tom Moulton Remixes
Various
Harmless

Of all the secret histories of black music uncovered by the indefatigable Numero Group label, this was one of the most alluring. The advent of affordable synthesizers in the 1970s enabled the birth of the home studio, and *Personal Space* told the story of the now forgotten soul stars and lover men making bedroom music in surburban US backwaters away from the metropolis. We said: "*Personal Space* opens a window on a hitherto unknown world of autonomic soul savants who – no matter how closely they adhere to the soul template – marched to heir own funky drummer." (March/337)

Before she got her first synthesizer, when concrète and tape works still didn't register as music in the public mind, Radigue undertook a brief but intense series of feedback experiments with two or three recorders running out of synch with each other, and this double LP compiled the most successful results. Given her non-musical sources, she happily accepted compiler Emmanuel Holterbach's job description of her younger self as a lover of sounds, and these early feedback works, she responded, "were innocent loves". We said: "Murky but engagingly decentred analogue soundworlds... These pieces exist... as key indicators of Radigue's work at a fertile and active time." (October/344)

The 40th anniversary of Philadelphia International Records prompted a host of retrospective releases, of which *Philadelphia International Classics: The Tom Moulton Remixes* was the most ambitious. Taking eight classic disco-era Tom Moulton reel-to-reel reworkings of Philadelphia International tracks, the Harmless label commissioned a further 16 mixes from Moulton and rescued another seven from the archive, creating a definitive set of Philly classics reworked by the godfather of the remix. We said: "The quality of his remixes (totalling well over 4000 to date) have ensured his place as dance music's most indispensable figure." (April/338)

Archive releases
of the year
11–50

11

Charles Mingus
*The Jazz Workshop Concerts
1964–1965*
Mosaic

12

Ruff Sqwad
White Label Classics
No Hats No Hoods

13

William Parker
*Centering: Unreleased Early
Recordings 1976–1987*
NoBusiness

14

Pyrolator
Inland
Bureau B

19

Sleep
Dopesmoker
Southern Lord

20

Smith & Mighty
*The Three Stripe Collection
1985–1990*
Bristol Archive

21

Gareth Williams & Mary Currie
Flaming Tunes
Blackest Ever Black

22

David Cain & Ronald Duncan
The Seasons
Trunk

27

William Basinski
The Disintegration Loops
Temporary Residence

28

General Strike
Danger In Paradise
Staubgold

29

*Time To Go: The Southern
Psychedelic Moment 1981–1986*
Various
Flying Nun

30

Ike Yard
Ike Yard
Desire

35

Black Rain
*Now I'm Just A Number:
Soundtracks 1994–1995*
Blackest Ever Black

36

Michael Chapman
Rainmaker
Light In The Attic

37

*Listen, Whitey! The Sounds Of
Black Power 1967–1974*
Various
Light In The Attic

38

Nico
The End
Universal/Island

43

The Shadow Ring
Remains Unchanged
Kye

44

Harry Pussy
One Plus One
Palilalia

45

John Carpenter & Alan Howarth
*Halloween III: Season Of
The Witch*
Death Waltz

46

Monoton
Monotonprodukt 07
Desire

15

Marshall McLuhan/Quentin Fiore/Jerome Agel
The Medium Is The Massage
Five Day Weekend

16

Cecil Taylor
Fly! Fly! Fly! Fly! Fly!
Promising Music

17

Bernard Parmegiani
L'Oeil Écoute/Dedans-Dehors
Recollection GRM

18

King Crimson
Larks' Tongues In Aspic
40th Anniversary Edition
DGM/Panegyric

23

Sensations' Fix
Music Is Painting In The Air
Rvng Intl

24

Witch
We Intend To Cause Havoc!
Now-Again

25

Daphne Oram
The Oram Tapes Volume 1
Young Americans

26

Electric Eden: Unearthing Britain's Visionary Music
Various
Universal

31

Steve Lacy
The Sun
Emanem

32

Pierre Schaeffer
Le Trièdre Fertile
Recollection GRM

33

This Ain't Chicago:
The Underground Sound Of UK House And Acid 1987–1991
Various
Strut

34

Drexciya
Journey Of The Deep Sea Dweller II
Clone

39

The Pin Group
Ambivalence
Flying Nun

40

Andrzej Korzynski
Possession
Finders Keepers

41

The Velvet Underground & Nico
The Velvet Underground & Nico
45th Anniversary Edition
Polydor/Universal

42

Rolf Julius
Raining
Western Vinyl

47

Zs
Score: The Complete Sextet Works 2002–2007
Northern Spy

48

Porter Ricks
Biokinetcs
Type

49

Qat, Coffee & Qambus: Raw 45s From Yemen
Various
Dust-To-Digital/Parlontone

50

Frank Zappa
Hot Rats
Universal/Zappa

Oren Ambarchi
2012 has been a hectic year with lots of travel, shows and projects. In the midst of it all, I was fortunate to experience some great concerts including: Fushitsusha in Tokyo; Charlemagne Palestine playing a private pipe organ concert in Kyushu; Rushford/Talia duo; Marco Fusinato's mindblowing set opening for Earth. Matt Middleton busting out one of the greatest guitar solos ever with The Aesthetics. Will Guthrie. Lasse Marhaug finally coming to Australia. Orcutt/Bishop/Corsano at Hopscotch, North Carolina. Keith Fullerton Whitman. Tetuzi Akiyama/crys cole. My four year old entertaining tram commuters with spontaneous renditions of AC/DC, Led Zep and McCartney. John Tilbury playing Feldman's *Palais De Mari* at Ilan Volkov's incredibly inspiring Tectonics festival in Reykjavik. Ilan invited me there to work with The Icelandic Symphony Orchestra, an experience I'll never forget. I was also fortunate to work with Mr Tilbury there and at Cafe Oto in London later in the year.

Other memorable collab shows were duos with Jim O'Rourke in Japan, trio shows with Jim and Keiji Haino in Kyushu/Tokyo, duo with Charlemagne Palestine in London ("drums! drums! drums!"), Afternoon Tea reunion in Berlin, Fire! Scandinavian tour, Merzbow duo in Sydney, theatre/dance projects with Benedict Andrews and Lucy Guerin, and premiering the live version of *Knots* with an ensemble in Melbourne.

Films: Friedkin's *Killer Joe* and Lanthimos's *Alps*. I also saw a bear on a beach in Winnipeg (!). And finally, listening to records with good friends and a good single malt is one of life's greatest pleasures.

Dylan Carlson
I have spent a significant portion of this year travelling – spending a month and a half from April to May in Northern England and Scotland making environmental recordings at sites of human/spirit interaction. Finding out that support for my more personal and, on the surface, outlandish projects is there (thank you to all the contributors who made my first foray into Kickstarter a success). Recording a Latitudes release of British songs with Teresa Colamonaco on vocals and Jodie Cox on guitar. An amazing trip to Suffolk to speak with a direct source of East Anglian toad bone lore was the absolute highlight to an amazing journey across the United Kingdom, a land and people I love dearly. Recording my first 7" (a

double) with the talented Rosie Knight (the Hackney lass). Seeing my friend, artist Simon Fowler, start his own music label, Small But Hard. Hanging out in Walthamstow with Peter, artist Marie Plum, Penny and Andrew. Matt from Falkeners. The Army Museum with artist Kathy Ward. *Battle Of The Eyes*'s amazing artwork. My first circumnavigation of the globe: Earth going to New Zealand, Australia and Japan. Then to London to begin first drcarlsonalbion tour of the isles, with Teresa on vocals and Rogier Smal on drums. During time off, meeting Clina, who took us to Tara and the hill of the Cailleach. Timmo's secret dolmen. Drew taking us to the Scottish folk archives in Edinburgh. Alice's amazing baking and hospitality in Glasgow. Looking for new methods of doing things, investigating digital recording and laptop musical applications (horrors – losing my Luddite card). Realising the technology is not the problem, but how it's used. Watching the death of the industry paradigm that has been in existence for 70 plus years. Labels and distributors and stores going out. Increasingly things will be self-produced and licensed or sold directly.

Touring will have to change as well. It will require audiences, promoters and bands to be willing to take risks. The 'different city every night' military campaign style is so destructive, environmentally and personally. Large amounts of fossil fuels and integration in the global economy are required. An attitude of an occupying army (the band versus everyone else). Playing venues run by large companies (Live Nation and Clear Channel). Instead, I would like to see residencies like in times past. Say three nights at smaller venues or different smaller venues. The band experiencing the environment of a place, interacting with people. Sets could vary and each experience would be a unique moment in time, the creation of a sacred space, for lack of a better term. Of course, the bands and promoters would have to forgo the idea of quickly recouping costs with one big show. Audiences would have to be willing to take the chance of which performance, or all of them; ticket prices would need to be less, otherwise it's just people getting rinsed.

Obviously it's a losing battle against downloading. But it will force bands to make items that are worth the investment of the audience. Hopefully live music will be restored to the forefront, and the privileging of recordings and objects lessened.

Rhodri Davies
Cons: Lol Coxhill's death. The US's treatment of Bradley Manning and continued use of drones. Composers writing to Sound And Music bemoaning their loss of privilege.

Pros: Celebrating my daughter's first birthday. Continuing duo work with John Butcher. Releasing a solo album with the alt.vinyl label. Playing with Mazen Kerbaj, Sharif Sehnaoui and Charbel Haber at the iconic Morden Tower. Playing a duo with

Paul Lovens. Getting soaked by the tide while burning a harp on Borth beach with photographer Bruce Cardwell. A trip to New York to receive a much appreciated Foundation for Contemporary Arts award. Experiencing La Monte Young and Marian Zazeela's Dream House and visiting poet Thomas Evans and family. Performing Eliane Radigue's *OCCAM I* in the reverberating acoustics of Emanuel Vigeland's Mausoleum in Oslo and being locked in the burial chamber alone for two hours. Seeing The Bohman Brothers play at the Royal Albert Hall and being part of Ilan Volkov's John Cage Proms extravaganza. Giving first performances of new pieces by Phill Niblock, Eliane Radigue and Philip Corner at AV Festival, Angelica and HCMF. Performing a live soundtrack for Fluxus films with the great Ben Patterson. Accompanying Harry Smith's *Early Abstractions* films at Tusk Festival.

Exhibitions: Benedict Drew The Persuaders, Jonathan Schipper Slow Motion Car Crash, Elizabeth Price HERE and Emma Hart TO DO.

Albums: Christoph Heemann *The Rings Of Saturn*, Charbel Haber *It Ended Up Being A Great Day, Mr. Allende*, :zoviet*france: *7.10.12*, Richard Dawson *The Magic Bridge*, Davies/Mukarji/Lazaridou-Chatzigoga *Outwash* and Matt Davis *Ghost/Light*.

Emptyset
Highpoints of the year were releasing *Medium* and completing *Collapsed* for raster-noton as well as presenting the *Fall Back* live recording by Roly Porter and Cynthia Millar on Subtext. Travels included spending time on a farm in West Virginia, visiting Norway and Sweden as well as performances at the Wysing Arts Festival, raster-noton's Electric Campfire in Rome, Semibreve, Unsound and Arnolfini, then finally ending the year developing an installation for the Architecture Foundation in London.

Records we enjoyed included Thomas Köner *Novaya Zemlya*, Powell *Body Music*, Lee Gamble *Diversions 1994–1996*, Andy Stott *Luxury Problems*, Max Richter *Vivaldi Recomposed*, Dome 3 on Editions Mego and Holly Herndon's debut album. Live shows of note included Carl Michael von Hausswolff at Sonic Acts, Kevin Drumm at Cafe Oto, both snd and Kouhei Matsunaga at the Shacklewell Arms, Roly Porter at Semibreve in Braga, Regis at Blackest Ever Black, Factory Floor in the Tate Modern Tanks and Demdike Stare in a synagogue at Unsound. Memorable exhibitions included Lis Rhodes at the ICA, Cerith Wyn Evans at the De La Warr Pavilion, Yuri Pattison at Space Studios, Elizabeth Price in the Turner Prize and Ryoji Ikeda at Hamburger Bahnhof.

Projects we are looking forward to next year include releasing a new record by Paul Jebanasam through Subtext and finishing our third album, developing a film installation for Tate Britain and performing at Kunsthalle Zurich.

Mark Fell

The cancellation of this year's Bloc festival halfway through the first evening was extremely disappointing. In my opinion Bloc is one of Britain's most interesting get-togethers, and what should have been a massive achievement turned out to be an unmitigated disaster. Although I'm sympathetic to the fans who lost out, I'm also supportive of the festival, which I thought was both well organised and well curated. From the beginning, the security around the event was insane. At the artist entrance, guards gave me a ridiculously thorough (and obviously pointless) search. Its only function was perhaps to demonstrate the idea of 'security' to an anxious troop of police officers assembled a few feet away. My hotel seemed prepared for a zombie holocaust – constructed, no doubt, on the fear of hordes of braindead ravers spreading their virus around the planet until humanity finally reduces itself to an amorphous blob of cold, spent flesh. Fear shifted from background to foreground, and onsite, shortly before shut-down, ludicrous comparisons were made to the Hillsborough disaster of 1989. Bloc occupied a precarious spatial and temporal position – at the heart of the 2012 Olympic site and weeks before the opening ceremony. The last thing Britain's capital needed at that point was death by overpopulation.

Weeks later, the opening ceremony came and went, offering a musical shadow of what should have happened a couple of kilometres south east. We should remember that, in its previous incarnation, this government passed a law, the sole aim of which was to criminalise rave culture. It made specific reference to music "wholly or predominantly characterised by the emission of a succession of repetitive beats"... ironic to see the same politicians badly role-playing a state-endorsed celebration of such musics. For me, Bloc's cancellation demonstrates two things: the massive popular audience for this kind of music, and how it is often met with a kind of institutionalised fear – framed as an object of anthropological rather than aesthetic interest. Best record of the year was V by KTL – amazing. Best festival was South Asian Arts (Leeds) summer solstice all-nighter – stunning performances of night ragas; I'll be there in 2013.

Luke Fowler

It's been an intense but rewarding year and things don't seem to be slowing down. As I write this I'm preparing for a concert with Jean-Luc Guionnet at the CCA and Richard Youngs at ZKM. The year began with the finalising of my two year portrait film of RD Laing, *All Divided Selves*, that was first installed in a collaborative exhibition with Toshiya Tsunoda at Inverleith House; having to deal with the Turner Prize as a result of this show was unexpected to say the least. I enjoyed having the opportunity to chat with Elizabeth Price and collaborate with 6a Architects on *Model For An Artists' Cinema*; that, I hope, with the film, will have a long life after the transient excitement for this year's shortlist fades into the next.

The rare opportunity to see two performances of Hanne Darboven's music in one year, with an equally wonderful concert by Yoshi Wada also at the AV Festival, left its mark. As did my second visit to the Greek countryside for the monumental Temenos screenings of Gregory Markopolous's magnum opus *ENIAIOS*, organised by his former partner, the equally exceptional film maker Robert Beavers.

I spent an unusually warm summer in Vancouver hanging out with the charming Hank Bull at the Western Front, mostly practising and composing. I enjoyed repeated plays of his great collection of Robert Ashley and Martin Bartlett records. I relished the chance to work with Josh Stevenson at the astounding Otic Sound, where I played my Small Serge system alongside their huge EMS Synthi 100. Otherwise an ongoing and fruitful musical collaboration developed with Richard Youngs, who adapted laments by Blake and Spitalfields silk weavers for my latest film on EP Thompson and the Workers' Educational Association. I have fond and funny memories of recording together with him and Toshiya Tsunoda, and also Heatsick at my studio. No idea if these tapes will ever see the light of day.

The campaign against Creative Scotland, with its neoliberal values and prescription of a market model to public arts funding, tainted an otherwise good year. Its ill-conceived decision to cut funding to the vital *Variant* magazine, as well as asserting an authoritarian and controlling yearly review of flexibly funded arts organisations (which are most of the places I work and gather in), and the frankly incomprehensible decision to ditch peer review for grants, raised the alarm all round.

As the double-dip recession bites, I welcomed the return of a social and politically engaged art. This was visible in the quality programming by Alex Sainsbury at London's Raven Row, whose APG show struck a deep chord, as well as equally interesting events by Scottish organisations Strickland Distribution and the indefatigable Arika. A good year for Tony Conrad fans, with the release of Brandon W Joseph's new book *The Roh And The Cooked* on his travels to Europe in 1972 and two amazing shows of his invented instruments at Galerie Buchholz in Cologne and Berlin.

Any misgivings I may have had about showing a feature length film in a gallery were thrown into sharp relief by a very attentive audience who sat through a two day retrospective of my films at the inspiring Vienna Film Museum. It was a strange experience to revisit 12 years of my life over those two bright autumn days.

I cannot forget the mesmeric experience of seeing Robert Ashley perform solo, paired with a successful reworking of his TV opera *Private Lives* by Alex Waterman, and finally travelling with Ben Vida, whose Pan record featured heavily in my soundtrack to the year.

Keiji Haino

Fushitsusha's October tour of Europe was very important to me – and I'd like to thank everyone who attended the shows. We toured with a different line-up from the albums, but I feel confident that we are gradually getting closer to the ideas I've been talking about for the past 20 years, in terms of the use of space (ma) and the music's dynamic range. Concentration on the midrange can lead to almost infinite extension of the upper and lower ranges, and I feel like I've found more effective ways to communicate that.

As always, I've been listening to an insane amount of music. My big discovery this year was June Tabor. There's a shocking freshness to her music – I get the strange feeling that it simultaneously fits and doesn't fit either daytime or nighttime. With people like her and Martin Carthy, I get really jealous of how they can put themselves into traditional material. I've also been going back to Italian symphonic prog to try to figure out why I always hated it. It would be better for me to find something to like in it.

The other big thing on my mind is these demonstrations against nuclear power. They stand around outside, then as soon as it turns ten o'clock, they all head off home and turn on their electric heaters. If you want to protest, change your lifestyle and stop using so much electricity! If we really want to get rid of nuclear power, we need to reduce our reliance on it. I'd like people to think about that more.

Laurel Halo

I like listening to and thinking about music in terms of keywords, blank vs not blank music. Because of this I thought I could be good at writing TV cues and sent some to a music library this year, but all my submissions were rejected – according to the company they weren't blank enough, they still sounded too much like standalone, 'real' music (this was probably a nice way of saying my cues were shit, though I could have sworn I nailed the forlorn yet hopeful prescription drug ad sound). "Cruise ship employee rape music", "gigolo exposé music", "Whitney Houston goodbye music" etc. It's not a 1:1 that less identifiable music is better, but keyword listening can help sort the felt music from the unfelt. How can you ever accurately describe in words what makes music felt? How can you keyword the contour or colour of intent? 2012's mass doomsday nervosa fueled some potent, wonderful music, yet there's a growing amoeba of flat, empty, brand-driven musics (literally Lana Del Rey for H&M) that rely on listeners who don't really care about what makes music music – that indescribable depth and grit, that undertow of fully charged vibrational force. Dead in the eyes/hearts/ears listeners are fuel for misanthropy. From this year I've loved a lot of new recordings (Jeremih, Cooly G, Usher's "Climax", Gatekeeper, Terrence Dixon, Peter Van Hoesen, Lee Gamble, Deepchord) and played alongside incredible artists (M Geddes Gangras, Dabrye, Jam City, Kuedo, Hieroglyphic Being, Ital, Demdike Stare, Hyperdub crew, Hippos crew, Pete Swanson, Slava, Teengirl, Sun Araw), all of which have that elusive, sublime grip. It feels good that no matter how noxious the content cloud becomes the wordless depth of musical spirit can't waver.

Mary Halvorson

2012 was a great year for live music. I heard amazing performances by Anthony Braxton, Bill Frisell, Kris Davis, Brian Chase, Wayne Shorter, Normal Love, Matt Mitchell and Dan Weiss duo, Extra Life, Jason Cady and Henry Threadgill, just to name a few. I also took part in tribute events for two of my guitar heroes: Jim Hall and Derek Bailey. Joe Morris – my guitar teacher and one of the most creative musicians on the planet – published an excellent book called *Perpetual Frontier: The Properties Of Free Music*. I formed two new bands: Thumbscrew (with Michael Formanek and Tomas Fujiwara), and Secret Keeper (with Stephan Crump). Much of my energy this year was spent composing and recording an album with my newly formed septet. I also started learning French, watched lots of basketball games and read five novels by Lionel Shriver. 2012 saw the release of many great albums including Ches Smith's *Psycho Predictions*, Jacob Garchik's *The Heavens: The Athiest Gospel Trombone Album*, Tim Berne's *Snakeoil*, Eivind Opsvik's *Overseas IV*, Michael Formanek's *Small Places*, Frank Ocean's *Channel Orange*, and The Melvins' *Freak Puke*.

Ian Helliwell

Another routinely disappointing Brighton Festival limped by in 2012 with its high ticket prices and vast amount of arts funding, leaving Brighton's vital annual events such as Cinecity and Colour Out Of Space struggling to function. Jeremy Deller and Nick Abrahams's workmanlike documentary *The Bruce Lacey Experience* was screened: a film that couldn't fail, given Lacey's irrepressible energy and fascinating career, though there was no critique of his slide into vapid New Age mumbo-jumbo, leaving his glorious robot-building days behind. It was valuable to have *The Lacey Rituals* double DVD set released; though very much a curate's egg, the irreverent 1970s *Human Behaviour* films stood out for me as truly displaying the singular Lacey vision.

Having loaned some props and tape loops, and spent an absorbing afternoon visiting the set, I was particularly intrigued to see *Berberian Sound Studio*. Peter Strickland's film was consistently arresting both visually and sonically, and I couldn't resist a smile at my oscilloscope's giant close-up cameo.

A visit to the Daphne Oram archive at Goldsmiths provided stimulating reading at this enlightening resource. I caught up on correspondence between Daphne and Roy Cooper, a week before an accomplished presentation at the Science Museum by Nicolas Helm-Grovas on Cooper and the Adwick School initiative in the 1960s, which introduced electronics and tape into the classroom.

At the start of 2012, with the FC Judd *Electronics Without Tears* album released, it was a pleasure to present my *Practical Electronica* film at Cafe Oto, and continuing this thread of research, I look forward in 2013 to finding a publisher for my A–Z book of early British electronic music composers.

Hieroglyphic Being

I do what I do to bring Positivity through my art and help better the world. Creativity is the most positive thing I can do. This is my redemption.

Books: Robert Charroux *100,000 Years Of Man's Unknown History*, Edgar Cayce *The Sleeping Prophet*, Andrew Tomas *We Are Not The First*, Erich von Däniken *Chariots Of The Gods*, Swami Panchadasi *The Human Aura*.

Films: *The Awakening*, *Kymatica*.

2013 forward: 1 Being a better being. 2 The world changing its vibrational frequencies 2 a higher state. 3 Looking 4 love or long live the flesh (lust). 4 Thankful 4 2012 & all entities in passing (rewind). 5 *Imaginary Landscapes #8* – 2×12" and CD out 5 February 2013 by Hieroglyphic Being.

Artists discovered: Demdike Stare, Deviere, Julia Holter, Holly Herndon, Giorgio Luceri, Hild Sofie Tafjord. Artists/genres rediscovered: Weather Report, Lalo Schifrin, Jaco Pastorius, jazz fusion, orchestral/cinematic/soundtrack music, Marcus Belgrave.

The come up: mathematicsrecordings. blogspot.com, soundcloud.com/ somuchnoise2beheard, Groovedis.com.

Collaborations: Holly Herndon, The Sun Ra Arkestra (Sun-Ra) Re-Interpetations, Chris & Cosey compiled by ? (Paul S U readin this)? Chanel von Habsburg-Lothringen (visual artist). Highlight of 2012: opening for The Sun Ra Arkestra @ The Barbican. Experimentation live @ Royal Albert Hall. Mentors: Adonis & Steve Poindexter. Thank U 4 all the haters and lovers of what I do 4 without U there be no me.

Julia Holter

2012 was the first year of my life that I spent a lot of time in a van with a bunch of dudes. It was wonderful actually, but my first impression of touring is that it produces a seemingly paradoxical combination of yearning for alone time and extreme loneliness. There were two records that I turned to over and over again while looking out the van window in these times of internal conflict, and it's funny because they both happen to be friends of mine. Laurel Halo's *Quarantine* did so much for me on a visceral level, and then beyond. I felt like I was ingesting the music or absorbing it through my skin. It's one of the most beautiful works I've heard because of its mercurial ability to evoke new experiences in a listener every time, and to feel so personal while passing through endless pathways of mysterious otherworldly imagery.

Nite Jewel's *One Second Of Love* (along with her track "Sister" on a 7" release this year) also continually supplied my van landscape with imagery – not so otherworldly this time, but more like the experience of seeing a photograph. As if little windows of alternate everyday realities were displayed on the van seats by way of Polaroids, each one from a different song. Her poetry is almost conversational in tone, but it never fully discloses everything; just expertly lingers on the right image/situation, repeats it and filters it through a bold and clear voice.

Listening to these pieces of music is exciting because it's clear that both of the people making them are impulsively writing what they want, without strategising. It's just coming out, thoughtful and well formed, but also with so much soul. For 2013 I plan to maintain my optimistic belief that the majority of people want to be allowed to experience their own music experience in their vans, and not be force-fed manipulative music. The dubstepped teenagers might like your 20 minute long musique concrète journey. Just put a lot of love into it and they'll probably be intrigued.

Eli Keszler

Settling into New York. Working on the *L-Carrier* installation with the large ensemble. Playing at Barbican/St Luke's with Mega Fortress and Reliquary House – climbing above the light trusses at the ceiling to install the piano wire. Driving around Europe with Ashley Paul and Geoff Mullen, and

finally seeing the Collection de l'Art Brut in Lausanne. Visiting the Parthenon. Biking around Berlin. Great concerts like The Flux Quartet at Paula Cooper Gallery performing Nono's *Fragmente – Stille. An Diotima.* Michael Tilson Thomas conducting Feldman's *Piano And Orchestra* at Carnegie Hall. Some new records for me, like Jakob Ullmann's *Fremde Zeit – Addendum*. Listening to early morning radio on WKCR in New York. Working on prints and drawings in the new studio. Cooking with the smoker in the backyard. Looking forward to next year – sketching a small orchestra piece, which is starting to settle in right about now.

Suzanne Langille

This was the year I found people. Social media has its vices, but it's how I discovered a new composer. Well, not new, but I'd never heard the music of Clint Heidorn of Los Angeles (*Atwater*, *The Oak Tree*) before connecting. Got him with Loren (Connors) for an Issue Project duet in Brooklyn and it was guitar haiku. It's how I 'discovered' visual artist MP Landis, a painter with a genuine connection to the id. He's part of our new *I Wish I Didn't Dream* release on Northern Spy, with a story by Kurt Gottschalk. It's how I first heard talented cellist Helena Espvall. It's how I reconnected with Isobel Sollenberger of Bardo Pond, a lovely soul and compelling voice. It's where I was mesmerised by the piano of Adam Casey of Melbourne (*The Boy Who Spoke Clouds*). And although I didn't find them there, I kept in touch via media with my favourite new blues brothers, Jozef van Wissem and Jim Jarmusch, those two tall dudes trotting the globe these days.

This is also the year I lost people. Some profound personal losses that no words can describe. On a gentler level, I'm not sure exactly when she left NYC and returned to Lisbon, but I've been missing that delightfully unique bassist Margarida Garcia all year. Finally, I miss the presence of Sonic Youth, although I expect that its fearless musicians will be heard in many different and new incarnations as we all move forward.

R Stevie Moore

Well, well, look at us here again already, end of the last, beginning of the next. Start here. One moore time, to be kind rewind.

For me 2012 represents naturally progressive personal growth, continuing the

wild new saga I'd suddenly started in 2011 at age 59. *The Wire* cover story (issue 340) changed my life. More world touring. More increased public acknowledgment of my musical worth. Felt good. Work and travel was mighty hard for this lazy old geezer, relentless at times. Venue extremes from small pointless gigs in beer taverns all the way up to killing it at Denmark's Roskilde Festival. And, even better than live performances in some ways, much new RSM vinyl was unveiled. New film documentaries forthcoming. My Bandcamp arsenal seems to be blowing up biggie. And now I'm out on the West Coast, recording euphoria with Jason Falkner.

Not much else I can currently recall... I loved discovering bands like Toy, Keel Her, The Vaccines and Civil Civic. Ariel's *Mature Themes* still be da bomb. Tim Burgess is a blessed angelic upstart. Saw no movies, read no books, ignored art and the media. Blame the weather. Here comes the flood. Wino potheads anonymous. Nashville rest stops and collection agencies. Still prefer my water sparkling.

Forgive I forget. Memory almost shot. Nevertheless not optimistic. Me, me, me... it's all about the gnarly narcissism. NJ dead end, global win/win sitch.

I'd like to thank the academy.

Pauline Oliveros

Oliveros@80 has been a year of celebration for me, with wonderful concert birthday parties. I am very thankful to all the venues in different parts of the world who have organised performances of my work, and to the Deep Listening Institute that has coordinated many new publications and communications.

I am also grateful to Important Records for releasing *Reverberations: Tape And Electronic Music 1961–1970*, a box set of 12 CDs of my work that mostly had never been released before. The packaging is extraordinary and reflective of that era, and is beautifully done. Additionally, I am grateful to my colleague Jonas Braasch, an acoustician and sonic architect who succeeded in simulating the amazing acoustics of the Dan Harpole Cistern, where The Deep Listening Band recorded 1989's *Deep Listening* on New Albion. The Cistern Simulation was a great birthday present, as we had dreamed of performing on stage with those acoustics this way since 1988. The dream came true, and more thanks go to Johannes Goebel, Director of Experimental Media and Performing Arts Center (EMPAC) at Rensselaer Polytechnic Institute, for programming Deep Listening Band and the Cistern Simulation for my birthday in May.

I am thankful to all my musical friends and collaborators for the increasingly deep musical experiences that seem miraculous. I salute my students, who are doing great things in the world and continue to teach me. I am grateful to be beginning my ninth decade of life with more activity than ever. It is fun and fulfilling. May it ever be so for all.

Pelt (Mike Gangloff)
Here in Poplar Hollow I'm trying to patch up a floor that some termites chewed on, but didn't quite get all the way through, and maybe that's a good analogue to how the year's been. On a personal front, the couple of years before this were pretty rotten, from Jack Rose's death to the bust-up of my marriage to a bunch of stuff I'm not going to bore you with now. So this year was all about saying yes – to travel and musical opportunities and really to the idea of love again, dramatic and over the top as that sounds. I had a lot of 'am I dreaming?' moments, like playing with Michael Morley or Michael Chapman, Steve Gunn or new pals Kelly and Pascal from Part Wild Horses Mane On Both Sides. I travelled across the Atlantic nearly as many times this year as I'd been in my entire life previously, and got in some fantastic music making with Dave and Vicky in Meitheal, with The Twigs in places like Le Viaduc in Brussels and the Fox & Goose in Hebden Bridge, and with Pelt, which has been lurching back into activity, though we never quit. Best of all, though, were trips in the spring and fall – to Ireland with Cara, the woman who's let me share her life this year, and to Pelt shows at Cafe Oto and Tusk with my Anglophile son Tycho, who's wanted to travel with me for years. It's been a year of shoring up, really. Because – to strain my metaphor even farther – even the wings of love can't carry you far if the floor is caving in.

Pinch
2012 has been a busy year for me. Powered on by the *Fabriclive* mix, and last November's LP with Shackelton, I've been carting my dubplates around the globe to shows in the USA, Russia, Japan and China as well as all across Europe and up and down the UK. I've released with Photek, worked on music with Roska, Deleted Scenes and with a longtime hero of mine, Adrian Sherwood, on a new LP set to drop next year.

Sometimes I forget how lucky I am to be in this position. I'll catch myself whingeing about having to take early flights or stay in shitty hotels and feel quietly pretentious. Usually that's when I wonder what it's all about these days – what's the point of 'it' all? In the earlier days of dubstep I was part of a fledgling community of misfits and urban music geeks. 'It' was all so clear to me – there was a sense of purpose, even an honour to 'it'. 'It' wasn't a race for more Facebook fans or Twitter followers. 'It' was about seeking

exciting new music-based experiences, shared by others with an equal thirst for 'it'. I've often worried 'it' is not there anymore.

I found myself standing in a darkened basement of a Bristol nightclub recently, swaying to the sounds of the Young Echo crew. I heard classics dropped seamlessly alongside their own fresh dubplates. I heard 'it' and I heard 'it' good. I felt happy. 'It' is an energy and an enthusiasm – the form it takes isn't the important thing to look for. This is a good thought for me to carry into 2013.

Simon Reynell (Another Timbre)
More than ever I feel that things in 2012 passed me by, because I spent so long immersed in Wandelweiser music, which can be like a drug that makes it difficult to hear anything else. So, onanistically, my highlight has to be the five days in midsummer when Jürg Frey and Radu Malfatti were here playing their respective instruments so wonderfully. I got a kick too from the number of musicians (young ones especially) now operating in that no-man's land that I like so much between improvisation and composed experimental music, an area that's currently so vibrant that it's hard to keep up.

Meanwhile I kept on trying to work out what it means to run a label in an age of digital distribution when more and more people expect to access music for free, and the way forward still seems clear as mud. But some excellent CDs appeared nonetheless. Leaving Wandelweiser aside, 2012 saw, among others, Sebastian Lexer and Christoph Schiller's *Luftwurzeln* (Matchless), Pascal Battus and Alfredo Costa Monteiro's *Fêlure* (Organised Music From Thessaloniki) and Jakob Ullmann's *Fremde Zeit – Addendum* (Edition RZ).

I also spent fruitful hours acquainting myself further with the music of two underrated English composers – James Saunders and Laurence Crane, but am aware that there must be so many others across the world whose music I haven't yet heard. In 2013 I must get out more.

Negatives? Musically nothing, but let's get rid of this mean-spirited and inept government.

Richard Skelton
Late last year, Autumn and I returned to the UK from the west of Ireland, settling in a small, narrow valley in south west Cumbria – a place so steep-sided that the sun barely breached the skyline all winter. The combined effect of altitude, sun deprivation and perpetual mist is

one of mild sedation. The world beyond the fell wall at times seems an indistinct blur.

Nevertheless, certain things have made it up the winding road: the Christine Burgin edition of Walser's *Microscripts*; the songs of Ivor Gurney; Hilma af Klint's *The Greatness Of Things* and KF Schobinger's *Verlorene Toden* (both Douglas Hyde Gallery editions); the choral works of Rautavaara; Peter Foolen's edition of Dick Cassee's *Grafiek*; Messiaen's *Turangalîla-Symphonie*; Chris Drury's *Algonquin* and Jonathan Pryce reading from *The Rings Of Saturn* in *Patience (After Sebald)*.

Cameron Stallones (Sun Araw)
"By severe contentions of friendship and the burning fire of thought."

We've all been young
We've all been old
We've all been sheltered from the cold
Come by my side and say what I think I
already know

Peter Strickland
Highs: Die Schachtel's magnificent *Prix Italia* box set, the BFI's series of ghostly DVDs, finally getting my hands on the Criterion DVD of *Carnival Of Souls*, the return of Robert Hampson and Main's reformation, :zoviet*france: on Soundcloud, Mark Moore's Scala mix, endless *Disco Discharge*, SCUM's cover version of "5-8-6", Ian Helliwell completing his FC Judd film, Dispokino's East European sonic fairytale collage, great finds on Death Waltz Recording Company, Finders Keepers, Eureka and Second Run DVD, the poliziotteschi documentary *Eurocrime*, snippets of music by Emeralds and Golden Donna, *O Is For Orgasm* by Hélène Cattet and Bruno Forzani, Michael Vorfeld's lightbulb collection, the tide in Portmeirion, discovering Dariush Dolat-Shahi through the Smithsonian Folkways rerelease, starting up my own Peripheral Conserve label again after an eight year lull, the Brothers Quay exhibition at MOMA, which almost had me on my knees. Books that I can't wait to read: Julian Cope's *Copendium* and Artemis Cooper's Patrick Leigh Fermor biography, film work/travel.

Lows: film work/travel, dropping a bottle of sesame oil down a marble staircase in a hotel in Brno on the first night of a Sonic Catering mini-tour, forgetting a suitcase on a train, not enough time for the people and things that matter, 'reform' being used as a euphemism for business interests over the NHS.

Pete Swanson
2012 has easily been the most hectic of my life. My album *Man With Potential* came out in December 2011 while I was in the middle of my first year of an extremely demanding academic programme. I was exiled to a far corner of Manhattan, haunting hospitals and learning the action of medications while my music career was getting defibrillated. I did manage to play a few shows this year, and I hope to get to Europe for a few weeks in January 2013.

My schoolwork has dictated a lot of my musical choices this year and I've been soundtracking my pharmacology cram sessions with the *Recollection GRM* series, the Dead-Cert catalogue, Ákos Rózmann, Lubomyr Melnyk and Laszlo Dubrovay. I also found the Blackest Ever Black and Downwards catalogues to be fantastic for late night research with their persistently driving pulse and modest movement.

I've been very impressed with the artistic resilience of the early 2000s Noise class, with Phil Blankenship, Ren Schofield, Dominick Fernow and Spencer Yeh successfully stepping into new sonic territory, and Aaron Dilloway and Jason Lescalleet continuing to be on top of the skree. Reissues from Gate, Harry Pussy and Shadow Ring only confirmed the supremacy of the 1990s Siltbreeze catalogue. Other 2012 fixations: Andy Stott, Chromatics, Gucci Mane "I'm Up", Holy Other, Traxman, Ike Yard, Silent Servant, *The Seasons*, BBC Radiophonic Workshop, Mark Fell, Scott Walker, Yeh/Lambkin live, Gate live.

It seems like 2013 is going to be busier and better than 2012. I'm ready.

Terror Danjah
The last 12 months have been my most eventful yet. The year started on a low: my older cousin died in Nov 2011, the situation dragged on and his funeral wasn't till Jan 2012. He was an older brother to me, a mentor – death in the family is a horrible way to start the year. Despite this, I completed my second album *Dark Crawler* on Hyperdub.

In October, I went on tour with the album across the world, visiting Japan, China, Spain and Sweden for the first time. On my travels, I've really got into the TV series *Sons Of Anarchy*, it's that good I watched season one to four within a week while I was in Japan. The people were amazing there too. Regarding events, the fourth Butterz & Hardrive rave was the biggest one to date, with DJ EZ, P Money, Skibadee, D Double, The Heatwave and the rest of my labelmates. The Bob Marley documentary film *Marley* was by far the best film I've watched this year, it's very inspirational.

Touch

30 years and counting, and in some ways we feel we have just started. Many lament the demise of music and its narrative as a cultural force, but our experience has been of an audience listening and observing more intently than ever. We've had the chance to revisit our work, with archive releases like *Liquid Music* with Fennesz and the confidence that our artists are at the top of their game – Philip Jeck taking his *An Ark For The Listener* to a new level of improvisational accuracy, Hildur Guðnadóttir proving herself to be a true adept while looking after a wild domestic transformation. And so on. The Touch 30 festival and double LP showcase is as vital to us as *Feature Mist* was in 1982. We are looking at ways to move the music publishing process into different dimensions with future activities. Listening and observing have to be closely linked to experience and education, and not made either expensive or immaterial.

Mike Harding Pros: Attentive and responsive audiences throughout 2012; brilliant performances by Spire live in Berlin, Jeck at Feeërieën, The Swifter at Cafe Oto, Bruce Gilbert at KHM, JG Thirlwell at EI, *Sea Polyphonies*, The Beam all-nighter… Also, freq_out 8, Hatufim, Cafe Scientifica, Vancouver, Hilary Mantel, NYC (both), WFMU, A & M Moore, and more…

Con: The death of Tom Lawrence.

Jon Wozencroft Pros: Magda, Anna and Maja, meeting Eleh in Berlin, Oren Ambarchi at Oto, the Preseli Hills with Paul Devereux,

sound seminars at the RCA. *HHhH* by Laurent Binet and *A Possible Life* by Sebastian Faulks, working with Jez Millar in Whitstable, meeting Andy, Miles and Sean (of Modern Love) in Seattle, a trip to Twin Peaks with Naut Humon and Geir Jenssen. Sitting next to Emptyset on the flight home and keeping optimistic.

Between the two: Chris Marker dying on his 91st birthday.

Cons: Austerity measures and neo-Stalinism, having to sell our family home, not having time to see new films, and Londoners being unable to walk in a straight line while looking down at their mobiles.

Cosey Fanni Tutti
2012 has been immensely fulfilling and challenging on many levels – just how I like it. Low points: the destruction and pain wreaked by the coalition government, the growing trend for the mass public display of grief, breaking my foot, the trauma of an MRI heart scan, and unnecessary tedious untruthful public mutterings.

But what really excites me is a tangible sense of an emerging change within music and art that has been missing for so long. The spirit of collaboration has featured highly this year, bringing with it a driving force and momentum

that energised and inspired me. Here are a few highlights from so many… Working with a multiplicity of remarkable people particularly the incredible Xeni Jardin on *Bioschismic*, which was a truly enlightening and emotional experience. I got taken by surprise by the success of *Transverse*, our collaboration with Nik Colk Void, when it received an overwhelmingly positive reception and a nomination for Best Art Vinyl 2012 Award. It has been wonderful breaking from studio recording and playing live. The palpable euphoria at Chris & Cosey shows and the moving AV festival tribute to Sleazy. What stands out as the highlight has been the completion of Sleazy's *Desertshore/The Final Report*. The project encapsulated so much, not only in honour of and the loss of Sleazy and consequently TG, but the affection and generosity of our collaborators has been beyond anything I've experienced before. What an amazing year! Roll on 2013 – there's much afoot…

C Spencer Yeh
What with everything going on these days, it's sometimes tough to remember why I'm doing what I'm doing, so please indulge some recollection and celebration:
– Caroling trio with Stine Motland, Ben Hall.

– Quartet with Okkyung Lee, Axel Dörner, Phil Minton.
– Dark basement duo with Tamio Shiraishi.
– Solo in a chapel, Oberlin, OH, solo at LAMPO with a younger self encased in video.
– Soundtracking home movies with Graham Lambkin at New Museum, NYC.
– Hired gun for Tony Conrad's NYC ensemble and Susan Alcorn's harmolodic countrywestern, telecommuting for Chris Goudreau and Dan Melchior.
– Both *1975* and CS Yeh's *Transitions* finally out, and why is orange my new colour?
– Launching the SSTUDIOS series with Dan Lopatin: one down, 2013 to go.
– Bringing the head of Lasse Marhaug to New England lobster, New Haven pizza, Baltimore crabs.
– 'Research trip' to Marfa Texas, checking the Big Bend.
– The CS Yeh Band.
– A reinvigorating reunion with cinema volunteering at Spectacle Theater, Brooklyn; cutting movie trailers, screening *Offshore Television*, and revisiting video circa 2002, including my Hair Police 'documentary'.
– Dietrich-deafened in the studio again with New Monuments.
– Sawyer/Stetson/Wooley/Yeh still not having a shorter name.
– Scary stuff: being 1/100th of the *Soundworks* at ICA London, being a No Fun stand-up comedian, being commissioned to compose for the String Orchestra of Brooklyn, and self-imposing a 'notes-only' rule.
– Making a new Burning Star Core live set I'm happy with – the key was getting my head out the ass of self-imposed 'rules'.
– As always, the people I am spoiled by, and honoured for being considered a peer. □

Views from the office

Loudness wars

Live, 2012 started with a clash between volume and location. In January, Kevin Martin's King Midas Sound were booked to play at the Bishopsgate Institute, built in 1895 as a concert hall and informal college for East London's workers. At the last minute, the line-up changed. Rumour had it that the King Midas soundcheck had been so loud that there were fears for the historic building's ceilings.

The question was, why would you programme such bass-heavy music in a clearly unsuitable space? For 2012 turned out to be a year of high volume in unlikely places, reflecting both a trend towards electronic music as extreme bodily immersion, and a confusion as to where best to experience it. If artists like Raime are, as Mark Fisher suggests in his 2012 critic's reflection, inhabiting an "unexplored space between Swans/Sunn 0)))/Ben Frost doomcore and post-dance music", where do you put them on, and what does the audience do when they get there? At the same Bishopsgate event, during Raime's opening set people stood facing forward, looking at the duo on a high stage and the Tarkovsky films behind them. It was not a Doom gig; nor was it any kind of dancefloor. A 19th century hall, then, might just as well be this unexplored space as anywhere else.

These were the kinds of places increasingly used by festivals such as Unsound, Mutek and Semibreve alongside club venues. Having a theatre or concert hall at their disposal allowed artists such as Roly Porter to work with visual artists and film makers to create ever more involving sensory experiences that have little to do with either traditional live music or DJ sets. Often, these sets were at a scalp-crawling volume, bass frequencies vibrating halls more used to orchestras. Being shaken by sub-bass is not a new experience for most of us, but to feel these vibrations sitting comfortably in the dark, with no directive to dance, no excuse to fidget – and no opportunity to find your own sweet spot in relation to the sound – made electronic music feel more than ever like cinema this year. This kind of live music is an extension of headphone listening. It feels private, not communal. In 2012 the discourse around it was of bodies overwhelmed by and choking on extreme sonics. We seemed to want to be a captive audience, one that needs blasting with a giant standing wave in order to remind us that we're real.

The dialogue between the post-dance and extreme music that Fisher cites goes both ways. When Swans reformed in 2010, Michael Gira spoke of the "the loudest band in the world" clichés that grew up around

the band's first incarnation. This year, the group toured a bludgeoning three hour set, the effects of which were similar to the accounts of sensory overpowerment that followed Blackest Ever Black's label night at London's Corsica Studios, which brought together some of Noise's old guard – William Bennett, Russell Haswell – with younger artists like Powell and Vatican Shadow. *The Wire*'s Jennifer Lucy Allan reported back to On Location as if from a war zone, citing rattling doors and a rattling chest, sonic fatigue from a "battering ram of beats and bass".

As Industrial and Noise tropes spread through the dance underground – and Noise artists continued to mine Techno and House – the results were exciting on record, but often confusing live. This year saw audiences standing or sitting still as dystopian booms shook buildings, transfixed by volume, flattened as well as aroused by bass, unsure of where the beat was, but reluctant to move around until they found it. Electronic music's stylistic boundaries were blurred; live, it seemed especially placeless. Perhaps high volume helped hold it together in 2012. Whatever your reaction to it, loudness is indisputable, something everyone can agree exists.
Frances Morgan

Digital futures

This was the year that digital became common currency for pre-release music. That's not to say, thankfully, that means any shortage of vinyl releases, or tapes – indeed with the likes of USB stick releases there's more formats on sale than ever before. But the way artists and labels spread the word about a coming album, and consequently the way many music critics hear records to be released, now tends to be digital, whether that's a Wetransfer download of a ZIP file, or a private Soundcloud link, or increasingly for major labels, some kind of proprietary third party streaming software which ties you to your computer as you listen.

The upside of this is there's more, and wider, music in circulation than ever before. Can't afford a vinyl release? Then there's scope for selling a digital download, or (why not?) simply giving it away for free on a myriad different platforms. *The Wire* inbox is full with pre-release music from the world over – finished releases, projects still in gestation, tantalising pre-echoes of music to come.

A possible downside, at least for the music writer, is that increasingly you encounter music for the first time as a set of MP3 files or a stream. Putting aside issues of digital fidelity, it means an album or 12" risks becoming yet more music files among the 1000s already on your computer, instead of a discrete object with its own artwork, sleevenotes and identity. Increasingly, music reviews are written from the music primarily rather than the object. In addition, the item you're reviewing sometimes can be subject to change, if record labels deem it necessary; the ever-changeable nature of the digital form can chip away at what used to be the solid, unchangeable identity of album, 12" or EP.

Of course, you could argue this is merely the damn critic's problem. In any case, music reviews in bygone years were never written from finished album copies. But it does reflect a wider situation where most albums are now released according to flexible, ad hoc schedules. A record company might test the water with a download, and then an LP edition is followed by a CD a few months later; a collection of killer CD-Rs gets rereleased in an official edition a few months later. The idea of a single release date, with the clamour and excitement of waiting for the moment a record drops, is becoming the exception rather than the rule.

Something is lost but something is potentially gained here, too. Labels are cutting their cloth to fit, and releasing only what they're confident they can sell. If this means multiple editions, perhaps each tailored differently, then record labels are making objects people will love and cherish. In these less plentiful times, we might finally be seeing music labels that are that little bit less wasteful, in terms of considering what really deserves a release, and only pressing up products that people really need.

Derek Walmsley

Planets collide

Across the Cross Platform and On Site sections in the magazine, sound and music are tools for understanding things that at first seem impermeable or unrelated. Sound waves are messy, they bounce around spaces and shake things up. And the way we think, talk and write about them echoes that mercurial nature. Sound is a direct route from a song through to a film, a video installation, website, or the design of a building. What is exciting in these sections of the magazine is seeing how the permeable nature of sound allows us to follow it through these different forms, ignore the border police of disciplines and think in new ways.

Works with sound as a main focus can be shown in an art gallery, but it isn't evident how one should understand them. For instance, film makers can see galleries as places for experimentation, as can architects, musicians and others – each discipline with their own histories to take into account. So, with all of these very disparate fields coming together,

skilled explanation is key. For instance, to be able to write capably about the sonification of scientific data about distant nebulae by a musician requires a large jump.

Predominantly these exploratory activities are packaged up neatly as art projects. But because they're presented in a white cube doesn't mean the artists are savvy to the obscurantist dialects of contemporary art, let alone care about them. It's a double bind: galleries can offer a place for experimentation, but – like that other planet-eater television, with its heavy handed commissioning and inflexible framing of the world – they can suck the life out of things, and impose their own language and values. An artist has opportunities to realise a new idea and even get paid for it, but at the same time what they make can become distant from their original intent. Somewhere in the process the artist becomes distracted by fitting their work into an art theory discourse, rather than developing their own take on the world.

Art and music proliferate into numerous forms, with no dominant schools, trends or worldviews. Some think culture reflects this catastrophy narrative of the world in the way it speeds uncontrollably through a vast number of profligate images and noisy hubbub. And it's partly this fragmentation that helps to explode venerable institutions and create new ones. Over the past year I've noticed an increase in artists and collectives using the internet and online platforms to skillfully communicate their ideas or host exhibitions. It's not new – nor will art and music ever exist solely online – but there is a renewed vigour to it that echoes the music world's digital exodus. So here instead of institutions, read platforms: new spaces where people are sharing their work and ideas, using it as an open sketchbook to try out ideas, or to try and start out the discussion in their own voices – itself something that brings a new set of urgent concerns.

Nathan Budzinski

Archive fever

Building a new website for *The Wire* this year raised many questions about the nature of what we do online, how the picture fits together, and how we connect and link it all back to the magazine itself. The communication from outside, often from PR agencies, shifted slightly. Where we once got asked to host tracks, now we're asked whether we'd like to 'premiere' something – a minor twist in the PR parlance, but one which underlines the problem of maintaining critical distance: at what point does posting something on the site become doing promo for an artist or label?

Twitter and Facebook continue as our main methods of daily communication to readers, although changes on Facebook make us less comfortable with that platform every day, with developments like paid post-promotion (which we do not use) now heavily pushed. Online news continues to be a vortex, with one site ripping off another, although link-back etiquette

between music sites has improved enormously.

This year crowdfunding projects cropped up on a weekly, if not daily basis, via sites like IndieGogo and Kickstarter. Dylan Carlson made over $35,000 for his drcarlsonalbion project on British folklore and faeries; A project to record and release saxophonist Giuseppi Logan made double its target, but Francisco López didn't even make ten per cent of his. This time next year, we'll be looking back on a year of Kickstarter in the UK.

The biggest issue for the online desk this year was the question of how to deal with audio and video content on the site. Should we, as a music magazine with a 30 year history, be operating like a magazine, or should we be treating the site as an archive? Digging to the depths of the old site, we found files posted a decade ago, like a tiny video of a pixellated Supersilent, and two minuscule audio snippets at 96 kbps, both of which are now, through improvements in computing, screen resolution and bandwidth, rendered antiquated. But we also found ourselves asking what would happen if a platform like Soundcloud shut down or was replaced by another technology, and looking for a solution where we still had some element of control over what we host online.

This decision comes down to the question of whether we embed content from third party platforms like Soundcloud and YouTube, or only work with audio and video that we can host on our own. The latter means we would be acting somewhat like an institution, taking the long view to preserve the text, sound and video on our site. The former means that we have a seemingly more immediate and proliferate connection with everyone on the Internet. A website like thewire.co.uk is effectively a magazine and an archive at the same time, a dynamic that needs to be constantly renegotiated.

Jennifer Lucy Allan

Charts

Mike Heron 15

The Real Bahamas In Music And Song
Various (Nonesuch Explorer)
Blind Boy Fuller
On Down (Matchbox)
John Cale
Paris 1919 (Warners)
Tahiti: The Gauguin Years: Songs And Dances
Various (Nonesuch Explorer)
JS Bach/Murray Perahia
Goldberg Variations (Sony)
Norman MacCaig
Nineteen Poems Of Norman MacCaig (Asis Audio)
Trembling Bells
The Constant Pageant (Honest Jon's)
Sleepy John Estes
Rats In My Kitchen (Gonna Buy Me A Mighty Cat) (Sun)
Georgia Seddon
This Little Bird (No label)
Nick Pynn
Afterplanesman (Roundhill)
Hariprasad Chaurasia/Brij Bhushan Kabra/Shivkumar Sharma
Call Of The Valley (Gramophone Company Of India)
Vashti Bunyan
Some Things Just Stick In Your Mind (Fat Cat)
George Harrison
Wonderwall Music (Apple)
Love In Motion
Ice House (Chrysalis)
Alasdair Roberts
Spoils (Drag City)

Compiled by Mike Heron, mikeheron.co.uk

Vias De Facto 15

Annie Gosfield
Almost Truths And Open Deceptions (Tzadik)
Michael Harrison & Maya Beiser
Time Loops (Cantaloupe)
LAND
Night Within (Important)
Dictaphone
Poems From A Rooftop (Sonic Pieces)
Trapist
The Golden Years (Staubgold)
Jason Lescalleet
Songs About Nothing (Erstwhile)
Anthony Pateras
Errors Of The Human Body (Editions Mego)
Andrey Kiritchenko
Chrysalis (Nexsound)
Nicholas Vasallo
Monuments Emerge (Innova)
Gareth Davies & Frances-Marie Uiti
Gramercy (Miasma)
Boris Hegenbart
Instrumentarium (Staubgold)
eRikm
Transfall (Room 40)
Emanuele De Raymondi
Buyukberber Variations (ZerOKilled Music)
Paul Corley
Disquiet (Bedroom Community)
Holly Herndon
Movement (Rvng Intl)

Compiled by Paulo Somsen, *Vias De Facto*, Antena 2, RDP, Portugal

15 Motion Memes

Christian Marclay & Otomo Yoshihide
Moving Parts (Asphodel)
The World Saxophone Quartet
Steppin' With (Black Saint)
Jimmy Lyons
Push Pull (Hat Hut)
Steve Lacy
Momentum (Novus)
Clifford Jordan & John Gilmore
Blowing In From Chicago (Blue Note)
Charles Tyler
Voyage From Jerico (Akba)
Sonny Clark
Cool Struttin' (Blue Note)
Herbie Hancock
Thrust (CBS)
David Sancious And Tone
Transformation (The Speed Of Love) (CBS)
Shannon Jackson
When Colors Play (Caravan Of Dreams)
Bobby Previte
Pushing The Envelope (Grammavision)
Mick Goodrick
In Pas(s)ing (ECM)
Dave Holland
Jumpin' In (ECM)
NWA
100 Miles And Runnin' (Ruthless)
Soul II Soul
Keep On Movin (Ten)

Compiled by Bobby Hill, WPFW, Washington DC, USA, wpfwfm.org

The Office Ambience

Marcus Valle
Vento Sul (Light In The Attic)
Emptyset
Collapsed (raster-noton)
François Bayle
50 Ans D'Acousmatique (INA Editions)
James Ferraro
Sushi (Hippos In Tanks)
Alasdair Roberts & Friends
A Wonder Working Stone (Drag City)
Bryan Ferry Orchestra
The Jazz Age (BMG)
Ruff Sqwad
White Label Classics (No Hats No Hoods)
Sun Ra
A Space Odyssey (Fantastic Voyage)
Karantamba
Ndigal (Taranga Beat)
Matmos
The Marriage Of True Minds (Thrill Jockey)
Joseph Hammer & Jason Crumer
Show Em The Door (Accidie)
Horse Lords
Horse Lords (Ehse)
My Dry Wet Mess
Stereo Typing LP (Brainfeeder)
Swindle
Forest Funk EP (Deep Medi Musik)
s_w_z_k
Variant & Empires EP (Tresor)

Compiled by *The Wire* Sound System. To hear a stream of our Office Ambience, go to thewire.co.uk. We welcome charts from record shops, radio shows, DJs, labels, musicians, bloggers, readers, etc. Email a top 15 to charts@thewire.co.uk

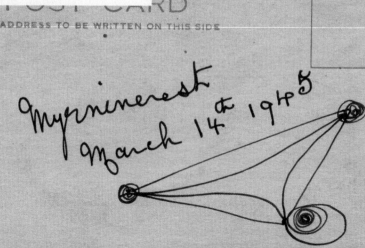

Madge Gill's postcards from the edge (see Cross Platform, page 28)

David Tibet Collection

Reviews Index

Aki Onda

Philip Lethen (Brothers Unconnected); Tim Soter (Aki Onda)

Alan Bishop...

... and Richard Bishop of Brothers Unconnected

Soundcheck A–Z

This month's selected CDs, vinyl and downloads

James Blackshaw & Lubomyr Melnyk
The Watchers
Important CD

"My deepest hope," pianist and composer Lubomyr Melnyk told me at the end of 2009, "is that other people will love 'continuous music' enough to learn to do it themselves." *The Watchers* reveals that English 12-string guitarist James Blackshaw has done just that. He and Melnyk actually met in October 2008, at a festival in Tallinn, Estonia, and immediately discovered an affinity. The pianist's characteristic voice leads the way on these four absorbing tracks; melodically sober yet cumulatively intense, and swarming with overtones. Blackshaw brings a different range of timbre, functioning at times almost like a tambura, enriching the drone that envelops Melnyk's stately phrasing.

The essence of Melnyk's conception of continuous music is that instruments generate energy; the priorities of more conventional playing are secondary to that fundamental transformation of the space in which the music is created. But it is ordered energy, not Dionysiac frenzy; its release demands rigorous physical discipline, akin to tai chi, a kind of athleticism and sustained concentration, not the romanticism of wild indulgence and flailing excess. Listening to Melnyk makes sense of Thomas Merton's observation that "Art enables us to find ourselves and lose ourselves at the same time". Listening to the beautiful music on *The Watchers* (which Important have also issued as a limited edition LP with a different tracklisting), you can hear that in Blackshaw he has found a kindred spirit.
Julian Cowley

Jeb Bishop & Jorrit Dijkstra
1000 Words
Driff CD/DL
The Whammies
Play The Music Of Steve Lacy
Driff CD/DL

There's a neat bit of poetic irony in the fact that a record devoted to the music of Steve Lacy, an American who spent most of his creative life based in Europe, has been released by a label run by European exiles who live in the USA. Driff Records is co-helmed by Jorrit Dijkstra, a Dutch alto saxophonist who relocated to the USA in 2002, and pianist Pandelis Karayorgis, who decamped from Greece to America in 1985. Lacy crossed the Atlantic to find an environment where he could make a living realising an expanded notion of what a jazz musician should be able to do; Driff's proprietors travelled in reverse simply so that they could play jazz.

While Lacy distilled everything to clear lines whose endings could be endlessly redrawn, The Whammies delight in disrupting his melodic progressions. The sextet, which include ICP Orchestra vets Mary Oliver on strings and Han Bennink on drums as well as Americans Jeb Bishop on trombone and Nate

McBride on bass, introduce discontinuities that magnify small facets of the source material. Bennink played with Lacy on some Soul Note releases in the 70s and 80s, but there's a lot more of what Kevin Whitehead called his wooden shoe timing here, with passages of pre-bebop swing abruptly piling up, then recovering their spring. And Karayorgis brings a cubist sense of angle and distorted dimension that's quite Monkish; Lacy, of course, never tired of analysing Monk's music, but Karayorgis's brash interjections play up the jaggedness. Dijkstra's occasional use of the lyricon, an early electronic reed instrument, not only redeems it from the crimes of its first champion, Tom Scott; he uses it to recast Lacy's bone-dry sense of humour into something earthier, especially when he and Bishop squelch as one on the marvellously muddy "As Usual".

Prior to The Whammies, the partnership between Bishop and Dijkstra has played out over three records with the latter's Pillow Circles and Flatlands Collective, but *1000 Words* argues strongly that they sound best working as equals. Each man brings one horn, a handful of tunes and a tableful of mutes. Instead of Lacy-like stark lines, they work in rhythmically assertive counterpoints and carefully graduated shadings, so that whatever one man does make's the other's playing sound better. On "Klopgeest" and "Standpipe", short spat-out notes and exquisitely elongated growls put the physical presence they've alluded to in larger groups front and centre. And the way Dijkstra illuminates Bishop's lyricism and pathos on "Ice" exudes a warmth and empathy that makes nonsense of the tune's title. The duo cover 12 tracks in under 47 minutes, rendering each performance with pith and clarity; one never feels like they're marking time before the next idea presents itself. While *The Whammies Play The Music Of Steve Lacy* does a swell job of personalising an august chapter in jazz history, the way *1000 Words* presents a fully engaged and engaging real-time dialogue is even more satisfying.
Bill Meyer

Broadcast
Berberian Sound Studio
Warp CD/DL/LP
Soundtracks are where so much contemporary film and television show their profound conservatism. It was via incidental music and scores in genre film and television that many were introduced to experimental music, and to affects and sensations that go far beyond the facile emotionalism of the typical soundtrack. The influence of horror movie soundtracks from the 1960s and 70s has always been evident in Broadcast's sound, and they tried their hand at producing a soundtrack of their own for Peter Strickland's recent film *Berberian Sound Studio*. The film-within-a-film conceit – an English sound engineer is taken to

Italy to produce the horrifying sounds for a low-budget exploitation movie – has a worryingly postmodern feel. Those worries are borne out by what Broadcast have produced here.

There's always been a thin line between some hauntology and postmodern pastiche, and here Broadcast veer too closely towards the latter. Hence *Berberian Sound Studio* is just what you'd expect – doomy organ, screams, malevolent whispers, breaths, heavily phased drums – and that's the problem. Their 2009 album with The Focus Group, *Investigate Witch Cults Of The Radio Age*, worked so well because Broadcast's tendency towards 1960s/70s simulation was subjected to Julian House's dreamwork scrambling. Here, the 70s simulations, artful enough in their own way, are presented straight. The result, sadly, doesn't evoke 70s Italian horror; it merely makes one think of already-overfamiliar period and genre signifiers.
Mark Fisher

Brokeback
Brokeback And The Black Rock
Thrill Jockey CD/DL/LP
Douglas McCombs founded Brokeback in 1995 to showcase his stark, elemental melodies on the Fender six-string bass guitar. Although the instrument was also the focal point of his contributions to Tortoise's early albums and an occasional embellishment in Eleventh Dream Day, the rock outfit he's played with since 1985, it was Brokeback's raison d'être. And while the project evolved from a shifting aggregation of studio confederates into a stable partnership with double bassist Noel Kupersmith, that focus never shifted.

But after the release ten years ago of their last record, *Looks At The Bird*, Brokeback seemed to fade away; when McCombs first convened the quartet that plays on *Brokeback And The Black Rock* in 2010, there had been no gigs for over two years. McCombs still calls the tunes and there's no mistaking his signature use of noir-ish reverb, but this time it's all about the guitars. Leading a classic beat combo, he plays more electric guitar than Fender bass. His melodies are as striking and defined as ever, but where they once felt noir-ish, now they're as expansive as the desert landscape on the album cover, and recorded in a way that takes up all available room. On a restrained air like "Tonight At Eleven", the reverberant halo around the guitars brings to mind Tom Verlaine's *Warm And Cool*; but when he turns it up on "Colossus Of Roads", McCombs sounds like he's aiming for Neil Young. And where previous Brokeback records had the gem-cut precision of studio creations, this one has a loose, lumbering gait that feels live even when overdubbed keyboards betray the fact that it's not. *Brokeback And The Black Rock* is a most successful reboot.
Bill Meyer

Brothers Unconnected
Unrock The House
Unrock 2×LP
Charles Gocher's death from cancer in February 2007 marked the abrupt end of Sun City Girls' 27 years on the very weirdest fringes of underground rock. Surviving members Richard and Alan Bishop announced that the group would no longer exist as a recording or performing entity. The following year they played out as the duo Brothers Unconnected, performing acoustic versions of Sun City Girls songs as a tribute to Gocher. They must have enjoyed it enough to make it an ongoing project, as this double LP captures all 80 minutes of a show recorded in Germany in 2011.

As a lyricist and wordsmith, Gocher is still a major presence. "Eyeball In A Quart Jar Of Snot" is a an unhinged monologue of deviant family relations, delivered here with the same tone of suppressed hysteria he originally used on *Horse Cock Phepner*; and "The Brothers Unconnected" – the piece after which the duo is named – is Gocher's scurrilous spoken word routine riffing on the Kennedys and Marilyn, which now sounds like a slightly age-worn product of the 20th century, like a verbal Pop Art collage from a pre-internet age. Still, it's a good deal funnier than the other spoken interludes in which the Bishops rant somewhat aimlessly about Israel, Holocaust denial, education and the European Union.

The album works best when the Bishops take themselves seriously as instrumentalists, with both playing acoustic guitar. On "My Painted Tomb" and "The Flower", they embrace their Lebanese heritage, sounding like a couple of Davy Grahams picking through thorny, microtonal raga folk. And "Wild World Of Animals" is a twanging 1960s spy-surf pastiche that showcases Richard Bishop's astonishing Moorish jazz chops. Like the best of Sun City Girls' albums, these instrumentals offer a glimpse into a parallel reality – one where oud virtuoso John Berberian was every bit as influential as John Fahey on serious-minded guitarists.
Daniel Spicer

Michael Chapman
Pachyderm
Blast First Petite LP
There was a time when you knew where you were with Michael Chapman. His distinctively slurred and world-worn vocals and artful fingerpicking were instantly identifiable. He was always too idiosyncratic and resourceful a musician simply to be filed under folk, blues, rock or any other single style, but broadly you knew in the past what to expect from the Yorkshire-born troubadour. Then the improvised drones, roaring feedback, metallic timbres and electric pulsations of last year's *The Resurrection And Revenge Of The Clayton Peacock* changed all that.

A new collection of experimental folk songs by **Alasdair Roberts** and co rescues traditional music from the realm of postcard nostalgia. By **Nick Southgate**

Lore of the land: Alasdair Roberts

Alasdair Roberts & Friends
A Wonder Working Stone
Drag City CD/DL/2×LP

In Don DeLillo's novel *White Noise*, two characters visit what is billed as "The most photographed barn in America". Watching fellow tourists snap the same picture-perfect postcard image that first made the barn famous, one observes to the other, "No one sees the barn. Once you've seen the signs about the barn, it becomes impossible to see the barn", before posing the existential question: "What was the barn like before it was photographed?"

Folk music exists behind a similar veil of hyper-observation. Each exercise in documentation, each phase of revival, is a distorting and distancing lens. As the music progresses towards being ever more superlatively and quintessentially traditional, it becomes less proximate and less vital to us. Folk music across the British Isles has been assiduously catalogued over the last 100 years, but the traditions recorded tell us as much about the hopes and dreams of the cataloguers as they do about the past itself. When it comes to regular folk revivals, styles are crafted which either wander into pastiche or stiffen so as to suffocate alternative interpretations. In traditional music we frequently only witness a gallimaufry of affectations and anachronisms and no longer hear the music at all. History is

always a construction, but tradition risks being mere confection.

Alasdair Roberts knows what is at stake if we are to peer behind tradition's veil and hear folk music as living and new. His attitude to the tradition is clear and iconoclastic. Speaking in *The Wire* 314, he commented: "I always talk about myself being an experimentalist rather than a nostalgist in terms of drawing on the past. I like the process of renewal rather than comfort. It's a myth, the whole idea of the rural idyll." That experiment started with his 1997 debut with nascent indie rockers Appendix Out, and the subsequent years of perfecting his musicianship combined with immersive scholarship have seen him wrestle tradition's dead hand from folk music's delicate throat.

Any attempt at renewal must know the past it desires to move beyond. Last year Roberts was resident at the University of Edinburgh's School of Scottish Studies as part of the Archive Trails project, which gave him access to the notes and recordings of legendary collectors Hamish Henderson and Alan Lomax. He has also recorded albums of traditional songs: *No Earthly Man* (2005) and *Too Long In This Condition* (2010). But it is his artistry as a composer, lyricist, guitarist and singer that is most remarkable. He is a master of scordatura (literally, mis-tuning) techniques on the guitar, finding voices

and moods for the instrument other players cannot. His singing voice carries a thick Scottish brogue that feels timeless, but its fragile edges and idiosyncratic intonations remain entirely personal. His is a living voice speaking of these times, not a hollow mouth echoing the sounds of the past.

Most importantly, he has become an exceptional lyricist. His themes are universal and mystical, yet never beholden to the images and phrasings of the past. The turning of the seasons and nature's cycle provide the backdrop, and he finds an inherent musicality in the vocabulary of the countryside. "The Laverock In The Blackthorn" chooses the Scots word for a lark over its blunter Anglo-Saxon name, and places the bird in the thorny tree that produces the bitter sloes harvested in winter and fermented into sloe gin drunk at weddings and wakes. This pairing is just one of many in an enchanting menagerie of creatures secreted poetically in the landscape of the songs. Elsewhere he mines a rich seam of biblical language for brimstone and fire but also grace and redemption, and elaborate rhyme schemes weld the words and music.

Given Roberts's mastery of song, it's no surprise that *A Wonder Working Stone* is in part a celebration of song itself. "*This song's made in anger, this song's made in love,*" Roberts sings on "Song Composed In December" over picked acoustic guitar,

the fiddle of Rafe Fitzpatrick, and Ben Reynolds's perfectly placed electric guitar licks. "The Wheels Of The World (The Conundrum)" turns over on itself as it builds to Roberts's warning of those "*Hoping to steal your old song from your people, to silence your song of one million tongues*", celebrating people whose "*hearts will never falter on the altars of the martyrs/Their art will not be bartered in the marketplace of dread*". His exhortation to "*Sing on, sing on, sing on*" is echoed by the chorus of the group, who then cycle into a round of the lines, "*These are the wheels of the world my friend, you must understand/For 2000 years they've been spreading destruction all over this land*". The warmth of this communal singing segues into the swirl of dance music on "Scandal & Trance", which opens with the refrain of "When The Saints Go Marching In" at a leisurely stroll before jigging into a Celtic tinged lament buoyed along by Stevie Jones's bass and Shane Connolly's drums. Its tale of ailing brides and bittersweet reversals closes on the reassuring chorus, "*All days will end in joy, they'll never end in evil*".

Each song on *A Wonder Working Stone* is a comparable experiment in tradition. The combination of Roberts's artistry and the exemplary ensemble backing him means the album succeeds in being a renewal, not a revival. This is the sound of new myths and new music being hewn from folk's stone. □

Pachyderm – taking its title from a generic term for a thick-skinned mammal – opens with a rising arpeggio ringing from Chapman's acoustic guitar. It's ripe with potential places to go, yet for the next 24 minutes his playing remains rooted within that same basic chord shape, with only slight variation and a touch of reverb to enhance the beating of the notes' decay. Virtually immobile, this music occupies its own space and draws you in. It's as sturdy and enigmatically self-sufficient as the elephant in Thomas Bewick's etching on the cover. The second side is an atmospheric remix by Robert Antony, embedding Chapman's unflappable solo in a flux of swirling and twitching electronics.

Discussing the unpredictable character of his own work as a sculptor, Pablo Picasso once pointed out that God had dreamed up the giraffe, then the elephant, then the cat – no fixed style, just trying things out. That neatly sums up where Chapman is now; following his *Peacock* and *Pachyderm* there's apparently a *Polar Bear* in the Blast First pipeline.
Julian Cowley

Éloïse Decazes & Eric Chenaux
Éloïse Decazes & Eric Chenaux
Okraina 2×10"

Recorded in Canada for a new Belgian label, this is a stylish release, spread across three 10" sides of vinyl and housed in the haunted woodcut designs of Gwénola Carrère. Éloïse Decazes is a French singer with something of the delicate hauteur of Josephine Foster. Her usual duo Arlt is upbeat enough, but here she aims for the lower-pitched melancholia of intimate traditional French song, and this midnight mood is sustained throughout. Traditional in this case means extremely old, and there's a medieval je ne sais quoi in the air, though Decazes and Montreal guitarist Eric Chenaux's approach is contemporary rather than academic.

Of the four trad songs here, the most captivating is "La Complainte Du Roi Renaud", a fox story woven around a hypnotic drone. Almost a lullaby, in other hands it could be a fierce bagpipe melody. Chenaux mixes acoustic accompaniment with hovering electric slide work, and adds subtle colour with harmonium or reed organ. The inventiveness of his *Guitar & Voice* (2011) is translated to this new release, including a non-orthodox guitar solo played by detuning strings at speed. Two contrasting "Contredanses" display Chenaux's bowed guitar, multitracked into a distant memory of a Purcell consort. A field recording of creaking trees underpins these two tracks. Beautifully produced and packaged, this is a quiet, melodic record and something of a gem. Does anyone still give music as a gift? This would make the perfect peace offering.
Clive Bell

Ducktails
The Flower Lane
Domino CD

The ten songs on the fourth Ducktails album (not counting a sackful of cassettes, CD-Rs, 7" singles, etc) glide by in just over 40 minutes. Ducktails started out as a solo project for Matthew Mondanile of Real Estate, but the sound has gradually evolved from its cheap Casio keyboard and drum machine beginnings to the glossy, po-faced retro pop of *The Flower Lane*, even as tracks like "Assistant Director" and "Letter Of Intent" continue to employ the bare-bones synth melodies and ultra-basic drum programming of the early days. There are many guests supporting Mondanile here; the group Big Troubles provide most of the instrumental backing, but guest vocalists pop up too, most notably Madeline Follin of Cults, who does a solid imitation of mid-1980s Stevie Nicks on "Sedan Magic".

The music is quite often blatantly derivative of the chart hits of 80s alternative acts like The Church, Crowded House, Aztec Camera, et al; softly sung, moderately catchy songs swathed in production designed to soothe and perhaps inspire a softly tapped foot. The occasional dab of heavily reverbed saxophone feels like a distinctly 80s touch, too. Still other songs combine monotone vocals reminiscent of The Jesus And Mary Chain with the strummed guitars of vaguely psychedelic acts like The La's or The Sundays. For a musician who was in college less than a decade ago, these are likely the sounds of early childhood. Without necessarily being part of any particular scene, on *The Flower Lane*, Mondanile is revealing himself as part of a generation for whom collage is the ultimate creative act, and cocooning oneself inside a warm blanket woven of gauzy, unexamined nostalgia is the artistic strategy of choice.
Phil Freeman

Brian Eno
Lux
Warp CD/DL/LP

The first draft of this review was not positive. It was nothing but a series of alternative titles for *Lux*: *Discreetly Wealthy Music*; *Music For Alain De Botton's Secular Temples*; *Music For The Room In Madame Tussaud's With Brian Eno's Statue In It*. Etcetera. So what is *Lux* first of all: his first solo album proper since 2005's *Another Day On Earth* after two recent collaborations for Warp, it originates from a commission to compose for the Great Gallery of the Palace of Venaria in Turin. Over the course of an hour and a quarter, piano, keyboards, strings and vibraphone (perhaps?) slowly spell out lullaby phrases that enjamb, and never find a full stop. The light is limpid, the reverb softly extending into the infinite. Elements come and go; the accents shift; the season changes; the record ends.

The press release calls it ambitious, but also an advance on his now-canonical Ambient works from the 1970s, which doesn't quite scream ambition to me. It's a very well crafted Ambient record: it keeps its head down, it tints the air, it would probably turn itself off when done and leap back onto the shelf for you if it could. But to borrow an idea explored by Eno in a column for this very magazine about electric-era Miles Davis, how much of its value, or its pleasure, lies in the fact that it's by Eno? If it wasn't by Eno, would anyone care or listen to it?

I don't think so, or not for very long. The move from Lux (light) to Luxe as luxury is one Eno almost invites critics to make here, but it's a crucial one: made from a position of luxury (financial and artistic), this is music as a luxury, like a warm bath or spa treatment. And it underscores what it is in late Eno that may lead to him being seen not as an arch-exponent of the modern but as a discreet throwback: the way so much of his later work, from the blandishments of Coldplay to his own music, is consolatory; comfort food. Rather than shock, radicalise or even simply invite the listen to rethink, it murmurs complacently to itself, and anyone wandering by the installation, everything's OK. And *Lux* is OK, while it's on. But that's all. And that's a shame.
Sam Davies

James Ferraro
Sushi
Hippos In Tanks DL/LP

Los Angeles based musician James Ferraro described his 2011 album *Far Side Virtual* as merely the overture to this new work, which continues his satirical – in his words, post-nihilistic – take on the zeitgeist. *FSV* was one of that year's most divisive records, with track titles like "Fro Yo And Cellular Bits", and a typical vocal sample, *"Richard Branson's avatar says hello"*. If you gave yourself up to its glossy daftness, this was the musical equivalent of a day in a beauty spa: mucho pampering but ultimately no one cares about you. Most records place great value on musical structure, but Ferraro seemed to chuck that out the window; tracks were intuitively flung together and then simply ended, like a jogger stopping for a phone call. This structural insouciance alone made it stick out from the herd.

If *Far Side Virtual* obsessed on 90s games and gadgets, *Sushi* is more centred in the present, and more focused altogether, as if Ferraro almost gives a damn. "Baby Mitsubishi" crams vocal samples and swooshing swords into a weird space to conjure up a neat satire on Rihanna-style pop. "Lovesick" is another intricate arrangement, the sugar-coated harp arpeggios underpinning a dead-eyed choir of squelchy mantras. "Powder" opens up a dark space, but then undercuts it with lip-smacks and flickers of cartoon voices.

Ferraro both critiques and delights in the void at the heart of music commerce and headphone culture. This music may be heartless and stoopid, but it serves to delineate his love-hate relations with that pop/gym/iPad thing we call life. "*Sushi* is designer," he says gnomically, "It's my darkness, it's just my life squeezed into my music." Another of his missions is to reclaim all rejected synth sounds from the bad taste dump, so the hyperactive wopwopwop and smashing glass of "Playin Ya Self" comes over like a hipster reworking of Sheffield comedy act John Shuttleworth, with his portable Yamaha keyboard.

The final two tunes may be titled "Condom" and "Booty Call", but here the album becomes more moody and exploratory. Ferraro mixes cool with cunning as he splashes wrong-key helium backing vocals across swooning

Andrew Chalk
49 Views In Rhapsodies' Wave Serene
Faraway Press CD

For the past five years, Andrew Chalk's music has been in a slow but steady state of change. The longform astral drones which have occupied him since the early 1990s have gradually come to be supplemented – and sometimes supplanted – by a new mode of playing. On 2007's *Time Of Hayfield*, as well as *The Cable House* and *Ghosts Of Nakhodka* (both 2009), individual sounds begin to appear – struck on acoustic instruments, and either worked into gentle pointillistic patterns, or allowed to resonate briefly before smudging into blurry drones. This small but important development became more obvious on two 2012 releases, *La Lumière Parfumée* by Elodie (Chalk's duo with Timo van Luijk) and Vikki Jackman's *A Paper Doll's Whisper Of Spring*, on which Chalk's influence is clear.

49 Views In Rhapsodies' Wave Serene at first sounds like a cryptic feint: a 54 minute album which contains no fewer than 49 tracks, about as many as on all Chalk's previous albums to date. Most of them are between 45 and 80 seconds in duration; the longest is 2'18". The instrumentation is almost exclusively organ and synthesizer,

from which waft forth brief curlicues of melody, chiming and reverberating delicately. They drift laterally or double back on themselves in soft eddies of movement. The tracks' apparent homogeneity is deceptive – close listening reveals continual shifts in volume, pitch and metre.

Their titles provide a veritable wealth of contextual clues about the ideas underpinning Chalk's work: wanderings through rural landscapes, surveying expansive vistas, communing with the Romantic sublime. The music now more than ever contrasts richly with such notions, sounding determinedly fragile and insular, all fragments of memory and emotional undertow.

Its limited instrumentation and ostensible narrowness of focus, however, shouldn't obscure that in its modest, self-effacing way, this is a radical album for Chalk. After all, not so long ago he would fill a 54 minute album with a single, monolithic drone composition – now he crams it with 49 featherlight miniatures which exude light and harmony. The evidence suggests that this hermetic artist, previously known for a singleminded focus, is undergoing a process of significant stylistic evolution.
Nick Cain

Fragile goods: Andrew Chalk

chords. Many would welcome more – indeed any – emotional involvement from Ferraro, and this more personal statement could point the way forward.
Clive Bell

The Bryan Ferry Orchestra
The Jazz Age
BMG CD

There always was something of the Cotton Club about Bryan Ferry, peacocking in front of his musicians wearing the sharpest tuxedo in town, intoning sad sweet songs with crazy rhythms, draping expensive eye candy on the front of his album sleeves and not caring a damn about the decadence. The question is, though, whether Ferry needed to make this point of connection explicit by having jazz pianist Colin Good repurpose 13 of his and Roxy Music's most bankable hits – "Don't Stop The Dance", "Avalon", "Love Is The Drug", they're all here – for an eight-piece jazz ensemble explicitly modelled on Duke Ellington's mid-1920s orchestra.

And the questions multiply. Is *The Jazz Age* anything more than a well-heeled vanity project? If Ferry wanted to open Roxy Music up, surely avant rockers or improvisors might have arrived at something more in keeping with the founding spirit of the group than this? In his Invisible Jukebox (this issue), Ferry puts the success of this purely instrumental record down to the "inventiveness and skill of the musicians". With Humphrey Lyttelton sidemen Robert Fowler (clarinet) and Alan Barnes (baritone saxophone), Chris Barber's drummer John Sutton and trumpeter Enrico Tomasso, a member of Bob Wilber's Ellington recreation band, the attention to period detail is impeccable. Tomasso or Barnes carry Ferry's vocal lines, retaining the

stylistic pretence as they mirror his original phrasing. "Just Like You" fades into a chiming piano chord like many a 78 rpm; the faux-Dixieland ending to "I Thought" doesn't quite convince though.

Another unconvincing aspect is highlighted by the melodic contour of "Avalon", which bends around a trademark Roxy chromatic incline that utterly refuses to march back in time. "Love Is The Drug" and "The Bogus Man" are both etched around Ellington's "The Mooche" and now the harmonic profiling is uncanny: ominous dirges shake hands across the decades. And if the question 'why?' is never quite answered, as stylistic cross-fertilising vanity projects by rock stars of pensionable age go, this one has bags of charm at least and is eminently listenable.
Philip Clark

Barry Guy/Glasgow Improvisers Orchestra
Schweben – Ay, But Can Ye?
Maya CD

Over six decades, until his death in 2010, Edwin Morgan's poetry explored science and science fiction, Scots versus English as a poetic language, violence as social communication, craft and technology, the death of Marilyn, socialism and nationalism ("Starlings In George Square" may be a reference to Stalin and to the brief Glasgow Soviet after the First World War), the kinship between the Scottish and Russian experience, and later his own previously unspoken but warmly hinted sexuality.

Schweben – Ay, But Can Ye? begins with Morgan's voice, ailing but strong and orphic, reading his own Scots translation of Vladimir Mayakovsky's "And Could You?". For non-Scots, the opening line will be every bit

as alien as the Russian original: *"Wi a jaup the darg-day map's owre-pentit."* The more interesting issue is whether the Glasgow Improvisers Orchestra perform in Scots, too, or in a lingua franca indistinguishable from improvisors in London, Chicago or even Mayakovsky's Moscow. Over ten years, GIO have developed a powerful compound language, an aural equivalent to Morgan's, that allows them to make powerful use of their own internal resources, coming from jazz, folk, classical music and points west, with steadily growing confidence.

Much of this has been honed in association with senior visiting players, notably Evan Parker (who started the ball rolling a decade ago at the Free RadiCCAls event), George E Lewis, Maggie Nicols and, repeatedly, with Barry Guy who devised and directed *Schweben – Ay, But Can Ye?* at the Stringfest double bass festival in Glasgow three years ago. The music is a pungent distillation of Mayakovsky's experimentalism, with deep lyricism alternating passages of jarring violence, soloistic individualism ambiguously rubbed up against a collectivist or universalising tendency ("Principals" and "Partners" is Guy's version of this). Hoarse prepared piano (harpsichord-like), cello, flute, trombone and guitar introduce the narrative. The vocalists have Morgan's poem for material and, in addition to Guy's graphic score (schweben means 'to float'), 13 Kandinsky paintings offer cues and potential interactions. A key element of the GIO sound, philosophy and way of getting along is the high (in comparison to London, even now) proportion of female members. Guy and partner Maya Homburger on Baroque violin offer a further instance of this balance and unity, not in a blandly yin-yang way but as a dynamic principle of the music.

Morgan speaks again at the end about what Mayakovsky meant to him, but it's all there in the poem itself, which underneath the delighted strangeness of the Scots speaks of freedom and improvisation: *"I suddenly smeared the weekday map/splashing paint from a glass.../And you/could you perform/a nocturne on a drainpipe flute."* Nocturnes, études, miniature symphonies in a post-industrial landscape and with the seemingly obsolete technology of the Western orchestra: that's what GIO do, and do it magnificently.
Brian Morton

Hamilton Yarns
Calm Down Grandad
Hark CD

Hamilton Yarns have been knocking around my adoptive hometown of Brighton for years now, and I've seldom paid them much attention aside from catching the odd support slot here and there. They've always seemed to be one of those doggedly amateurish pseudo-avant indie outfits who didn't know when to quit (there are plenty of those in Brighton) and would eventually expire onstage in the middle of some ramshackle improvisation for trumpet and glockenspiel.

Who'd have guessed that they had it in them to produce an album as confident and compelling as *Calm Down Grandad*. Whatever Hamilton Yarns were lacking when I've seen them perform in the past, they seem to have developed in spades, and the result is a form of beautifully layered, free-breathing electroacoustic pop that has something in common with Birmingham's Pram, albeit for the most part without the crepuscular eeriness. Then again, perhaps it would be more accurate to state that they now sound an awful lot like Robert Wyatt sitting in on a *Hong Kong In The 60s* session, such is their slightly creaky appeal.

Though little more than sketches, the songs are engaging and remain just the right side of twee, while the use of environmental sound is inspired, woven in and out of and between songs, often giving the impression that a shuttered window had been flung open onto the seafront mid-session. If in the past Hamilton Yarns sounded like they were trying a bit too hard, well, somewhere along the line they stopped trying and started being. Either that or I missed the point completely and they've always been this good. In which case, more fool me.
Joseph Stannard

King Crimson
Larks' Tongues In Aspic 40th Anniversary Edition
DGM/Panegyric 13×CD+DVD+Blu-Ray

I'm sitting here with a box containing 15 discs that expand on an original studio album that lasts 45 minutes. Such is the mystique surrounding King Crimson's 1972–73 output that the scale of this set, while doubtless absurd to many, represents some kind of Holy Grail to worshippers at the

church of Fripp (Jamie Muir diocese). *Larks' Tongues In Aspic* marked a stirring new direction for Crimson as they moved away decisively from both the symphonic pomp of their early music (1969's *In The Court Of The Crimson King*, the following year's *In The Wake Of Poseidon*), and the tentative Keith Tippett-abetted jazz shadings of 1970's *Lizard* and 71's *Islands*. The shambolic jam band boogie purveyed by the 1971–72 touring group, as documented on the notorious *Earthbound*, was also consigned to the dustbin of history the moment the new five-piece line-up played its first gig.

That gig is included here, an October 1972 Frankfurt club performance recorded in rough but just about passable fidelity. Guitarist Robert Fripp's new cohorts – distorto-bass titan John Wetton, the limber, crisp drummer Bill Bruford, violin colourist David Cross and the Improv percussionist Muir – lurch with reckless abandon through embryonic versions of the yet to be recorded *Larks' Tongues* material, and more importantly, throw themselves with total commitment into an hour's worth of improvisation, driven ever forwards by the manic energy and invention of their secret weapon Muir, the galvanising influence on

the group during its 1972–74 period even after his early departure to attend a Buddhist retreat. It's the Improv angle that ensured this incarnation of the group was able to escape critics' post-1976 rock dinosaur cull (what you might call the progrom) and have its work assessed in the context of electric Miles and Can rather than Camel and Jethro Tull. Released in early 1973, *Larks' Tongues In Aspic* ironically features less free playing than the post-Muir albums. The first part of the title track has a short passage of high energy group improvisation in between more rigidly composed sections – the only time the group really sound like their onstage improvising selves. Nevertheless, it remains an astonishing piece of music, ranging right across the dynamic range from the impossibly delicate thumb piano introduction through to its bludgeoning six-chord riff. "The Talking Drum" rides a mesmerizingly minimal groove, with Cross and Fripp's uncoiling modal lines pulling it inexorably towards hysteria; while loose and open-ended in compositional terms, the track nevertheless follows a template laid down over the previous six months of live work. The second part of the title track, meanwhile, is a tight, Bartók-like chamber rock piece that takes a snippet of

violin melody from part one and explores its rhythmic properties exhaustively and with immense power.

The vocal tracks are far less satisfying, veering between the mildly lumpen ("Easy Money") and the somewhat cloying ("Book Of Saturday" and "Exiles"). The *Larks' Tongues* box includes a CD of outtakes from the album sessions that offers revealing glimpses of the process of recording, with certain passages rivalling the finished album in power. Steven Wilson's new mix of the album adds weight and presence to previously thin-sounding sections, and his unpicking of the elements that comprise the beautiful coda to "Larks' Tongues In Aspic Part One" on the disc dedicated to remixes is fascinating, highlighting the clever use of spoken word tapes that predates similar work by Eno (who had recently initiated a longstanding working relationship with Fripp) on *My Life In The Bush Of Ghosts* by six or seven years.

In addition to studio material, the box collects all known live recordings of the Muir-era group, each restored to the maximum fidelity possible for cassette recordings made in the early 1970s. The biggest draw is the long awaited appearance of the live TV session recorded for the German show *Beat*

The frantic vocal cut-ups of **DJ Spinn** tap into black pop's long history of using the voice to subvert Western language systems.
By **Tony Herrington**

DJ Spinn
Teklife Vol 2: What You Need
Lit City Trax DL

This is the second collection of tracks to be released by Chicago's Lit City Trax, a label, or maybe data dump is a better way to describe it, launched by Rashad and Spinn, two of the most outward facing and prolific producers in the defiantly parochial Footwork scene (the others are Traxman, Spinn and Rashad's contemporary, and Young Smoke, who is almost half their age).

Spinn's ten track *Teklife Vol 2: What You Need* follows in the considerable wake of Rashad's 20 track *Teklife Vol 1: Welcome To The Chi*. The fact that both collections carry the same title is significant. It underlines how Footwork's scene mentality is morphing into the kind of brand identity that can turn MCs and DJs into CEOs; reasserts the ghetto sensibilities of its producers (even – or maybe especially – those who have become members of underground dance music's international DJ set); and demonstrates that these self-same producers are wholly conscious of the fact that their entire existence is technologically determined, by the sampler, the sequencer and the internet.

Where *Welcome To The Chi* was generically expansive (and Traxman's *The Mind Of Traxman* was lumpenly progressive, and Young Smoke's *Space Zone* was rigorously conceptual), *What You Need* is symphonically soulful. Compared to Spinn's earlier stripped-down dance craze tracks – "Bounce N Break Yo Back", "Down Low", "If U Ain't Jukin'" – some of it sounds

Ashes57

Club just a few days after that debut gig. Only a short excerpt was ever broadcast – a rather tense, stiff take on "Larks' Tongues In Aspic, Part One" that has been circulating on the web for a number of years. More than half an hour of extra footage is presented here; there's an unconvincing take on "Exiles", featuring Wetton's unpleasantly strained tenor vocal and an extended improvisation that lacks finesse but makes up for it in white knuckle energy. It's here you have a sense of why the group generated so much purple prose among those who witnessed them live. The fierce concentration of the players is electric to watch, and Muir's madcap theatrics add an element of visual mania that is entirely suitable for this most wired of musics.

Nevertheless, in documenting this six-month period so exhaustively, some of that famed mystique has been slightly tarnished. My assumption has always been that Muir's influence on Crimson's practices gradually dwindled the more time elapsed after his departure. The group's final work in this incarnation was brutally exciting – see the USA live album – but the improvisations had settled into familiar patterns that in some way parallel the uninspired groove workouts of the understandably maligned Earthbound group, albeit with a juggernaut power and breathtaking technique. One would assume, then, that the Muir era would have been about a rock group genuinely operating without a tightrope, bringing in processes inspired by the likes of Muir's previous collaborators Derek Bailey and Evan Parker – in effect something closer to what Henry Cow went on to achieve in the same period. But these live tapes reveal a group who repeatedly default to an admittedly thunderously exciting but ultimately safe rock vernacular, as if it's Muir who has gone further in accommodating the imperatives of a rock group than vice versa. It could well be the case that it took a Jamie Muir-sized hole to unlock the creative potential of Crimson rather than the man himself.
Keith Moliné

Lithuanian Sound Art
Various
Gintas Kraptavicius CD
Gintas K
Gintas K
Copy For Your Records MC

"Away with dodecaphony, polyphony, harmony and cacophony!" wrote Vytautas Landsbergis in a 1966 manifesto. "We must learn to marvel at truth. We shall again have aesthetic pleasure in such simple acts as drinking water, spitting into a well or blowing our noses." During the 1990s, Landsbergis was Lithuania's first post-Soviet head of state, but during childhood he was a close friend of Jurgis Mačiūnas, who later initiated Fluxus. These two releases from Gintas Kraptavicius show some of the imaginative ways in which the current crop of Lithuanian experimentalists are working with sound beyond the conventional terms of music.

Andrius Rugys's *Äūgir gir gir gar gar gar (garsas)*, which opens the sound art compilation, confronts full on the challenge of finding art in the practices of everyday life. A rowing boat trip on a lake near Vilnius. Oars creak, water drips, birds tweet, two passengers sing a folk song. Another piece, by SALA, captures the fizz of fermentation during the brewing process. But there's no formula governing these ten pieces. Antanas Dombrovskij's *NNN broken jazz* is a sonic cicatrix of cranky synths, blown plumbing pipes and sampled vocal improvising. Vytautas Jugurtis's *Hi Fi* is a grainy, crackling computer composition.

Lina Lapelyte's *PAR* is an atmosphere conjured up live at London's Cafe Oto, using violin, electronics and environmental sound recordings. Arturas Bumsteinas even ventures over the border, into song.

If Gintas K's own contribution, *a seeping flow of popping granules, melodic fragments and gassy blasts*, leaves you wanting more, his ear-catching cassette, limited to 50 copies, features five sprightly digital improvisations in a comparable textural vein. All enjoyable alternatives to spitting in a well.
Julian Cowley

Radu Malfatti & Taku Unami
Radu Malfatti & Taku Unami
ErstLive CD
Keith Rowe
September
ErstLive CD

Ten years to the day after the Twin Towers collapsed, Radu Malfatti and Taku Unami played as a duo, followed by a solo set from Keith Rowe, at The Stone in downtown Manhattan. Released on the ErstLive imprint of Jon Abbey's Erstwhile label, is it any coincidence that Rowe took the decision to actualise his material in retrospect with a unashamedly emotive album title,

positively Baroque. But like Rashad, and despite – or like I said, maybe because of – all the international clamour and glamour, Spinn sounds like he is still making tracks to rock neighbourhood dance circles, which is why his music retains its vernacular power (unlike that of Traxman and Young Smoke, who diffuse it to fit an album format – neither of the *Teklife* volumes are albums, they're collections of tracks, a distinction which is philosophical rather than semantic), and why it still sounds more urgent and vital than most other electronic music you are going to hear this month (including all those rather desperate Footwork hybrids being pumped out by producers from outside the scene such as Machinedrum, Addison Groove, Ramadanman et al).

As ever, the tracks are short and to the point, flying past in a blur of clipped and looped vocal samples and multidirectional machine rhythms, each one doing that Footwork thing: dismantling the House prototype and building it back up into constructions whose surfaces warp and bend like the stainless steel shell of Frank Gehry's Pritzker Pavilion – an alien spaceship landed in the midst of Chicago's Millennium Park.

"Dey Comin'" is stark and minimal and deploys Footwork's key rhythmic tropes: snare triplets that sound like someone hitting the keys of an amplified typewriter, accelerated hi-hat paradiddles, offbeat or oddly syncopated bass pulses, plus synth drones that modulate between two or three pitches. On "Let Me Baby" Spinn introduces another Footwork trait, the way it mines the archive of the upwardly mobile soul and R&B of the 1970s and 80s for vocal samples and instrumental moods, and then uses these to set up dramatic shifts in the music, in this case the way the line *"If you just come to me…"*, a soul man's seductive promise, cues a vertiginous drop into a double time rush where all the components in the track are mobilised to induce total mania on the dancefloor.

But rather than its delirious energy and extreme frequency range, from sub-bass to needling highs, which is what hits you in the clubs, in the reflective sensorium of headphone listening, Footwork's approach to vocal sampling is what defines its aesthetic, and on *What You Need* the defining mood of that aesthetic is poignancy.

"4 A $5 Bag" turns a sample of a hoarse black American male voice discussing a drug deal into a tenebrous rhythmbabble (all the voices here are distinctively black). The title track suspends, distorts and atomises the ululating voice of an R&B diva, so lyrical sentiments are replaced by a more complex set of emotions. On "Over There (Getting It)" dance circle exhortations are clipped and looped into lines of richocheting sibilants and consonants – rather than denuding these inner city voices of personality, this has the opposite effect, amplifying their humanity by exposing their lack of agency. "Dance Floor Packed" loops the end syllables of a similar chorus of voice samples so they sound like a stuck CD, pitchshifting them through a hellish stuttering chorale, before easing them into oblivion dub-style in a hearse of echo. "Do My Dance" interlocks multiple vocal samples so they dramatise a typical call and response routine in which a strong female voice taunts and mocks a chorus of dumb male braggadocio, sentiments which are further rendered inert and impotent by the way Spinn cuts and loops them so they never resolve (in such a context, anyone who finds lines such as *"nothing but shaved pussy in my iPhone"* offensive, or from another perspective, ironic, deserves all they get).

Were they to bother checking for it, aficionados of the literary avant garde may hear echoes here of the way sound poets like Henri Chopin, Åke Hodell and others used the technology of the typewriter and the tape recorder to blast apart and reassemble language to reveal something febrile and atavistic. Having said that, it would be risible for anyone to suggest these tracks are selfconscious exercises in avant garde linguistics. But it would be equally patronising to say this variable was merely a by-product rather than an actual function of the music's imperative to rock the house and, like all black pop, define itself relative to both earlier innovations and its own immediate reality. Beginning with scat singing, and its transmutation of the voice into a generator of pure sound and emotion, as well as the street corner word games and vocal routines such as the dozens, which became some of the foundation stones of rap, black pop has been defined as much by vocal science as rhythmic complexity and instrumental intensity. And Footwork takes vocal science further out than any black pop since electro. To get all philosophical on it, Footwork's use of sampling embodies the latest technologised iteration of a vernacular form of semiotics in which black music articulates then subverts the mendacity of Western language systems which are insufficient to express true lived experience. Or to get all musicological about it, in the hands of a producer like Spinn, grounded in Chicago's urban music traditions, Footwork puts the blues back into machine music, a fact underlined here by the eerie use of Auto-Tune on "She Turnt Up", which distorts a soul man's solipsistic lament into a more profound alien plaint (a technique mirrored on *Space Zone* by Young Smoke's equally eerie revival of the vocoder).

Of course, this is the kind of talk that is greeted with snorts of derision from the kind of white hipsters who never want to think about what they're hearing in black music and why. But there is nothing random about Footwork's sampling of black voices – these are African-American archetypes, from star-crossed lover men and women to self-deluding gangbangers, stuck, as Larry Neal said, "on the meanest, most gut level of human existence", and Spinn's sampling of them feels deep and empathetic.

As that old white bluesman Walter Benjamin once put it: "To understand a linguistic entity it is always necessary to ask of which mental entity it is the direct expression." And in its radical application and expansion of vocal science, Footwork is the direct expression of black producers talking it like they walk it. □

September, while Malfatti and Unami clearly prefer to let their names speak for themselves? I think not. Rowe's 34 minute improvisation is a conscious reflection upon, and commemoration of, 9/11; Malfatti and Unami might well have played the same set had it been 12 September or 11 October.

That said, someone – Abbey? – has decided to register the Malfatti/Unami set as a consequence of time and place. The CD begins and closes with conversation; a few minutes of vividly miked audience hubbub keeps you guessing before the musicians amble into the performance area, and 50 minutes later, the improvisation concludes with Malfatti and Unami discussing whether they're finished or not (all in explicit contrast to *September*, which nearly squeezes out the first sound in its relish to get going). And the CD has a resonance that the performance probably didn't. Hearing instrumental sound crumble into rubble and dust, framed by the external ambience of New York City cabs, passers-by and the trash being collected, dredges up unavoidable associations.

If Malfatti and Unami's incidental relationship to the surrounding environment is broadly Cageian, Rowe's set purposefully summons New York City life into his piece via his trusty radio. EMF's "Unbelievable" rips through the surface, a reminder of the sort of pop, you suspect, that Dubya and Sarah Palin had on their iPods. Rowe's radio also captures copious 9/11 chatter from local radio stations, while his guitar and contact microphone interjections are brusque, jarring and unruly, even by his austere standards.

But another thread running through *September* completely changes the terms under which he normally works. Rowe arrived with a pre-loaded recording of 19th century Czech composer Antonín Dvořák's second piano quintet. The symbolism could hardly be more pointed. Dvořák's cornerstone *New World Symphony*, written when he relocated to New York in the 1890s, is filled with nostalgia for the old country and curiosity about the new; his quintet similarly ruminates on memory and regret. Its presence – and in long chunks – gives Rowe's structure intense narrative urgency; something precious from history gets trashed, the present wonders what to do.
Philip Clark

Man Chest Hair
Various
Finders Keepers CD
When Stack Waddy is the most famous group on a compilation, you know you're in the realm of true obscurity. *Man Chest Hair* gathers rarities, demos and studio outtakes from 17 early 70s Manchester groups, nearly all of them working variations on blues rock, biker boogie, and/or hamfisted prog. Animal based group names (Urbane Gorilla, Greasy Bear, Savory Duck) abound, as do fuzzed-out guitars, drums that thud like cardboard boxes and blasts of sub-Uriah Heep organ. Naturally, it's mostly a boys' club, though a few women show up – JC Heavy's "Is This Really Me?" features a vocalist who sounds like a teenage Shirley Bassey with an occult obsession. The only group featured twice are

Plasma, a heavy instrumental outfit; "Seven Stairs" offers Steppenwolf-esque riffing, screaming guitar leads and phased drums, while "Hazel Time" (a CD bonus track) is a funkier, strutting tune.

Like early 1980s hardcore, this type of rock dwelt within a narrow set of aesthetic boundaries, with only small differences to tell groups apart. Greasy Bear had acoustic guitars and a vocalist reminiscent of Black Oak Arkansas's Jim Dandy Mangrum; Socrates packed horns; Savory Duck had synths, medieval-ish melodies and lyrics about dragons; The Way We Live's vocalist (heard on the awesomely titled "King Dick II") sounded uncannily like Jack Bruce. Indeed, they were doing their best Cream imitation, and it's a pretty good one. *Man Chest Hair* is full of small-time groups offering their take on the work of more successful peers, and consequently is strictly for 70s rock obsessives. But it's a fun listen and an interesting bit of history.
Phil Freeman

Monopoly Child Star Searchers
The Garnet Toucan
Underwater Peoples LP
These are lean times for Hypnagogic pop. Leading lights such as Ariel Pink, James Ferraro and Ducktails have veered away from tape hiss toward cleaner production and clearer intentions. Others, like Sam Mehran of Matrix Metals/Outer Limits Recordings, seem to have cleared out altogether. But Spencer Clark, Ferraro's former partner in The Skaters, is sticking to lo-fi, at least when he records under his Monopoly Child Star Searchers moniker. *The Garnet Toucan* is the final instalment in what he calls a romance audio trilogy, and it's filled with layers of reverb and murk. Often it feels like Clark tied his sounds to a rock and tossed them into the ocean, and we're only getting glimpses through ripples on the surface.

Clark prefers an interstellar metaphor, claiming that *The Garnet Toucan* "uncover[s] the symbolic animal's transfiguration into the outerzone of infinite space". It's apt, as his music often mimics the echoed, analogue blips associated with the space race technology of the 1950s and 60s. Those decades have other echoes here too. Unlike some of his H-pop peers, who are more obsessed with the 1980s, Clark as MCSS reaches back to the early electronics of Raymond Scott, the radio experiments of Henry Jacobs and the hermetic art of The Residents. As with those pioneers, Monopoly Child Star Searchers' music carries the spark of discovery, as if Clark were mixing chemicals in a lab, eager to find out which will melt into each other and which will cause explosions. In that respect, his work is less about pop culture memory than abstract sonic exploration.

Some may find Clark's evocation of old innovations to be simply mimetic, and there are moments where *The Garnet Toucan*'s primary appeal is nostalgic. But more often than not, his variation on this style – bright loops, swelling rhythms and wavy synth flourishes – is idiosyncratic and oddly moving. The way he makes everything enthused and wired gives *The Garnet*

Toucan a tangible rush of blood. This aspect of his music is matched currently only by the endless inventions of Black Dice and the recent explorations of Brian Pyle aka Ensemble Economique. Like them, Clark isn't just inhabiting a form, he's furthering it, filling its outlines with a kind of colour and personality it hasn't previously contained.
Marc Masters

Norbert Möslang
indoor_outdoor
Ideologic Organ DL/LP
A former member of Swiss electronic duo Voice Crack with Andy Guhl, Norbert Möslang has always been vitally concerned with inside and outside states, not in the jazz sense of metrical/harmonic/melodic music versus free, but in a quite literal opposition between adjoining acoustic spaces. He once told me that hearing voices through a wall was more interesting than actual conversation. Here he has wired up the windows of an art gallery in order to record the world outside. This might be read as sly commentary on the role of the artist, shut in the Platonic cave of self and able to sample reality, or the Forms, only through the insulated blubble of remote noise. He has also taken recordings from a Swiss marina – reminiscent of Luc Ferrari's *Presque Rien No 1* (see Boomerang, this issue) – and processed the sound using his armoury of 'cracked everyday electronics', a form of glitch aesthetic executed on the kind of gear that even the charity shop won't take on safety grounds. The effect of all this on the title track "indoor_outdoor" is both strange and strangely calming, an aural equivalent of shut-in syndrome, but with no associated anxiety. One listens to Möslang with an evenly suspended attention. No part has priority over any other part. There is no shout of meaning, no sense of dramatic development or, perish the thought, climax. The music unfolds, and its naturalism quite comfortably takes the place of melody, harmony, metre or any other structural element.

Not (quite) so, however, "hot_cold_ shield", the only other track here. It was recorded seven years after "indoor_ outdoor", in Quebec, not Switzerland, and in collaboration with Toshimaru Nakamura's no-input mixing board. The approach is considerably more violent and confrontational, and to that degree more predictable and tame. It offers sound art as a kind of quasi-political manifesto – the effect is of competing slogans being shouted at sufficient distance to lose the actual words – rather than Möslang's usual patient evocation of the world as inners and outers, peopled by insiders and outsiders, and agreeably unknowable.
Brian Morton

Manuel Mota
Rck
Dromos 5×CD
"Bon qu'à ça" was Samuel Beckett's typically laconic response to the question "Why do you write?" – and no English translation ("that's all I'm good for") can do justice to its terse, trisyllabic minimalism.

Dead end: Jon Mueller

Jon Mueller
Death Blues
Hometapes/Taiga CD/DL/LP

It could be argued, surely, that all successful art is a response to and comment upon human mortality. Undeterred by the possibility of stating the obvious, Milwaukee based percussionist Jon Mueller presents this album as the latest facet of an ongoing multidisciplinary project – also called *Death Blues* – that "addresses the inevitability of death as impetus to become more present in each moment". If you can detect a whiff of the self-help guru in that mission statement, you'll be unsurprised to learn that Mueller – as well as running the Crouton record label for ten years until 2009 and collaborating with artists such as Rhys Chatham and z'ev – has also carved out a parallel career as a motivational speaker and writer on "creativity and new business approaches", with an explicit mission statement to help connect people and ideas.

Up to now, *Death Blues* has largely taken the form of a written manifesto and an event in November incorporating live music and attended by hooded acolyte-vocalists including Marielle Allschwang, of whom Mueller's website informs us: "The scent at her station was a top note based scent, May Chang, which corresponds with the color green. She held the Shoofly quilt block pattern, signifying guidance and direction."

It's possible to discern the influence of Alejandro Jodorowsky's quixotic masterpiece of acid astrological surrealism, *The Holy Mountain*, in this harmless New Age bunkum and, indeed, the album starts with what sounds like a homage to Don Cherry's 1973 soundtrack, with loose twangs and wordless vocal moans creating an atmosphere of meditative expectation. From this wafting preamble, however, the rest of the album takes a sharp turn into a rigid grid of bludgeoning repetition and iron insistence: basic 4/4 drum patterns supporting funereal block-rock riffs unwaveringly thumped out on strings that loll halfway between a berimbau and a detuned bass. The album's sole lyrical content comes around ten minutes in – a single shout of *"right now!"* – leaving us to glean Mueller's entire message from a disappointingly featureless, tightly regimented musical landscape.

So, how does this represent the celebration and opportunity of each moment? Is the whole project an interactive parable encouraging the listener to find spiritual meaning in the crushing banality and mechanistic drudgery of modern life? At the very least, it provokes questions that lie at the heart of the uncertainty of existence: Is anything interesting going to happen? When is it going to end?
Daniel Spicer

There's the same 'this is what I do' matter-of-factness to the music of Manuel Mota, a singular figure in the post-Fahey continuum of Improv guitar heroes, who rarely performs outside a small circle of friends and has released only a handful of recordings, many on his own hard-to-find Headlights imprint, in a career now entering its third decade.

Charting the evolution of Mota's playing, whether on acoustic or electric guitar, is no easy matter. While one can clearly hear, on successive albums, Taku Sugimoto composing himself into near-silence, and Loren Connors stripping the blues to the bone and wrapping the skeleton in a shroud of hum and hiss, drop the needle on any of the tracks in this handsome five CD box, which contains concert recordings from Lisbon, Ljubiana and Paris along with 11 tracks recorded in Mota's own home, and you could easily mistake it for something he released a decade ago. There's a little more space in the music these days, for sure, but Keith Rowe's observations on Mondrian in *The Wire* 206 come to mind: "[He] just basically did the same thing. Even after the seismic change of going to live in America, his lines just thickened up a bit."

It's well nigh impossible, especially on a guitar, to avoid references to the repertoire you've grown up with, the memory written in the fingers – think of Alan Licht's tasty jam band licks, Derek Bailey's Webernian bebop – but there's very little in Mota's playing that reveals the blues rock he was weaned on. It's deceptively cool, studiously avoids excess and seems remarkably relaxed, yet once you start listening you're absolutely spellbound – check out how the ambient

murmur and rustle of the punters at Lisbon's Zdb artspace on disc three quickly subsides into rapt attention.

Now that many improvisors arrive at the gig with a bagful of compositional caveats and thou shalt nots, it's refreshing to come across what used to be called in-the-moment playing, where the slightest accident, the tweak of an effects pedal catching the resonance of a harmonic, can send the music off in an entirely different direction. Fellow guitarist and Dromos labelmate Tetuzi Akiyama sums it up well in his affectionate mesostic that consitutes the sleevenotes: "the hands fooling/encounters new thoughts/after logics abandoned/bringing the distance/toward us away."
Dan Warburton

Aki Onda
Cassette Memories Volume 3: South Of The Border
Important CD/DL

As a child, Aki Onda was shown Super 8 footage of Mexico by his father, who was there as a member of the Japanese hockey team during the 1968 Olympics. This kicked off Onda's lifelong fascination for the country. Later on, a viewing of Alejandro Jodorowsky's mystic Western *El Topo* added further fuel to his fantasies. The third volume of his *Cassette Memories* series is comprised of recordings he made in Mexico using three cassette Walkmans. Two of these ceased to function properly along the way. Nevertheless, he continued to use them for their intended purpose.

The implications of this decision are obvious and fascinating. Field recording

is seldom a simple act of documentation – it inevitably involves elements of improvisation, processing and editing. But here, Onda presents us with a reality further modified by the functional quirks of the machines themselves. The title of the series therefore takes on an added significance: these memories are flawed, damaged, semi-present beyond even the usual limitations of the format. One must surely wonder, then, what was his motivation in continuing to use broken recording equipment?

It seems likely that Onda realised that he had chanced upon a way to recreate his private, mythic Mexico while employing fragments of the real thing. This methodology allows us to share a subjectivity which encompasses not only memory and lived experience but also preconception. It's highly effective, but it isn't always pretty. For instance, the marching band that opens "The Sun Clings To The Earth And There Is No Darkness" is gradually overwhelmed by the massed chirrups of a vast flock of birds. It's a violent, disturbing sound, gaining in density until it begins to overload the listener's head, blocking out rational thought. Which is apt, as rational thought would appear to be the last thing on Onda's mind. Taking cues from Jodorowsky while demonstrating awareness of his own outsider status, he consciously locates himself in the role of magic realist amid a landscape heavily foreshadowed by dreams. In his hands, therefore, the cassette recorder – broken or otherwise – becomes a shamanic tool for the manifestation of other realities.
Joseph Stannard

Pere Ubu
Lady From Shanghai
Fire CD/DL

Pere Ubu may be a group, but there's definitely one man in charge, and that man is David Thomas. He's conducted business like a cinematic auteur, weathering commercial insults and tinkering with Ubu's signature sound as necessary to articulate his recurring visions of a fading America and the hapless mopes who drive its highways at night. So what should we make of him naming a record after an Orson Welles picture that utterly failed in its appointed mission to be a modest money maker, only to be hailed decades after the fact as a masterpiece whose brilliance transcended studio meddling? Since Thomas produced and wrote the record, there's no interfering outsider to blame. And since it's the best Ubu release since *Tenement Year*, blame isn't really an issue, although the characters that speak through Thomas's songs are burdened with guilt and doubt.

The album is probably best understood by looking at its immediate predecessors. *Why I Hate Women* tried to translate pulp fiction author Jim Thompson's noir-ish vision into music, and *Long Live Pere Ubu!* was a gruelling reimagination of Alfred Jarry's dada play as a rock opera. Both were, like so much Ubu since their late 1980s Phonogram era, unabashedly verbose; *Lady From Shanghai*, on the other hand, requires the music to do more heavy lifting than it has on any Ubu album since 1980's *The Art Of Walking*. Popcorn-jittery beats and decisive basslines drive the satisfyingly direct melodies, which

Kathrine Berger

Folke Rabe
What??
Important CD

What is the shape of space? Modern science proposes multiple models. Some say it's curved, others that it's bent or elliptical or hyperbolic or, in the closest we come to any kind of consensus, approximately, infinitely flat, where space goes on forever, endlessly outwards, a kind of phantom barely-deviating forwards. It's a model that would seem to revolutionise our own personal experience of space. If the circumference is truly nowhere then the centre is everywhere, meaning every individual can just as easily be taken as the centre of the universe, a head-swimming concept that would confuse personal, microcosmic experiences of space with impersonal, macrocosmic ones. The UK sculptor Rachel Whiteread's life-sized casts of the insides of rooms, houses and towers seems caught up in this same personal/impersonal dialectic. They turn space inside out, revealing the impermeable within the permeable, the penetrable within the impenetrable, while underlining the paradox that lies at the heart of the subjective experience of space. Concrete poetry, let's call it.

The music of the Swedish composer Folke Rabe, like the gridlocked post-Hendrix rock minimalism of San Francisco power trio Blue Cheer or the invasive third ear soundings of the composer Maryanne Amacher, works a similar concrete magic. I've lived with *What??*, his 1967 recording of barely fluctuating electronic drones, for many years and listened to it in many different spaces: in a caravan in the corner of a field in County Clare in Ireland; in a cottage in the village of Portmeirion in Wales where the cult 1960s television series *The Prisoner* was filmed; in a converted shop-front in the Fishtown area of Philadelphia in the company of the late guitarist Jack Rose; in the countless flats and houses and tenements I've flitted between.

A late 1960s electronic masterwork by Sweden's **Folke Rabe** turns space inside out with its evocation of ever-changing emptiness. By **David Keenan**

It's strange to recall all the personal associations I have with this music, associations grounded in the specifics of time and space, even though on a first encounter it can seem impersonal and austere. *What??* never sounds the same, although paradoxically it's one of the most unchanging and elementally profound works to come out of the first, groundbreaking era of minimalism. It's a music that seems made of the stuff of memory, yet it refuses autobiography, insisting instead on an endlessly renewable moment.

From its titular confession of incomprehensibility, through to its original enigmatic pairing on a 1970 Wergo split LP with *Proteinimperialism* by Bo Anders Persson – a member of the Swedish drone rock groups International Harvester and Träd Gräs Och Stenar – *What??* has long been a totemic work, a sort of event horizon for early minimalism. Realised in the electronic studio of the Swedish Radio in Stockholm in the late summer of 1967, here it's given its first full outing since Jim O'Rourke's 30th anniversary edition on his own Dexter's Cigar imprint.

There is no obvious movement or change in the piece; it seems to simply exist, to occupy the room, to sit there and not so much vibrate as shudder or shiver, slightly. Its elongated, deliberate, barely-detectable pitch changes are incredibly sexy – a slow striptease that gives way to a slow striptease that gives way to a slow striptease, an aching, eternal disrobing.

Rabe favoured electronic over acoustic drone sources because of their "enormous, tireless endurance", and *What??* is an experiment with time as much as space. He was interested in how time interacts with and alters the overtones in a sound, for example his fascination with the fluctuating overtone activity in a dying piano chord – in other words how time 'plays' sounds, which runs into his confessed interest in monotony. But for Rabe, monotony takes on another meaning, as an obsessive focusing on moment-to-moment experience, and additionally as a way to decode the specific nuance of the present, how the present holds within itself a poetic idea of the past, or how our own poetic concepts of past and future might be modulated by the nuances of time itself.

What?? poses a question; a question that is unanswerable outside of the context of its own unfolding. Where are you, it asks, right now? There are two versions included here: the original piece and a half-speed rendering. If the original comes over as an exercise in highwire suspense, the equivalent of being creepy-crawled in slow motion, where you wake with a start to find that the furniture in the room has been rearranged, then the second, slower piece feels like having the floor pulled from beneath you altogether. Heard straight after the first, it's vertigo-inducing, the equivalent of a crude zoom shot, a power chord from the guitar of Leigh Stephens, a moment of reality-disordering close-up that drops your stomach like a helter-skelter.

Eternal music is not a music that sounds forever, despite its promise. Rather it is a music that sounds the ends of space, the limits of space, which allow us to conceptualise it. Rabe consistently talks about getting *inside* the sound, and what we find there is not emptiness itself but endless shells, redolent of emptiness, fields where emptiness might manifest or suggest itself, but never, quite, the experience of emptiness itself. The music of Folke Rabe, like the moulds of Rachel Whiteread, like the music of Blue Cheer, makes the inexplicable explicable and underlines the most primal combination, the ultimate duet: that between time and space – reverberant in space, expressive in time, but ultimately expressive of nothing, really, except variations of itself again and again. *What??* remains one of the great modern musical koans. What?? it asks. What?? And the answer is, not this, again and again and again. □

Folke Rabe (left) with Bo Anders Persson, late 1960s

are buffeted by Robert Wheeler's contrarian analogue synths squalls.

Ubu don't so much recreate their signature sound as break off pieces of it to use in a new construction just as Frankenstein-like as the garage rock/musique concrète collision of *The Modern Dance*. While Thomas hasn't entirely abandoned narrative, his lyrics here often recall that record's incomplete, telegraphic missives. But if *The Modern Dance* was a love poem to a decaying urban landscape, this is a collection of confessions delivered by men who are coming to the realisation that they are the butt of some sick joke; *"The truth hurts"*, complains the protagonist of "Lampshade Man", but there's no escaping it. I wouldn't go so far as to call *Lady From Shanghai* a masterpiece, but it's a rich and layered work that refuses to be easily summed up.
Bill Meyer

Michael Pisaro
Tombstones
HEM Berlin DL/LP

Michael Pisaro has a teaching job title to envy: The Roy E Disney Family Chair in Musical Composition (Roy was Walt's nephew) at the Herb Alpert School of Music in CalArts. Pisaro is perhaps the most simpatico and articulate spokesperson for the Wandelweiser Composers Ensemble, who have been working with notions of silence and the implications of Cage's *4'33"* for two decades now, and cross-fertilised with Improv more than any other school of composition. *Tombstones* – like Bowie's *Pin Ups*, perhaps – is Pisaro's look back at pop. It's a set of 20 song scores, nine of which are presented here, each one containing a moment lifted from a popular song, placed under Pisaro's microscope. In practice the listener doesn't hear these as quotes, though it's intriguing to be told that the descending chords of "Silent Cloud" include a snippet from The Beatles' 'Julia', like a homeopathic tincture dissolved in the music.

Pisaro's ensemble has E-Bowed guitars (including himself), harmonium, strings and percussion. Everything is spectral, vibrato-free and very slow. Of course the challenge for the musicians is to make this glacial pace seem natural, and by and large they succeed. The four women singers have poise and vulnerability, and avoid the chilly correctness of most contemporary performance. The warm, hazy ensemble sound is key to the record's success: the group move in a loose-limbed fashion. The scores, included here, make it clear performers have some freedom in timing, and occasionally a part sounds improvised, like the ghostly string sound that makes a big contribution to "Silent Cloud". The pop references (Dylan, DJ Screw and co) may be a tease, but once a piece like "New Orleans" hits its stride, this is just beautiful and haunting music.
Clive Bell

Silver Pyre
AeXE
Sedgemoor CD/LP

The cover photograph of *AeXE* depicts a sight familiar from my childhood: a stretch of the Dorset shoreline, rebranded by the tourism department in the years since I moved away as the Jurassic Coast. Silver Pyre's Gary Fawle grew up in the neighbouring county of Somerset and has left and returned several times, most recently during the making of this, his debut album. This dual identity as native and outsider offers him the perfect perspective from which to evoke both the familiarity and strangeness of the South West's landscape: fields dotted with abandoned farm equipment whose rust lends them a prematurely antique air; lanes swallowed by the vigorous summer growth of ancient hedgerows; the mix of birdsong and humming pylons, and prehistoric tors sharing the horizon with *"leaden skies by industrial tumuli"*.

Musically, the album recalls both of the inquisitive, intricate mid-1990s electronica of The Black Dog and the introverted pop of Talk Talk or Disco Inferno. The former manifests itself through tactile environments built from rounded, Acid-flavoured beats and playfully repeating synth melodies (Fawle was assisted by Tom Bugs on programming); the latter comes through in Fawle's warm, unaffected tone and prose-like, near-whispered lyrics from shifting, ambiguous narrators whose egos often merge with personifications of their surroundings. "Urn Reconstruction" finds him corroding in tandem with some unnamed archaeological relic – *"Maybe it's better I'm further away and the flame has less oxygen"* – while on "Born Metallic" he sympathises with the land's obsolete industrial architecture. *"Why do I stay standing here?/The weather's changing regularly over me/I'm rusting here"*, he sings, as chattering rhythmic motifs evoke a past busyness that contrasts with the narrator's inertia.

It may be the favourable bias of a fellow West Country yokel speaking, but *AeXE* induces a far more palpable sense of connection to history than that offered by any tourist brochure, presenting a world lived through many timescales, from the geological pace of eroding hills, through the seasonal cycles welcomed on "Harvest" (*"elderflowers, witch-hazel [...] first colours forming"*) to a restless anticipation of a future that may require moving away.
Abi Bliss

Slomo
The Grain
Trilithon CD/DL

It's with a wry chuckle that I consider using the words 'long awaited' in relation to the third release by guitarist Holy McGrail and synthesist Howard Marsden's Slomo project. Of course! What else could it be? Having established their modus operandi with two albums of slowly unfolding drone, *The Creep* (2005) and *The Bog* (2008), long awaited could serve as an apt description of their entire aesthetic. Check the tags on their Bandcamp page and you'll come across the term agricultural doom, which, along with a quotation from the Cornish harvest festival tradition known as 'crying the neck' (which signals the cutting of the last handful of corn) on the sleeve, gives an idea of their current preoccupations.

Whatever its thematic provenance, *The Grain* is a supremely eerie listen. The 42 minute title track is no exercise in flatlining inertia, but a sonic approximation of organic growth in which Marsden's low-end synth swells and seethes while McGrail wrings baleful squalls from his guitar. The sense of rural isolation cultivated is comparable to the one conveyed by Alan Lamb's field recordings of abandoned telegraph wires (collected on 1998's astonishing *Night Passage*), while the mood of mossy melancholy recalls recent Brit-drone excursions such as Mordant Music's *The Tower* and Eric Zann's *Ouroborindra*. This kinship is especially apparent on the 25 minute second track "Against The Grain", with its processed clicks and creaks.

The Grain appears just as the jumble of ideas and imagery identified as Hauntology seems to be infiltrating the mainstream, with variable results. It would be a shame to see such a potentially flexible aesthetic reduced to a byword for quirkily nostalgic electronic pop, hammy horror and a fusty, tweedy (though internationaly marketable) idea of Britishness. With their thorough and deliberate exploration of the folklore and landscape of these isles, McGrail and Marsden remind us that there are more adventurous and expansive ways of channelling this current. Against the grain indeed.
Joseph Stannard

The Sonic Catering Band
A Gourmet's Slumber
Peripheral Conserve CD

Although no pumpkins were hacked to death in the making of *A Gourmet's Slumber*, this compilation of rarities dating from 1996– 2011 from The Sonic Catering Band reveals that founder member Peter Strickland's fascination with the messy business of recording food stretches back far longer than the explicit vegetable violence dealt out by Foley artists in his recent film, *Berberian Sound Studio*. Strickland and fellow musicians (the nebulous line-up also includes core members Colin Fletcher and Tim Kirby) have made the chopping, crushing, frying and boiling of a variety of foodstuffs the basis of their compositions, recording each stage of the preparation of a variety of recipes before collectively eating the finished dish.

Occupying a middle ground somewhere between field recording and more intricately arranged musique concrète, their approach results in a magnification of the small-scale violence of cooking, using close-up recording, sampling and effects such as delay to draw listeners' awareness to the brutal chemistry wrought on a molecular scale by the dicing of cucumber or the sizzling of fat in a pan. Despite the jokey air of track titles such as "Interculinary Dimension", the atmosphere is dehumanised, with the sensual experience of eating being notably absent: in that track, a Balkan soup with walnuts and sheep's yoghurt becomes a cold symphony of drones, while in "Frostbite", the creation of a rich vanilla

Ben Bennett
Spoilage

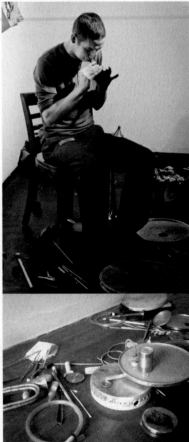

label.experimedia.net/025

ice cream focuses upon the metallic rhythms of eggs being whisked over a seething pan of boiling water. "Refrigeration" features no recipe at all, but amplifies the hum of that most unobtrusive of kitchen appliances to an abrasive storm of overtones and crackle.

With its keen ear for capturing unnerving details within familiar rituals, *A Gourmet's Slumber* surpasses the novelty of its premise, providing a satisfying, if hardly epicurean, listen. Indeed, Strickland concedes in his sleevenotes to there being little correlation between the tastiness of a dish and the quality of its sonic footprint – "our more refined tracks only conjure memories of upset stomachs or burnt meals" – in which case it's fair to conclude, given the track's richly detailed soundscape of spattering oil droplets and evaporating liquids, that the borscht soup of "Peristaltic" was a particularly unpleasant one.

Abi Bliss

Spaceape
Xorcism
Hyperdub CD/DL/12"
Rather than just a performer, Spaceape has always been a role – or perhaps more an instrument – played by Stephen Samuel Gordon. Appearing on almost all Kode 9's productions, Spaceape is an assemblage of the stentorian pronouncements of Prince Far I and Mutabaruka with science fiction and post-Deleuze theoretical tropes. In an echo of On-U Sound's encounter of Jamaican millenarianism and grim British industrial/post-punk nuclear fatalism, in Spaceape the cyborg qualities of the reggae vocal are processed through British pirate radio culture.

Now, it seems, the player and instrument are less distinct. The publicity for this release mentions Gordon's name for the first time, revealing that he has lately been living with a rare form of cancer, a condition reflected in the lyrical themes of radiation and collapse in Kode 9 & Spaceape's *Black Sun* album. The voice, too, has shed almost all of the arch patois inflexions and we must assume is closer to Gordon's own speaking voice. Yet it takes us no closer to the real person. For all the sense that there is agonisingly intimate autobiographical detail here, the best thing about the seven short tracks on this EP is that they never give us an easy way in. Partly it's the Haitian rhythms and voices that constitute the only backing which hint that we're listening to someone not speaking to us but engaged in a private ritual. It's also the precision of Gordon's delivery, writing and production – however conversationally inflected the tone might seem, the precision lifts it miles above the slam poetry it superficially resembles, and the sense of artifice removes *Xorcism* from mere attention-seeking confessional. Or perhaps simply it's those alien and cyborg tendencies manifesting for real. Whatever the truth, *Xorcism* is a fascinating and unexpected development.

Joe Muggs

Colin Stetson & Mats Gustafsson
Stones
Rune Grammofon CD/LP
The most immediate impression of this short series of improvisations between avant garde superstar saxophonists Colin Stetson and Mats Gustafsson live at the 2011 Vancouver Jazz Festival is that at least the duo format restrains Gustafsson from the hysterical masculinism of his work with The Thing, while unfortunately reining in Stetson's more adventurous explorations around the bass saxophone, as heard on his *New History Warfare* recordings, as well as his much publicised collaborations with the likes of Arcade Fire, David Byrne, Godspeed You! Black Emperor and others.

I will confess to having developed an allergy to Gustafsson's tone – maybe Michel Foucault could explain just what's going on there – at the Jazz Em Agosto festival in Lisbon some years back, but still wonder what, beyond turning the volume dial up to Spinal Tap's 11, The Thing did that diverse ensembles and individuals such as Don Weller's Major Surgery, Trevor Watts's Amalgam, John Surman solo or with SOS or Evan Parker in any setting, not to mention numerous North American icons besides, hadn't done decades earlier. But unlike Gustafsson's work with the likes of Jim O'Rourke or Sonic Youth, which often seem mainly about deafening or scaring the audience (an effect lost on this onetime regular at Throbbing Gristle, Test Dept and Einstürzende Neubauten events), here he is forced into a conversational and even discursive interaction with Stetson. Baritone and bass saxophone (chiefly) exploit the full range of each instrument and beyond, veering from the comical to the menacing, with moments of both delicacy and grace, impersonating other instruments and even producing hypnotic machine-like pulses.

I would have liked to have heard more of the otherworldly effects Stetson coaxes from his centenarian bass saxophone, but this is an eloquent and fluid exchange between two skilled instrumentalists. However, every time I play this record, the spirit of Ornette Coleman's 53 year old *The Shape Of Jazz To Come* appears in the room. Has nothing really changed in avant garde jazz since 1959?

John Gill

Touch. 30 Years And Counting
Various
Touch CD/2×LP
In 2007, Touch co-founder Jon Wozencroft published a piece in *Tate Etc* on the cover art of Joy Division's *Unknown Pleasures*. The "black enigmatic textured item", emblazoned with a pulsar's white radio waveform, "this freezing of time over an unimaginable distance", crystallised the group's "sound and space", the almost cosmic coldness and force of their work, recorded in a studio and during a historical moment that slipped between analogue and digital sound. Touch's aesthetic (partly determined by Wozencroft's simple, exquisite design) floats in the same enigmatic space. The drift of pure sound – from gamelan to field recordings to circuit-board eruptions (in the case of the laptop music of which the label was an early adopter) – is bounded, interrupted and made possible by materiality: instrumental playing, design, technology.

This 30th anniversary compilation, presented as four long tracks that stitch together new pieces by current Touch artists, acts as a kind of complement to the ongoing reinvestigation of the label's archives (a new reissue series started recently with a vinyl edition of 1984's *Islands Between*), and a magnificent, twilit drift through this interzone. The mixed format of the album renders each new sound as a surprise, with such contrasts as important as individual pieces. The first side fades from a recording of water at Pont Saeson, Pembrokeshire, into Fennesz in his anti-romantic late style, hovering bass noise slipping into firefly trails of treble over the sound of cavernous reverb. Side two (the CD mimics the LP's one track per side arrangement) starts with what sounds like a wiretap, its vocal booty cut up by retransmission. (Eleh's piece for piano and sub-bass that follows is less interesting than BJ Nilsen's subsequent field recording from Gower Street, near where I used to study in London – scaffolding, police sirens, uncouth voices.)

Even on their own, some of these pieces possess wonderful sonic drama. Chris Watson's location recording of a major railway terminus, "Brussel-Noord", recedes into pools of (presumably architectural) reverb, as if luxuriating in its own shifting layers of sounds. Mika Vainio contributes a fascinating solo guitar piece, alternately stripping the instrument to pure signal and grappling with the shimmer of E-Bowed timbres. Oren Ambarchi's "Merely A Portmanteau" is a beautiful laminate of guitars (and possibly cello), its scree and splinters of noise taking on an almost elegiac tone, a lament for the physical, the haptic itself.

Wozencroft himself pays close attention to these subtle problems and opportunities of listening and media: writing on early cassette culture, he has remarked, "Imagine for a moment that they are the human form of digital – every time you copy something, what you lose in the mechanical process you gain in the particular rituals of dedicated attention and distribution." Here, opening side four, Philip Jeck's obliterated atmospheres of fret brush and vinyl crackle – haunted by the memory of the physical medium, the tone arm and turntable, that prevents it from sounding endlessly – segues into a particularly lovely piece by Francisco López, in which Colombian and Peruvian birdsong are encroached on by what might be air traffic or lowering electronics. By the sound of things, Touch are as seductive and vital as ever.

Dan Barrow

The Boomerang

New reissues rated on the rebound

Louisa Mark

Louisa 'Markswoman' Mark
Breakout
Soul Jazz CD/DL
Carroll Thompson
Hopelessly In Love
Soul Jazz CD/DL

Lovers Rock is music you want to climb inside and live in forever. At its best – and this new Soul Jazz series has been launched to cherrypick the highpoints of the style – Lovers Rock offers something unprecedented outside the briefest of moments in disco, New Jack Swing and 1990s R&B – a dynamic push and pull between women's and men's desires and dreams, with neither side reduced to two-dimensional sex objects.

It helps that the music itself has, for want of a better description, a masculine and a feminine side. The group for Louisa Mark's 1981 album *Breakout* was made up of the kind of stellar players you suspect might not have come together if there wasn't a strong female voice to unite them – alongside UK reggae multi-instrumentalist and Lovers Rock pioneer Dennis Bovell was the underrated roots group The In Crowd, plus the legendary Jamaican outfit The Heptones. The music is superlative, with clear, metronomic rhythms opening up huge, calm spaces in between for synthesizer cuticles and vibraphones to play.

But the bittersweet story of vocalist Louisa Mark is most striking. She was nurtured by Bovell through talent contests and club residencies in the mid-70s. In 1975 her debut recording session, with Lloyd Coxsone, yielded "Caught You In A Lie", widely regarded as the first Lovers Rock single, made when she was just 15, after which she dropped out of music for a couple of years due to contractual issues. Playing the romantic lead at such a tender age at the behest of music svengalis rightly rings alarm bells these days, but the title of her debut song is significant – "Caught You In A Lie" underlines how Lovers Rock took women's points of view and hinted at female knowledge that had to be hidden from domineering men. Sometimes the narratives are of doomed romance, and there's an awareness that sometimes even lies themselves are seductive.

By the time of *Breakout*, Mark was still just 20, but it would in retrospect represent the zenith of an abortive career. There's already a sense of experience in the songs, and a complex nostalgia for simpler times which you suspect she half-knew didn't exist. "People In Love" begins *"Night is the time for love"*, as if Mark was channelling a Billie Holiday torch song with Teddy Wilson's Orchestra, a mood crucially qualified by the next line: *"… and the kids are sleeping all*

right." Mark's voice is a little like Holiday's in the way her pitch and timing feels loose and intuitive, and some of the emotion comes from her not quite hitting a note, or overshooting it in sheer excitement.

Breakout is a staggering record for such a young singer, with each track a minor epic of heartbreak and redemption, and even when the endings are not happy, there is a sense of stark clarity here that at least represents some kind of hard-won enlightenment. "Moving Target" is sonically bittersweet, cramming in a spectrum of texture and scale, from thundering electric bass rig to tiny hand percussion. *"Ten years from now/Will you still hold my hand?"* Mark asks, as if she knows the answer already, but is enjoying the fantasy while it lasts.

Carroll Thompson was a friend and contemporary of Mark's, and *Hopelessly*

In Love emerged the same year. It's a less immediately striking set, with Thompson's straighter voice plotting simple narratives of breaking up and making up on songs like "I'm So Sorry". While Thompson wrote some of these songs herself, there's an odd sense of her fulfilling a straightforward male fantasy of the young girlfriend under metaphorical lock and key – a fantasy that's less about sex and more about control and perpetuating male power structures. "No, You Don't Know", however, is Lovers Rock at its complex best. Thompson's confession, *"I may have your child/But I know I'm not your wife"*, sounds abject, but the succinct and frank chorus, *"No, you don't know/How to love me"*, hints at the kind of female desires, moral and sexual, that are hidden in much pop music.
Derek Walmsley

Crime & The City Solution
A History Of Crime: Berlin 1987–1991 – An Introduction To Crime & The City Solution
Mute CD/DL

A straightforwardly chronological sampling of the last three Crime & The City Solution albums (1988's *Shine*, 1989's *The Bride Ship* and 1990's *Paradise Discotheque*), plus "The Adversary", their posthumous contribution to the soundtrack of Wim Wenders's *Until The End Of The World*, this 71 minute disc is an ideal entry point to an underappreciated group.

Crime was formed in Sydney in 1977 by vocalist Simon Bonney, and its status as the mirror-world Nick Cave & The Bad Seeds (Australian moves to London then Berlin, borrows a member of Einstürzende Neubauten, wallows in fever dreams of

Gothic Americana) is decisively confirmed here, except that songs like "Free World" and the half-Country, half-Metal (no, really) "I Have The Gun" had more raw throbbing vitality than anything the wildly posturing Cave has ever put his hand to.

The key to the sound of Berlin-era Crime was the balance of elements: Bonney's theatrically mournful or overwrought voice; Bronwyn Adams's keening, almost Tony Conrad-style violin; Alexander Hacke's barbed wire guitar; Chrislo Haas's droning keyboards; Thomas Stern's rumble/clang bass; Mick Harvey's minimalist drumming. The songs get a little softer, a little glossier as the disc goes on, and Bonney's vocal persona shifts from that of a post-punk bellower to a crooner like Morrissey (and on the jazzy "The Adversary" – upright bass,

brushed drums – a Leonard Cohen-esque groaner), but it's all clearly the work of a group with a singular vision. The elliptical lyrics are always enveloped by the music, which surges and thuds, never ceding the spotlight or becoming a mere backdrop. Bonney, Adams and Hacke have recently reincarnated Crime with new cohorts, but the compelling music they produced during this period would be ripe for rediscovery even if that weren't the case.
Phil Freeman

Sandy Denny
The Notes And The Words: A Collection Of Demos And Rarities
Universal 4×CD

Sandy Denny's trajectory saw her pass through The Strawbs, Fairport Convention

and the underrated Fotheringay as well as various form-shifting alliances in a productive solo career. Like Gram Parsons, the revered avatar of Cosmic American Music, hers is a stepping-stone career of golden touches – however brief Denny's involvement with a particular group, it seemed to be pivotal both to that act and folk music at large. Denny's personal and professional lives were erratic, dogged by alcohol and other substances as well as the inevitable tensions of working with lovers and boyfriends (Trevor Lucas finally becoming both husband and producer). This combination of traits produced an unusually high number of abandoned demos, shelved projects and discarded recordings as events overtook her music.

This treasure trove has been mined

before, and there's nothing previously unreleased in this box – Island's exhaustive 19 CD *Sandy Denny* box set collected all known recordings and demos. This slimmed-down box set collects the cream of the hard-to-find material, much of it only otherwise available in that wildly expensive and deleted set.

It's a strong collection. There are occasional completist-only moments, for example the a cappella take of "Lord Bateman", but there are no half-takes or scratchy home recordings. There's an alternative rendering of Denny's most iconic track, "Who Knows Where The Time Goes". The greatest interest comes from tracks that illuminate both her own history and that of the song itself. A stormy acoustic version of "Autopsy", with its line *"Why must you bore me to tears?"* never crueller, is presented before it was electrified on Fairport Convention's *Unhalfbricking*. Also stripped back are tracks from Denny's final album, *Rendezvous*. In a quest for a breakthrough album, the 1978 production aimed to ride the lucrative AOR coat tails of Fleetwood Mac and co. Here songs like "I Wish I Was A Fool For You" emerge from the slick fug, and "I'm a Dreamer" in particular is reinstated as a lynchpin of her development.

Nick Southgate

Luc Ferrari
Presque Rien
Recollection GRM DL/LP

Luc Ferrari is unusual among European electroacoustic composers of the period in retaining a strong element of naturalism and narrative in his soundscapes. His first experiment with this approach was *Hétérozygote* in 1963, a stereo tape piece with 'anecdotal' use of realistic sound, concrete images conjoined with abstract sounds and structures, listeners invited to supply their own 'anecdotes'. He took this further on *Presque Rien No 1 Lever Du Jour Au Bord De La Mer*, a strikingly literal evocation of early morning in a fishing village which nevertheless retains an air of mystery. Ferrari's description of *Presque Rien Avec Filles* is "A Tuscan landscape, an Alsatian forest, girls passing from afar, *and the rest is my secret*". The payoff line, often overlooked, moderates the simple pictorialism of these pieces, which are somewhat reminiscent of listening to the audio track of a rapidly-cut movie from the ciné vérité or Dogmatic Realism era.

Ferrari is always looking for surprise, the way a creaking gate might be mistaken for birdsong, especially when repeated, or footsteps seeming to generate a rhythm that is more apparent than actual. "I love the sound that betrays small uncertainties," he says, using natural and untempered sound as a form of structural dissonance. This is highly affectionate as well as effective/affective music, done with tremendous craft and grace and a Beckettian ambiguity about the creator/narrator – Ferrari's first musique concrète piece *Étude Aux Accidents* was realised in 1958, the same year as *Krapp's Last Tape* – or even the sense of self; other pieces include *J'ai Été Coupé*

and *Je Ne Suis Perdu*. The 'passing show' is always more interesting than the auteur's I, but the auteur's eye and ear have become a single organ.

Brian Morton

Goodiepal
Narc Beacon
Fonal CD/DL

Goodiepal's 2001 debut *Narc Beacon* is an album of sharp, textured fragments which burrow their way under the epidermis of your imagination. Like much of Goodiepal's output, and indeed the confrontational persona that he has maintained for the past decade or so, *Narc Beacon* is aggressively synthetic, designed to agitate and provoke. While there are some correspondences to Dan Deacon's manic dayglo electro, Parl Kristian Bjørn Vester employs frantic melody, not to unite its audience in collective Walt Whitman reverie, but as another means to destabilise the listener's equilibrium. On "Icon Dub", the lulling serenity of the tune battles with wraithlike swirls of sound to produce something like seasickness. Similarly the standout track "Kirby's Dream Land" (which I'm hoping is a reference to the pioneering comic book artist Jack Kirby, whose infamous 'krackle' effect finds an echo in Goodiepal's crunchy sonics) wobbles and vomits like a drunken robot trying to sing itself sober.

Joseph Stannard

Bruce Langhorne
The Hired Hand OST
Scissor Tail LP

Bruce Langhorne was a Greenwich Village regular and busy session guitarist in 1960s New York, contributing to a stack of records including Dylan's *Bringing It All Back Home*. When the phenomenal success of *Easy Rider* triggered a wave of indie movie commissions, Langhorne landed the job of scoring Peter Fonda's 1971 film *The Hired Hand*. In keeping with the film's low-key melancholy, Langhorne dialled his music all the way down to produce this desolate masterpiece, perhaps the loneliest film score ever.

Assembling guitar, banjo, recorder, harmonica, organ and fiddle, Langhorne plays everything himself, but the pace never stirs beyond a doomed amble, and the mood is introverted even compared with *Pat Garrett & Billy The Kid* (the other Dylan album featuring Langhorne). A borrowed Fender Twin Reverb amp makes a major contribution, ghosting eerie echoes around the banjo. Langhorne's violin is gnarled and troubled, but his guitar spells out simple figures defiantly. High piano notes stand for raindrops, and a recorder wails into the wind while somewhere a piece of loose metal rattles. It's the West seen as Purgatory, its characters endlessly moving on, but Langhorne conjures beauty from the pain.

Clive Bell

Ivo Malec
Triola, Ou Symphonie Pour Moi-Même
Recollection GRM DL/LP

In 1990, composer Richard Barrett described Ivo Malec's stereo tape piece

Triola as "one of the most powerful and fascinating works in the entire field of electroacoustic music". It's hard to argue with that. Electronic music ages badly, but the Yugoslav composer's 'symphony for myself' is now 35 years old and still pungently fresh. Malec turned to the work after a layoff from music, and used the break, and his research at the Groupe de Recherches Musicales and under Pierre Schaeffer, to 'relearn' his trade and, as he has suggested, to settle a score with himself. The piece combines artificial/electronic sounds with found elements which are entirely denatured in this context. As deeply influenced by surrealism as Olivier Messiaen, Malec is nonetheless drawn to that school's more disruptive elements. The result, alternating between a kind of spluttering fury and Messiaen-like stillness, has the quality of a dream – Barrett referred to "Magritte-like friction" – in which reliable signifiers are hard to locate. The piece does, however, follow an approximately symphonic three-movement structure – triola = triplet – though it lacks obvious thematic development. It's a one-off, even in Malec's exotic catalogue.

Bizarra comes from a little earlier, in 1972 and shortly after the orchestral *GAM(m)MES*. It is in every way more conventional in its juxtaposition of imaginative 'swamps' inspired by Isidore Ducasse, Comte de Lautréamont, and the clean, hard-edged, scientific rigour of an electronic music studio. It's scarcely a dull piece – Malec, now 87, doesn't do dull – but its contrasts are more predictable and its soundworld has a slovenly obviousness, as if the composer set up the situation and then simply went for lunch.

Brian Morton

Only 4 U: The Sound Of Cajmere And Cajual Records 1992–2012
Various
Strut 2×CD/DL/2×LP

Beset at home by the Windy City's growing acceptance of hiphop and shady business practices, and increasingly marginalised by the inexorable niche-ification of dance music and the rise of rave in Europe, Chicago House circa 1992 seemed to be in its death throes. Then, out of nowhere, came the twin calling cards of some guy calling himself Cajmere that reasserted Chicago's primacy. The first of these was "Percolator" – a ferociously minimal, mesmeric and funky track (in the truest sense of the term) that relocated Rotterdam's 'poing' to a Southside community centre dance-off. "Brighter Days", meanwhile, featured the full-throated singer Dajae on top of an infinitely malleable rhythm bed that enabled it to become perhaps the decade's definitive vocal House record.

Equally adept at stripped-down jack tracks, fathoms-deep late night ambience and maximalist diva garage, and blessed with George Clinton's sense of humour and outrageousness, Curtis A Jones (aka Cajmere and Green Velvet) almost singlehandedly rescued House music from the blahs in the early 90s. Jones's

records – like the hilarious club chat-up "Chit Chat" or the playground fierceness of "LaLaLaLaLa (Nside My Mind)" – fizz with personality, even the instrumentals and seemingly more generic Garage records (check the percussion on "Feelin' Kinda High"). More important for the dancefloor, though, was Jones's rhythmic sensibility, which finds the funk in everything from Nitzer Ebb to 1920s big bands.

In addition to his own work, Jones's labels, Cajual and the trackier Relief, were instrumental in spawning the careers of Glenn Underground, DJ Sneak, Gemini, Boo Williams and Johnny Fiasco, thus creating the foundation for the third wave of Chicago House. *Only 4 U* collects the bulk of Cajual's classics (but where are Glenn Underground's "Detroitism" or Cajmere's recent disco re-edits?), including Gemini's anything but smooth jazz-House odysseys "If You Got To Believe In Something" and "Le Fusion" (which could be an early Mo' Wax record), Dajae's nearly as good follow-up to "Brighter Days", "U Got Me Up", and Braxton Holmes's scintillating gospel House anthem "People Everyday". Shame this isn't a retrospective of both Cajual and Relief, but *Only 4 U* nevertheless bears fine witness to the rebirth of Chicago House.

Peter Shapiro

Yeast Culture
IYS
Art-Into-Life LP

If there's been a more lavishly packaged reissue of a total obscurity released in recent months, I'd love to see it. Unless you spent time in the late 1980s memorising names from the RRRecords mail order catalogue or decoding the reviews section of *Bananafish*, the name Yeast Culture won't mean much. It was the project of a Seattle based individual named Marc Schomburg, who released a small handful of cassettes and one LP, *IYS*, before abruptly ceasing activity. Art-Into-Life's deluxe reissue is wrapped in a gatefold sleeve, secured by not one but two belly bands. Inside is another gatefold, which folds out into a four-panel square. Both sleeves are heavily silkscreened in expressionist splashes of turquoise, green, red and black. The album is pressed on 180 gm vinyl, with handpainted centre labels.

The artwork doesn't stoop to anything so prosaic as identifying when or how the music was created. A 42 minute piece, it appears to combine processed field recordings and electronics into jittery looping patterns of rattles, scratches and clicks, whose rhythms and shapes continually shift within a narrow dynamic range. The appeal of *IYS* lies in the uncertain provenance of the sounds, which seem both insectoid and digital in nature, and the static nature of its structure and pacing, both of which remain uniform throughout. These features certainly mark the album as unusual for the time, but whether Art-Into-Life are justified in bestowing this degree of importance – and so hefty a price tag – on its rerelease is another matter entirely.

Nick Cain

Julius Hemphill
The Complete Remastered Recordings On Black Saint & Soul Note
Cam Jazz 5×CD

Julius Hemphill's membership between 1976–89 of The World Saxophone Quartet, which was that most unusual of things, a commercially successful avant garde jazz group, has tended to overshadow his status as one of black America's greatest 20th century modernists.

In *The Wire* 312, Wadada Leo Smith claimed that the project of America's post-war black avant garde had stalled because it had failed to build the kind of institutions necessary to genuinely alter its environment. Existing between 1968–72, The Black Artists' Group of St Louis was briefly one such institution, and Hemphill was one of its principal architects. With a membership that included male and female dancers, poets, actors and visual artists as well as musicians, all combining in multiple community-oriented projects, BAG was a more inclusive organisation than Chicago's Association for the Advancement of Creative Musicians or Los Angeles's Underground Musicians' Association. It was in the context of BAG that Hemphill scored large scale compositions for multiple ensembles, co-directed the metaphorical experimental film *The Orientation Of Sweet Willie Rollbar*,

and helped stage the elaborate black masques *Images: Sons/Ancestors* and *Poem For A Revolutionary Night*. To paraphrase critic Robert Palmer, as quoted in Benjamin Looker's 2004 history of BAG, *Point From Which Creation Begins*, such initiatives absorbed then subverted Western modernist aesthetics in order to mobilise "a multiplicity of incantations, symbols and ritual actions which [expressed] the unity of one world of black culture".

The Afrocentric cultural politics, conceptual audacity and urgent delivery of these and other BAG projects would be distilled by Hemphill into records such as 1972's *Dogon AD* and 1975's *Coon Bid'ness*, which contained some of the most stark and original jazz of the time. *Dogon AD* was recorded while Hemphill was still in St Louis. *Coon Bid'ness* was produced in New York, after BAG had dissolved and a number of its musician members had made the move to Gotham, where they participated in what now feels like the last stand of America's black avant garde, performing alongside exiles from the AACM in the repurposed lofts and warehouses that clustered in the derelict SoHo district of Lower Manhattan.

The earliest of the five albums contained in this box set, *Raw Materials And Residuals*, was recorded in 1977 during the twilight of the lofts. As much as Suicide's

first album, also produced in 1977, it now feels like a quintessential document of a particularly tense New York moment. Taped at the end of a year marked by the Son of Sam murders, the burning of the Bronx and the citywide blackout, the searing multidirectional melodic and rhythmic attack of Hemphill's alto, Abdul Wadud's cello and Famoudou Don Moye's array of Sun Percussion enact a sonic analogue of a city wired on claustrophobic nervous energy.

Three years later, Hemphill and Wadud were on the outskirts of Milan, with drummer Warren Smith and trumpeter Olu Dara. Like many of their contemporaries, they had come to Italy to record at the Barigozzi studios of Giovanni Bonandrini's Black Saint and Soul Note labels, which since the mid-70s had provided a European refuge for musicians whose art brought little honour back in Amerikkka. Perhaps as a consequence, the music on *Flat Out Jump Suite*, despite that title, is more reflective and expansive, though no less compelling, for this is still an art of exiles, and on "Mind (First Part)" and "Body" especially, one that is suffused with the blues.

By 1980 Hemphill and Smith were back in New York where they recorded *Chile New York: Sound Environment*, the sonic component in a still existing sculptural installation by ceramics and visual artist

Jeff Schlanger which was exhibited in response to the 1973 CIA-backed coup which overthrew Chile's democratic socialist government, led by Salvador Allende, and installed the military dictatorship of Augusto Pinochet. In a space charged with reverb and punctured by Smith's dramatic interventions on timpani, vibes and tuned percussion, Hemphill's overdubbed saxophones and flutes vocalise long ribbons of melody that weep and moan and fray at the edges. Ripped out of context, the music sounds abstract but deeply felt, and the project restated Hemphill's commitment to the kind of politicised public intermedia art he had once made under the auspices of BAG.

A decade later, *Fat Man And The Hard Blues* (1991) and *Five Chord Stud* (1993) were recorded in more prosaic circumstances, after Hemphill had been ejected from The WSQ and formed a new saxophone sextet. As a consequence it's hard not to hear both records as a continuation by other means of The WSQ's dynamic raids on the blues continuum – this is vivid, intense music animated by swaggering R&B, swing-era saxophonics, eerie spirituals and dissonant multiphonics. Due to ill health, including diabetes and a heart condition, Hemphill conducted but wasn't able to play on *Five Chord Stud*. He died in 1995 aged 57. □

Julius Hemphill, 1977

Gérard Rouy

A box set of recordings by the late saxophonist **Julius Hemphill** reasserts his position in the front line of the black avant garde. By **Tony Herrington**

The Columns

Frances Morgan on a lost NZ outsider document, 90s math moves, and Persian poetry

The Garbage And The Flowers
Eyes Rind As If Beggars
Fire CD/DL/LP

The original release date is 1997, but these songs were recorded earlier in the decade. Some sound older, relatives of early Flying Nun. Older still is this Wellington, NZ outfit's main blueprint, The Velvet Underground, here evoked in various ways, from the fragile "Sunday Morning" charm of "Love Comes Slowly Now" to a rackety, almost unlistenably warped live take of "Nothing Going Down", all scraped violin and "European Son" guitar scree. There's a tendency to view NZ psych of this period as having no contemporary analogues, but I hear Kendra Smith's Opal (later Mazzy Star) and Guild Of Temporal Adventurers in Helen Johnstone's hymning of a "Rosicrucinn [sic] Lover" and psychedelic stream-of-consciousness rhymes on "Carousel". Most songs stumble from the speakers through a pleasing mass of fuzz, feedback and reverb, although this isn't as well judged as the balance of scuzz and sweetness you hear on, say, Alastair Galbraith's *Talisman*. That said, Johnstone and guitarist Yuri Frusin still record under the same group name, and a recent 7", "Alamo Rose", is very similar to the material here, indicating a pretty stable aesthetic. Perhaps this long-lost outsider document is more design than accident after all.

Horse Lords
Horse Lords
Ehse CD/DL/LP

Microtones are this Baltimore math rock quartet's secret weapon. But if I've just made Horse Lords sound like the driest rock proposition of the month, it doesn't take deep knowledge of Just Intonation to work out that something's enjoyably odd about Owen Gardner's modified guitar on these two instrumentals that owe as much to Terry Riley and Malian griot as they do to Don Caballero. The alien feel of the tuning holds the interest through "Wildcat Strike"'s long but too tentative guitar/percussion build, and the group ramp up the polyrhythms and bring in some rough electronics and snaking sax for a joyful and awkwardly funky of percussion breakdowns and *Reed Streams* squawks. On "Who Taught You To Hate Yourself", they abandon a metronomic workout for a hazy guitar/synth interlude, which feels a little generic right now; oddly, it's the 90s math moves that feel freshest.

Li Jianhong
1969
Buh CD-R

Recorded in 2008, this missive from one half of Chinese Noise duo D!O!D!O!D! initially

Jessika Kenney

seems a little ephemeral, possibly an offcut from one of Li's many projects that's been picked up by this small Peruvian label for a limited release. Yet its two pieces, presumably improvised, are more focused than a CD-R of solo electric guitar squall would lead you to expect. On the title track Li pushes the guitar not only in volume but in taste, daring the listener to become immersed in an uncomfortably dense sonic field of itchy distortion and long seesawing tones, from which a lead line tries to worm its way, coated in excess wah pedal slime. In calling his other, similar piece "Revolution Is Only A Sad Illusion", perhaps Li, a key figure in Hangzhou's experimental scene, is hinting at the absurdity of rock's supposed radical potential. He certainly puts it through the wringer here.

Jessika Kenney & Eyvind Kang
The Face Of The Earth
Ideologic Organ DL/LP

The deep scholarship of vocalist Jessika Kenney and Eyvind Kang, on viola and setar (an Iranian lute), is not in question, but few of their listeners, this one included, will have more than a glancing knowledge of all the poetic and musical traditions referenced on their second duo album. How much does this matter? After all, that they are so comfortable placing songs based on Persian ghazal and Javanese kidung side by side, in the same way Latin poetry and Tibetan music informed their last release *Aestuarium*, suggests that Kenney and Kang want us to hear patterns beyond and behind these traditions. With the physical release there are apparently "reading cards" for the listener to play with, "to become a participant in the creation of meaning", but with just a download to hand, the temptation is to luxuriate in exotic affect, in the faultless planes of Kenney's voice, its weighty viola and percussion accompaniment on "Tazaf" and the delicate plucked strings on "Kidung" mirrored in vocal whirrs and trills. By "Mirror Stage", electronics have crept in and Kenney's voice is multiplied and manipulated into a minimalist composition that recalls Meredith

Monk's *Dolmen Music*, which also imagined ancient orders of language and meaning. Kenney and Kang treat their source material with more subtlety than Monk, but she's often a good reference point for the nervous listener, a reminder that leaps of imagination and interpretation can be off, but never really wrong.

Peepholes
The Overspill!
Upset The Rhythm CD/DL/LP

Underground musicians approximating (appropriating?) pop's sheen then scuffing it with human imperfection is an increasingly well worn process. But London/Brighton duo Peepholes' almost-pop songs are played live, on synth, vocal and drum kit, and thus come unstuck not via deliberate digital smearing but in real time, clumsy fills tripping up neat keyboard melodies which contend with the extra rhythmic ripples of drummer/vocalist Katia Barrett's heavily reverbed singing. This differentiates it from the Hypnagogia of the last few years and, despite the Gothic boom of Barrett's voice, the spectre of Witch House. Instead, *The Overspill!* is more akin to early Human League, Joy Division or even, on "Lion", a DIY Japan (Carlisle is fond of his synth's flute and marimba settings); mainstream reference points, but dragged into some new shapes here. Buried in the lo-fi delivery is some accomplished songwriting that has gelled over the group's numerous EPs and CD-Rs. This is their first album, and they expand accordingly with the 14 minute "Living In Qatar", which ends unexpectedly in pulsing Cluster/Eno territory.

Richard Pinhas, Merzbow & Wolf Eyes
Victoriaville Mai 2011
Victo CD

Last year Byron Coley described this set from Canada's Musique Actuelle festival as a "mesmeric pile of racket", and also remarked approvingly that, aside from obvious sounds like John Olson's sax, it was hard to tell who was doing what. This clearly recorded document of the quintet's hour-long set (one 47 minute track plus an encore) allows for a little more clarity to emerge – Nate Young's vocal, low in the mix then roaring out, is a disquieting presence; different qualities and textures in the many electronics used, from gnarly analogue noise boxes to harsh laptop swoops, can be picked apart if you feel inclined. But what really hits home is, as on their collaborative album *Metal/Crystal*, how controlled and listenable said pile of racket is, how slowly and delicately it builds and how intelligently communicative this process is. 15 minutes in and we're still at a slowly shifting, almost kosmische velocity, and the wall of distortion at the set's peak is soon dismantled to reveal some crystalline Heldon-style guitar vistas from Pinhas. An onslaught of high volume static, drone and sax blowout is saved for the well deserved encore. □

Rory Gibb on digital weedsmoke, music to tie dancers in knots, and a swarm of metal hornets

Beneath
Illusions EP
Keysound 2×12"

The sense of foreboding that pervades Beneath's music has become a rarity on British dancefloors, making his *Illusions* EP a welcome prospect. Despite throbbing along at House tempo, the main touchstone here is 2003–06-era dubstep: rasta chat riffs on DMZ, while the rushy, rough 'n' tumble drum programming of "Wonz" recalls Oris Jay and Toasty. But though early UK Funky and Jungle also hang heavy in the mix, these six tracks rarely feel backward-looking. Indeed, there's a purity to the way they remain rooted in long-running aspects of UK club culture – pirate radio, the symbiosis of British and Jamaican sound system musics – where many contemporaries have diverted from that lineage towards straight-up House and Techno. The tracks on *Illusions* crackle like live urban infrastructure: voices addled with radio static, Tube tunnel rumble and hiss, marimbas that reverberate like drips in a drainpipe. It all culminates in a blistering remix of Balistiq Beats' "Concrete Jungle", where clustered kicks power a ferocious Grime/ragga MC turn from Jamakabi. Six minutes in, it explodes in a salvo of sub-bass squelches, the sound of London's underbelly violently forcing itself upward from basements and warehouses to flood the streets.

Kahn
Dread/Midnight Blues
Deep Medi DL/12"
Kahn & Neek
Backchat
Hotline DL/12"

Kahn's range is impressively broad; the Bristolian's work this year has encompassed body-shock Grime, two-step and rip-roaring electronic dub. His debut 12" for Mala's Deep Medi suits the label's sub-bass and space remit: "Dread" hinges around a gruff Rasta vocal, decayed to the point that it sounds piped in from another era entirely, and "Late Night Blues" consists of sparse, yawning sub and Rider Shafique's languid chants. While most purist dubstep now adheres to an ethos based around high production values (the so-called 'dungeon sound'), the untreated feel of Kahn's tracks is a refreshing return to the raw energy of the genre's early days. Neek collaboration "Backchat", the inaugural release on new label Hotline, is harsher still. Essentially Grime slowed to 120 bpm, the lower tempo intensifies its effect, with each kick hitting with enough force to distort everything around it. It shares a vocal – *"if you diss badman you get shot"* – with B side

"Dubchat", which allows the original's fury to fizz outward through a sparser beat.

Karenn
SHEWORKS004
She Works The Long Nights 2×12"
Of all the styles to have come back into fashion (was it ever in?), it's been surprising to witness the recent proliferation of abrasive Industrial Techno across dancefloors raised on dubstep and House. Although Karenn – London based producers Blawan and Pariah – are nominally at the forefront of a younger generation exploring these territories, there's actually something so self-contained about their music that it's hard to imagine it fitting into any dancefloor ecology outside the twisted minds of its creators. On this six-track EP, the duo whip up a kind of construction site Techno concrète: sub-bass rumbles like a cement mixer, hi-hats and snares crumple like sheet metal, what little melody is present arrives as a hollow whine, like girders screeching in the wind. The density of these building materials is offset by deftly syncopated rhythms, which retain traces of the frenetic drum patterns that defined Blawan's earliest releases. The results are surprisingly funky despite their extreme low fidelity. Around "Clean It Up"'s monolithic kick/snare axis swirls a junkyard's worth of percussive detritus, adding swing to its unstoppable forward momentum, and "A Room Full Of Fuck All" offers some respite by slowing proceedings to a nauseous crawl. The whole thing sounds like it was recorded in a dustbin, lending it as least as much in common with lo-fi hardcore punk and noise rock as with most contemporary Techno.

Laurel Halo
Sunlight On The Faded
Hyperdub 12"
Laurel Halo's *Quarantine* wasn't quite like anything else released in 2012. By pitting her unprocessed voice against unforgivingly synthetic music, she highlighted both her own vocal imperfections and the uncanny glossiness of their surroundings. "Sunlight On The Faded" pulls the same trick, though outside the album context it loses some of *Quarantine*'s disorienting power. It's all tension and no resolution, with Halo's clipped delivery tugging against a woozy backdrop whose rhythms are half obscured by clouds of digital weedsmoke. A dub version reveals that far from hanging in stasis, "Sunlight" is in fact travelling at immense speed. Freed from the anchor of her voice, a rush of cymbals drags powdery strings, insectoid clicks and muffled kickdrums along in the slipstream.

Mala
Stand Against War/Maintain Thru Madness
DMZ 12"
Humour and seriousness co-exist in the music of Digital Mystikz' Mala. His more

recent work, though, has erred strongly towards the latter, occasionally to its detriment. He's best at his most playful, and these two older tracks, unearthed from the depths of the DMZ dubplate archive, are among the best he's ever released. Devastating in its simplicity, "Stand Against War" is up there with dubstep's all-time great tracks, powered by subs that thwack like helicopter rotors. A delicate oriental melody – summoned straight from 2003-era sino-Grime – threads through in fits and starts, lending the whole construction an unearthly tranquillity. "Maintain Thru Madness" feels psychically heavier, but is crafted with the same lightness of touch; its plunging conga rolls and airhorns channel the spirit of parties long since ended.

Phat Chex
Can't Stop/Git Da Funk
Apple Pips DL/12"
The two tracks on Phat Chex's debut 12" tap into the same UK/Berlin crossover region that characterised Apple Pips' early releases. Reverbed chords gather like stormclouds, while the rhythms beneath alternate between fevered motion and periods of highly charged stillness. Despite its languid feel, "Can't Stop" is deceptively tense, with percussion swung to the point that it shadowboxes around the beat: kickdrums spring from heel to toe without ever landing quite where they're expected, before occasionally broadsiding defenceless dancers with a well aimed snare hit. Over on the flipside, "Git Da Funk" releases all that built-up anxiety in a hailstorm of hi-hats and hammered piano chords.

Sensate Focus
2.5
Sensate Focus 12"
The playful streak running through snd's rave reductions extends to Mark Fell's solo material, and in particular this year's Sensate Focus vinyl releases. What's so striking about this series is the way it imagines club music not as a sequence of peaks and troughs, but as a living and breathing ecosystem in a continuous state of flux. Changes to the trajectory of a chord or the angle of a snare's attack ripple outwards through the mix, glancing off other elements and affecting them in turn. Equally impressive is the seemingly autonomous manner in which they unfold, as though Fell needed only supply an initial hit of activation energy before allowing the track's finely balanced architecture to ferry motion from place to place. The latest, *2.5*, contains Fell's most club-friendly Sensate Focus productions to date. You could almost imagine adventurous DJs dropping "X" in a club and allowing its spring-loaded kick, sub and snare patterns to tie dancers in knots. "Y"'s rubber ball bassline, handclaps and sing-song voices make such astonishingly complex club music sound like child's play. □

Steve Barker on Black Ark gizmos, Peaking Lights in dub, and Yabby You anthologised

Breadwinners
Dubs Unlimited
King Spinna CD/DL/LP
The Breadwinners is the project of North West England's Alan Redfern, who brings together a series of guests including the legendary Big Youth. His all-analogue Bakery studio is equipped with hardware associated with Lee Perry's unique Black Ark sound, in particular the Mu-Tron Bi-Phase and Roland Space Echo. Since 2006 he has produced hundreds of tracks, the best of which are presented on this debut all-analogue album. Certainly from the opening track, "The Breadwinner", where the mix is pure Black Ark, there's a confidence and conviction that's rare in most new dub sounds. When "Dub Rock" kicks in, you'd swear you were going into Studio One's "Real Rock". But there's innovation here, too, especially from his own cultured flute and sax playing, best evidenced on the tune that could easily have been issued by Augustus Pablo's Rockers label, "KT's Ital Stew", with its beautiful flute embroidery. Apparently Big Youth toasted the closing track "Joy" on his first take, and the tune sounds like a long lost classic. An impressive debut.

Barry Brown
Right Now
Greensleeves CD
Barry Brown was a graduate of Bunny Lee's 1970s roots machine, and this limited release on the Time label back in 1984 is a real find, elevating his journeyman status to a higher league. Produced by Jah Screw and engineered by the legendary Barnabas, the set was recorded, voiced and mixed at Channel One Studios in Kingston. The original album is now extended with eight complementary dubs showcasing both the mighty Roots Radics and Lloyd Parkes's We The People Band. Also included is the in-demand non-album sound system favourite "Mafia", plus a special bonus of Tristan Palma's "Nuh Shot Nuh Fire", a deejay take on Brown's "Jukes And Watch".

Digitaldubs featuring YT
Sound System Culture/Dub Echoes Riddim
Mazumba DL/7"
When British toaster YT declaims, *"to fully enjoy these tracks you need a big stack of 18" scoop bin, some midrange and some tweeter"*, you feel like ditching your MP3 system forever, and when he praises the van drivers and box lifters, this booming tune really lifts your heart. The track is all over the net, but the vinyl comes to the UK via Glasgow's Scotch Bonnet distribution and should be snapped up immediately,

as it's destined to become a self-fulfilling landmark in Britain's sound system culture.

Keith Hudson
Torch Of Freedom
Hot Milk CD
Still more admired for his groundbreaking work as a producer rather than his output as an artist, this debut release from the Hot Milk label concludes the revival of the legendary Keith Hudson's solo output with the first reissue of his *Torch Of Freedom*. At once alluring and idiosyncratic, Hudson's vocal delivery and choice of material is at its most extreme on this quasi-showcase set – the vocals are not followed by strict dubs but curtailed instrumental noodlings that play with the structure and lyric of the original tune rather than performing a de/re-construction job. Released in 1975 on Brent Clarke's UK Atra imprint, the set is notable for the extreme ache of "Like I'm Dying", a retread of the great "Melody Maker" rhythm and probably best known from the vocal version "I'm Alright" – deep, treacly, foreboding, reggae at its most menacing. Also here is "Turn The Heater On", famously covered by New Order. Musicians in Hudson's Soul Syndicate Band include Carlton and Family Man Barrett, Earl 'Chinna' Smith, Robbie Shakespeare and Candy McKenzie.

Peaking Lights
Lucifer In Dub
Weird World DL/LP
Wisconsin based Peaking Lights, aka Aaron Coyes and Indra Dunis, graduated to the sun-speckled California campus of Not Not Fun for a cassette-only release of their *Imaginary Falcons* in 2009. Their dub intentions were proclaimed following 2011's *936* album with a series of remixes including one from Adrian Sherwood. This time it's a partial dub companion to their recent *Lucifer* set – two tracks are dropped, with dub edits by Coyes and mastering duties from Sonic Boom. This kind of sacramental melding of psychedelics and dub has been skirted around for years – many have threatened and Jah Wobble has come close – but the strands of classic pop, tribal House and Krautrock evident in *Lucifer*'s influences are woven seamlessly here. The whole thing could easily be ingested as one long energy pulse, with six long waves of throb and flow. "Beautiful Dub" best represents the feeling: a slow ride into a desert sunset.

Ramon & The Crystalites/Bongo Herman & Les Crystalites
Golden Chicken/Move & Groove
Dub Store Japan 7"
There are many weird moments in reggae, and this is one of the weirdest: an idiosyncratic minor chord organ instrumental by Derrick Harriott's house group The Crystalites. Central to this track is the inimitable Spanglish intervention of Ramon The Mexican (aka Owen George

Anthony Silvera from Waltham Park in London), the resident deejay for Harriott's Musical Chariot Sound System. On "Golden Chickens" Harriott cannot resist a dig at fellow producer Lee Perry, making reference to The Upsetters' "Sipreano": *"Sipreano, Sipreano, so you think I'm counting my chickens before they hatch, eh?/But they are hatching – golden chickens, too!"* This track plus more Spaghetti Western stuff can be found on the Trojan compilation *For A Few Dollars More (28 Shots Of Western Inspired Reggae)*. A binghi bomb explodes on the flip, with Bongo Herman and Les punching the skins while a winding R&B sax from JoJo Bennett graces the unrelated rhythm.

Seekers International
The Call From Below
Digitalis Recordings DL/LP
One of the first hauntological dub albums to emerge over the past few years. Seekers International (aka SKRSINTL) have been spectral inhabitants of the blogosphere for some years since their NinjaRiddimXcursions and YARDFLEX manifestations, and claim to represent "the ital vein of the mysterious yet undeniable TRANSMOLECULAR sound family". "Touch Riddim" opens the set in orthodox manner, with a vocal rip from Perry's "Cloak And Dagger", but quickly floats into a more ethereal rhythmic dimension suspended between the airier moments of Chain Reaction/Burial Mix and Sun Araw. "Droplets Riddim" could easily be a looped intro from an early 90s Nervous or NuGroove 12". But overall the tendency is for deep-shadow dubwise riddim repetition. Dancehall peeks into "Large it Up (Ver 2)", but it's the more Echospace-inflected tracks such as "AllWaysdub" and closer "Even Though" that seal the space-dub deal.

Yabby You & Brethren
Deeper Roots: Dub Plates And Rarities 1976–1978
Pressure Sounds CD/DL/LP
Its 15 years since Blood & Fire's definitive Yabby You compilation *Jesus Dread*, and at last here's one fit to set alongside it, released in cooperation with the late producer's family. Many of his singles were pressed in tiny numbers in the 1970s, and included here are tracks from King Miguel, Barrington Spence, Prince Pampado and Smith & The Prophets, all typical of the producer's meditations on life in Kingston. Of most interest, though, are the nine dubplate mixes from King Tubby, creating a deeply meditative mood. These range from newly discovered tracks like Don D Junior's "Milk Lane Rock" to mixes of classic rhythms like the Black Ark's "Jah Vengeance" ("Dub Vengeance"), "Conquering Lion" ("Open Your Heart") and the dub of the classic "Deliver Me (From My Enemies)" ("Deliver Dub"). The kind of excellent run-through of fresh mid-1970s roots, vocals, dubs and instrumentals that's getting more and more difficult to source. □

Sam Davies on mossy trampolines, crisp analogue fudge, and sonic vandalism

Vladislav Delay
Kuopio
Raster-Noton CD/DL
12 months after his first album for raster-noton comes Vladislav Delay's second, and like *Vantaa*, *Kuopio* is preoccupied with the notion of depicting the Finnish landscape through sonics that melt together Techno, dub and Ambient into an unexpectedly pictorial language. And once again Sasu Ripatti pulls it off – *Kuopio* is thoroughly and evocatively penumbral, a record of half-light, with strange terrains stretching off around the listener, its outlines softened by a weak, distant sun. But landscaping conceits aside, there's so much else to *Kuopio*: the multiple, decentred parts, moving in and out of each other to create a subtle, kaleidoscopic tumbling together of melody and harmony. Or the way Ripatti organises texture, timbre and rhythm so that his sensuous, finely detailed, spongy pads retain a vibrant, tensile strength – like a series of trampolines carpeted with moss.

FaltyDL
Hardcourage
Ninja Tune CD/DL/LP
Hardcourage, Drew Lustmann's third album as FaltyDL, finds him moving away from his previous Garage reference points; to which my instinctive response is, what's wrong with Garage, and get back to the Garage. But *Hardcourage* justifies the departure. Cutting loose from Garage's rolling shuffle seems to cut Lustmann loose at the level of composition: tracks develop more tangentially and spontaneously than before. With a couple of exceptions (the enveloping gloomy Deep House of "Finally Some Shit/The Rain Stopped" and the crisp analogue fudge of "Kenny Rolls One"), the album's signature move is to borrow the communal ecstasies of club music to express the warm afterglow of romantic love. Occasionally the heart-on-sleeve approach goes awry, as on "She Sleeps", with its cameo by the singer from Friendly Fires – "Straight And Arrow"'s Todd Edwards-style cut-ups are a far better use of vocals. But largely the album pulls off its attempt to impersonate the sun bursting through the clouds (see "Bells").

Emptyset
Collapsed
raster-noton DL/12"
raster-noton feels like the ideal home for Bristol's Emptyset and the unrelenting rigour with which James Ginzburg and Paul Purgas build and demolish sonic architectures. This new four track EP reads almost as a response to Kangding

Ray's *Pruitt Igoe* EP for the label. Here, as there, the music is pulverised as much as pulverising: sounds pounded to dust, their white noise vapour caught hanging in the reverb, while the rubble rains down on subterranean bass foundations. Strange, though, what even such stark, ground-clearing abstractions summon up – there's always a ghostly imprint of funk left in Emptyset's most mathematically minded artillery blasts, and there's a ritualistic, ceremonial quality too, even if only that of the hushed countdown preceding an orgy of municipal demolition.

Russell Haswell
Factual
Editions Mego LP
Although all six tracks here are excursions into "real-time, one-take, analogue-digital modular synthesis", it feels like a slightly miscellaneous, disconnected collection. It hints at whole Haswell albums as yet unmade, or begun and then discarded. So "BLACK METAL INSTRUMENTAL INTRO DEMO" riffs on BM's blast-beat kicks, firing them out before decimating them in sad isolation, swamps it all in scorched distortion, then loses interest. "KILLER SNAKEHEAD" picks up on the current underground dialogue between Techno and Noise (see also Container, Diamond Catalog, Dungeon Acid) – an idea that's half-continued on "RAVE NIHILATION", and its incinerated synth arpeggios – but again Haswell's attention wanders. *Factual* is never less than a blast though, with "URBAN nO!se" and its seething can-of-worms static, and "RECORD SHOP DAY" and its 'garbage disposal through Auto-Tune' chatter topped off by "SHEFFIELD", a classic chunk of live Haswell, in which he designs then obliterates a rollercoaster arc of purest sonic vandalism.

NHK'Koyxen
Dance Classics Vol II
Pan DL/LP
On paper, the idea of Kouhei Matsunaga – sound artist, collaborator of Asmus Tietchens, Merzbow – making a record called *Dance Classics Vol I* suggested something about as recognisably of-the-dancefloor as Florian Hecker's *Acid In The Style Of David Tudor*. But the results, while never less than aslant in their intersections with dancefloor currents, were authentic and often fascinating, the title meant as self-deprecation rather than genre vandalism. *Vol II* continues in that vein and improves upon it: its execution crisper, its ideas that much more realised. Techno, electro, even hiphop are taken apart and reprogrammed into new shapes that are best described as unbalanced: a loop that feels a beat too long; an arrangement zeroed in on what might typically be a background part; a sound twisted past breaking point. Dance classics perhaps not, but an excellent way of coaxing jaded ears to listen afresh. □

Julian Cowley on meaty Colombian cuts, Ghanaian disco, and worldly Thai pop

Diablos Del Ritmo
The Colombian Melting Pot 1960–1985
Analog Africa 2×CD/2×LP
Wganda Kenya's "El Caterete" sets the flavour and the standard for this uplifting 32 track compilation of mainly 70s material, drawn from the inexhaustible musical vaults of Colombia's Caribbean coast. A meaty Latin party cut steeped in African marinade, it's an entirely natural, organic mingling of ingredients rather than a calculated fusion. This selection, packaged with a 60 page illustrated booklet, is a lovingly researched celebration of the region's spirit. Supple electric bass, crisscrossing percussion, exultant voices, electric guitars and punchy horns distil the tropical everyday into irrepressible dance music. It's delivered with unflagging energy and abundant variety, ranging from pounding Afrobeat to shuffling and snaky local variants of cumbia. The exotic as lived and breathed.

Drop On Down In Florida
Various
Dust-To-Digital 2×CD + Hbk
From the opening of Robert Dennis's "Early One Foggy Morning" to the closing voices of the Sacred Harp Singing Convention, *Drop On Down In Florida* testifies that music can be a hub of community. Blues are sung with encouragement from family and friends; gospel lays bare the bonds of shared faith. Listening to the mournful voices of Richard Williams or Ella Mae Wilson, you sense that these black singers have found viable ways, in the Florida sunshine, to come to terms with the troubles in their lives. But at the heart of this set, recorded at the end of the 1970s, issued initially on vinyl and now housed in a beautifully produced 200 page book edited by Dwight DeVane and Blane Waide, is Moses Williams, aka Door Man or Haywire Slim. A migrant labourer with a whisky gruff, dirt-track and tin-shack lonesome voice, Williams accompanies himself rowdily on a woozy self-made one-string instrument, his bottleneck reeling out that low yo-yo stuff while he growls undiluted outsider blues with raw brilliance. His presence makes this a release not to be missed.

Guelewar
Halleli N'Dakarou
Teranga Beat CD
Karantamba
Ndigal
Teranga Beat CD
Royal Band De Thiès
Kadior Demb
Teranga Beat CD
Gambia, Africa's smallest country, has a discography to match, but Greek DJ

Kiki Gyan

Adamantios Kafetzis and his Teranga Beat label are committed to broadening the picture and have unearthed some unusual material in the process. Guelewar flourished in the early 1970s, developing music around traditional circumcision songs. The group reformed a decade later and *Halleli N'Dakarou (Children Of Dakar)* was recorded live at a club in neighbouring Senegal in 1982. The performance has the feel of a sprawling rock jam with funk chops, meandering guitar solos, gloopy bass and vocals delivered in Wolof. It was recorded direct to a four channel reel-to-reel, so the balance and overall quality of the sound is far from ideal, especially when Moussa N'Diaye's doodling Mini-Moog is over-exposed. An odd mix, but worth hearing.

Karantamba were fronted by Guelewar guitarist Bai Janha. *Ndigal* is a less erratic live recording, made in Senegal in 1984. Janha mentored this outfit and his playing provides the sturdy focal point for their vigorous percussive patterns and confident vocals. Although steeped in American rock and funk, Karantamba's music is altogether more cohesive, purposeful and resilient, if less idiosyncratic, than that of Guelewar.

Kadior Demb, by Senegalese nine-piece Royal Band De Thiès, has inexplicably remained unissued since 1979. Adam Seck and James Gadiaga's declamatory vocals surge over bright rippling guitars, incisive horns and driving hand-drums. A distinctive and disciplined group who work intriguing, rhythmically off-kilter variations on the region's mbalax dance style. A compelling find, and certainly the pick of this batch.

Kiki Gyan
24 Hours In A Disco
Soundway CD

"Disco Dancer", "Keep On Dancing", "Disco Train", "Sexy Dancer" – the titles flaunt Kiki Gyan's commitment to a musical style that is, as Peter Shapiro calls it, "all shiny, glittery surfaces". Ghanaian Gyan formerly played keyboards with Osibisa, and during the late 70s was a highly sought-after rock session musician. Touches of African percussion flutter around the glinting mirror ball of his

polished take on disco, but essentially these seven sleek grooves, recorded between 1978–82, are cast in the well-trodden international language of the dancefloor. Synthetic strings, falsetto vocals, slap bass riffs and disembodied handclaps abound; glimmering signifiers that speak only of play and display. Gyan, made wealthy through music, later experienced a grim personal descent into drug abuse, poverty and squalor. He died in 2005. *24 Hours In A Disco*, on the other hand, is a pristine moment, preserved in its own stylistic perfection.

Youssou N'Dour
From Senegal To The World
Nascente 2×CD

Now that Youssou N'Dour has become a film actor and United Nations Goodwill Ambassador, has been awarded an honorary doctorate by Yale University and elevated to ministerial status in the government of his native Senegal, this is a welcome opportunity to get to know him through his music once again. *From Senegal To The World*, collecting hits and rarities from the 1980s, shows him at a pivotal point in his creative life. The first CD presents music made in Senegal with his groups Étoile and Super Étoile De Dakar. There's nervy, dynamic excitement running though those guitars, percussion and horns, trying out contexts for the grace and soaring energy of N'Dour's youthful voice. That exhilarating sense of the music scrambling to rise to a vocal challenge is far less evident in the late 80s material gathered on the second CD, where N'Dour's singing is steadily subsumed into increasingly lavish production and framed by mainstream rock priorities. It's far less satisfying, although "Diabaram", the lovely closing track, with its quietly plashing cymbal and Ryuichi Sakamoto at the keyboard, does justice to that astonishing voice.

Nung Lamyong Kularbseemuang/ Chanpen Dennapa
Kati Sorn Jai/Lam Toey Dai Lao Leaw Luem Mia
Paradise Bangkok 7"

Devotees of Thai pop will recognise the marvellous "Kati Sorn Jai" from the Sublime Frequencies compilation *Siamese Soul* (2009), credited to Lam Yong and translated as "Lessons For Life". Now DJs Chris Menist and Maft Sai have revived this durable late 70s number on their Paradise Bangkok label, well worth tracking down. After an opening flourish of sweaty brass, "Kati Sorn Jai" is pared back to skeletal percussion and a delectably unyielding, cheesy organ and bass riff. The clinching ingredient is Lamyong's vocal – sultry, sinewy and unambiguously worldly. On the B side is Chanpen Dennapa's "Lam Toey Dai Lao Leaw Luem Mia", an engaging slice of South East Asian power pop boasting some of the funkiest phin (lute) playing you're ever likely to hear. □

Andrew Nosnitsky on a chef turned rapper, ratchet-clap party starters, and the sound of soul trap

Action Bronson
Rare Chandeliers
Vice DL

Action Bronson sounds like Ghostface Killah. He not only bears a vocal similarity to the Wu-Tang legend, but every dimension of his rap style. He flows like Ghost, he drags his syllables like Ghost. When he brags, he uses Ghostian turns of phrase like *"Catch me in the…"* When he breathes, he wheezes like Ghost. But apparently the 'No Biting Allowed' sign that Masta Ace posted on the door has long since rusted over, as Bronson has been warmly embraced by the hiphop underground. Maybe this is because Bronson's appearance as an unapologetically obese white man makes him ripe for Tumblr reblogs, or because his 'chef turned rapper' narrative strikes a chord with the hip foodie generation. *Rare Chandeliers* was produced entirely by The Alchemist, whose beyond-sparse drama loops are always welcome, but Alc has already produced better songs for the actual Ghostface. So it is unclear why this album – or the rapper who made it – needed to exist.

Future
Pluto 3D
Epic/Freebandz CD/DL

With its kaleidoscope of sustained kickdrums and impassioned Auto-Tune gurgles, Future's *Pluto* was one of rap's strangest successes last year. In acknowledgment, his label gave it one of those almost pointless bonus track reissue repackagings that have become all too common. While the new version corrects some of the organisational problems with the original tracklisting, and adds three new songs – the highlight being "My", on which Future's cracking voice somehow turns *"porky"* and *"Porsche"* into two words that rhyme – it also needlessly replaces some standout tracks with star-studded remixes. It shouldn't come as a surprise that Kelly Rowland, P Diddy and Ludacris can't handle the atmosphere on *Pluto*. Drake and Snoop Dogg couldn't, either, on the original version (they remain here). Future might be the only young rap star who is capable of making hits without any co-sign, and yet all his hits keep being retroactively bogged down with celebrities.

Personal & UnkleLuc
The Wild EP
No label DL

In a crowded landscape of fashion-fabulous avant garde poseurs, Miami producer/

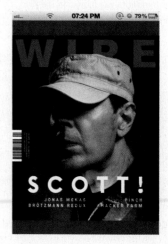

rapper Personal and graphic designer UnkleLuc have produced a genuinely experimental rap project in *The Wild*. It's so experimental, in fact, that its first third is basically unrecognisable as hiphop. Instead, it's a sheer muck of Industrial plod and sound collage, from which rapping emerges eventually, first in the form of cameos from Spaceghostpurrrp and Robb Banks and later in a mess of unidentified, multitracked and distorted word blurs. Unlike Purrrp's recent efforts, *The Wild* is not a lo-fi affair by any means. Personal built something sophisticated and stunning, then destroyed it from the inside. It's like a warped interpretation of Kanye's *My Beautiful Dark Twisted Fantasy*, one where the darkness affects the beauty and not the other way around.

Earl Sweatshirt
Chum
Odd Future DL

Right before Odd Future's press buzz hit critical mass in 2010, Earl Sweatshirt, their youngest and most talented rapper was unceremoniously sent away to a Samoan boot camp. After turning 18 earlier this year he's finally re-entered the fold as a star, but to weirdly subdued fanfare. Partially this is because of his own relative silence. He's dropped a smattering of guest verses since coming home, but "Chum" is his first fully formed solo song, and that means a lot. Writing songs – ones with ideas and structural integrity – is Earl's greatest skill, and he delivers here. He's wisely dropped the rape fantasies of his pre-Samoa work, leaving just the densely penned multisyllabic rhymes and raw introspection: *"Get up off the pavement, brush the dirt up off my psyche."* His performance is numbed as a stylistic choice, which does raise some questions about his technical abilities, but for now the words themselves are more than enough to compensate.

Tree & 110% Pure
Trillin' EP
Gutter City DL

With his *Sunday School* EP, Chicago rap and production eccentric Tree developed a sound that he has coined 'soul trap', whose characteristics are best described as what would have happened if J Dilla had been given access to Lex Luger's drum kit. The tape was well received critically, but otherwise almost completely eclipsed by the more aggressive drill sound that teenage rappers like Chief Keef have popularised. With *Trillin'*, Tree forgoes his own productions in favour of those from producer 110% Pure, whose instinct leans more towards trap than soul. And so the short shot *Trillin'* feels like a purposeful statement. Tree is busily proving that he can run with the youngins, and that his Scarface-like rasp is just as equipped for synth-heavy 808 drama as for soulful laments. □

Philip Clark on the missing Trane, common-cold triads, and Ballardian Improv

John Coltrane
Complete Live At The Sutherland Lounge 1961
RLR 3×CD

John Coltrane's 1961 two-bass quartet – adding bassist Raphael Don Garrett to the classic McCoy Tyner/Reggie Workman/Elvin Jones line-up – was never officially documented, but this decidedly unofficial release has a fundamental problem. Recorded into what sounds like rubber band threaded through a frying pan, there's plenty of saxophone, piano and drums, but the bass end of the acoustic spectrum is essentially missing. And so I can't tell you how Workman and Garrett carve up the space between them, although as Coltrane dummy-runs "Greensleeves", which would feature in the *Africa/Brass* sessions a few months earlier, and revisits "Cousin Mary", "Bye Bye Blackbird" and "Blue Train", the extra bass activity doesn't result in any audible seismic structural shocks. That said, any Coltrane fan who would turn their nose up at this material probably isn't worthy of the name. As he played Chicago's Sutherland Lounge in March 1961, he was psyching himself up to join Impulse! and, compared to the Village Vanguard uproar of only six months later, two tryout "Impressions" – apparently the earliest existing versions – feel speculative and gentlemanly. But it's telling to (almost) hear Coltrane adding satellite voices to his quartet, a policy that, from *Africa/Brass* to *Ascension* and beyond, unfailingly upped the ante.

Charlotte Hug & Frédéric Blondy
Bouquet
Emanem CD

"*Bouquet* is more likely to appeal to connoisseurs of Grisey, Xenakis, Cage and Feldman than to listeners weaned on Coltrane, Sanders and Ayler," argues *The Wire*'s Dan Warburton in his sleevenotes, an observation which, while undoubtedly true, omits to mention that the sort of musician minded to perform Grisey, Xenakis and Cage probably couldn't do what Charlotte Hug and Frédéric Blondy do here. Because Hug and Blondy dig deep to find primary sound sources of their own, a way of thinking about music that has led Hug to experiment with loosening her bow – all four strings on her viola available in an instant – while Blondy combines a knows-no-limits keyboard technique with keen-eared foraging inside the piano. At 73 minutes, *Bouquet* is a long listen but there are few longueurs: once the point has been established,

and that timbral meeting point surfaces, they either fizzle out or simply stop. But the longer "Sombreuil" is underpinned by Blondy bowing the piano strings, carefully divining harmonic points of convergence for Hug's viola. The sounds are unreal, and a proper acoustic riddle. But it's important to remember, as the notes italicise: "*no overdubbing or electric modification was used.*"

Albert Mangelsdorff Quintet
Live At Audimax Freiburg, 1964
Jazz Haus CD

Before Albert Mangelsdorff hooked up with Peter Brötzmann during the late 1960s and cultivated his trademark multiphonic trombone technique, he led this honest-to-goodness jazz quintet, which responded with lightning certainty to the American mother music. "Now Jazz Ramwong" has Charles Mingus flowing through its veins, "Set Em Up" could have graced the opening of many a period Blue Note album, while bassist Günter Lenz and drummer Ralf Hübner nail "Rakhahs" to the harmonic floor with a funky modal vamp. And yet Mangelsdorff's quintet clearly had loftier ambitions than merely hacking it as a lowly repertory band. Tenor and soprano saxophonist Heinz Sauer spoke fluent Coltrane, his discursive soprano solo on "Okaka" motivated by aspiring to get inside, rather than matching, Coltrane solos note for note. And Sauer's tenor reconnects the Coltrane of "India" back to source as the group wade into an epic reading of Ravi Shankar's "Theme From Pather Panchali" – a whole two years before The Beatles made referencing Shankar de rigueur. With the group's studio albums all in purdah, here's a window into a largely forgotten moment in the evolution of European modern jazz.

Neil Metcalfe/Guillaume Viltard/Daniel Thompson
Garden Of Water And Light
FMR CD

In 1925, the French architect Gabriel Guevrekian unveiled his so-called Cubist Garden – officially: *Jardin D'Eau Et De Lumiere* – at that year's Exposition Internationale des Arts Décoratifs. Designed to refract light around smaller triangles encased within a larger three-pointed structure, this model of how to funnel material through space is clearly not lost on Neil Metcalfe (flute), Guillaume Viltard (bass) and Daniel Thompson (guitar). An oddball moment occurs at around the 14 minute mark: during the extended first track Metcalfe drops in some stylistically incongruous swing-inflected flute lines and Thompson responds with common cold triads; otherwise every understated pluck, floaty breath and remote strum have the intricate inner choreography of flickering, waltzing shadows. An exceptionally charming record.

The Remote Viewers
City Of Nets
RV CD

The Remote Viewers have serious form when it comes to albums with menacing titles that read like scraps from JG Ballard's writing table. *City Of Nets* is the follow-up to previous releases *Nerve Curve*, *Sinister Heights* and *Control Room*, and sitting Davros-like in the centre of proceedings is John Edwards, whose drum programming actually sounds surprisingly pukka when compared to his intentionally polite, larky basslines. The title track is very London: I hear Ian Dury's Blockheads, The Jam and Loose Tubes. But then a piece like "Dark Threat" is, you feel, basically the theme from *Cagney & Lacey* performed by a saxophone section who can't be arsed to make the grade, and backed by a drummer who thinks he's backing bandleader Harry James. Staffed by musicians normally associated with free Improv – Caroline Kraabel, Sue Lynch, Adrian Northover, Rosa Lynch-Northover, David Petts – once again Ballard comes to mind: a music that ruminates on the everyday from the outside, where it's happy to remain.

Sleeping In Vilna
Why Waste Time
Ayler CD

Hiphop artist Mike Ladd (formerly of The Infesticons and others) provides and intones the words; improvisors Carol Robinson (clarinet), Dave Randall (guitar) and Dirk Rothbrust (drums, percussion) create a sonic backdrop on the fly. Ladd's lyrics rail against Western consumerism and war, although his sensuous love song "Marvelling" adds another dimension. In "Past Chaser", Ladd's lyrics get strangled by the musicians' dense and relentless onslaughts. Nevertheless, this is poetry and jazz like I'd always hoped it could be.

Juma Sultan's Aboriginal Music Society
Whispers From The Archive
Porter CD

Percussionist Juma Sultan has slipped through history's net presumably because history has no clue how to deal with a onetime Jimi Hendrix sideman whose muse led him to seek out Archie Shepp, Sonny Simmons, Kalaparusha Maurice McIntyre and Fire Music. Not that this music – culled from Sultan's own apparently vast archive of recordings made in New York City during the 1970s – sounds too much like generic free jazz, either. The Aboriginal Music Society knitted Latin and African percussion into extended structures that bathed in post-Coltrane mysticism while grabbing back key signatures and countable grooves. The opening track, "AMS", recorded in February 1978 at Rashied Ali's Alley, is rooted in a long, transcendental percussion intro which grounds citrusy solos from saxophonist Art Bennett, regular Sultan collaborator Ali Abuwi on oboe and pianist Kasa Allah. □

Nick Cain on camel crickets, dripping taps, and blank synth drones

Joke Lanz

Three Legged Race
Persuasive Barrier
Spectrum Spools LP

Bee Mask
When We Were Eating Unripe Pears
Spectrum Spools LP

With Hair Police apparently on hiatus, Robert Beatty seems to have been focusing on graphic design as much as music, working up a succession of terrific sleeves for labelmates Eric Lanham, Outer Space and others. *Persuasive Barrier* is the full-length vinyl debut of his Three Legged Race solo project, following the usual dozens of cassettes, 7"s and CD-Rs. It's an idiosyncratic hybrid, surveying a range of disparate styles and studiously mangling them: deadpan, half-speed exotica-style études; wobbly UK DIY-esque electronic chiming and bleeping; and a couple of more clangorous electronic blasts, "Permethrin I" and "Permethrin II".

Another exercise in stylistic tourism, if a less singular one, Chris Madak's third album for the label as Bee Mask occupies itself with 60s concrète and electronics, re-rendered in spacious fidelity with a glossy digital sheen. Its seven tracks run together into a 31 minute suite; the majority of them mutate continually in an organic linear flow, sucking in a broad range of electronic sounds and feeding them through all manner of modulations and filtering. Some intriguingly awkward juxtapositions and clunky segues pop up on "Pink Drinq" and "Fried Niteshade", helping to keep the album's momentum from becoming too smooth.

Marc Behrens
Unit
And/OAR CD

This 42 minute document of a sound installation was recorded in a warehouse space somewhere in Germany during 2009. Its set-up plays off control and randomness: various sounds were played through speakers suspended a few centimetres above two floor-mounted frame drums, causing the drums to resonate. The sequence of the recordings – of cymbals, camel crickets in China and Tibet, stones being rubbed or ground together – was created with an aleatoric script. Once the piece's limited conceptual appeal (recordings generating sound from an instrument, rather than vice versa) has worn off, *Unit* becomes a dourly episodic listen, with a scattering of sound incidents separated by long gaps. As ever with these types of recordings, much is lost in the translation to CD. Seeing the installation in situ would doubtless make for a much richer listening experience.

Ulises Carrión
The Poet's Tongue
Alga Marghen LP

Ulises Carrión's biography makes me wonder if he'll one day turn up in thinly fictionalised form as a bit character in a posthumously published Roberto Bolaño novel. After relocating to Amsterdam from his native Mexico in 1975, he opened Other Books & So, a shop-cum-gallery dedicated to artists' publications. Released on cassette in 1977, *The Poet's Tongue* comprises six text based works, all recorded at the Institut voor Sonologie in Utrecht, which share a "refusal of discursiveness", as Carrión put it. Their elevation of idea over result is consistent with 1970s conceptual art. In "Hamlet, For Two Voices", a man and a woman take turns naming a character from the play; for much of "Aritmética" a male voice repeats the phrase *"uno mas"*, varying his pacing and inflection. Others use strategies more reminiscent of sound poetry. On "45 Revoluciones Per Minuto" a voice counts in Spanish *"one revolution, two revolutions, three revolutions"* and so on all the way up to 45, as a pop song plays in the background.

Philip Corner
Coldwater Basin No 2
Alga Marghen LP

You wait years for a recording of water running from a tap into a sink in New York's Lower East Side sometime in the 1960s, and then two come along within a year of each other. A late 2011 Alga Marghen micro-edition, *Coldwater Basin* treated us to not one, but two 20 minute recordings of said liquid in said domestic setting. The one-sided *No 2* offers a 14 minute follow-up. If the sound source hadn't been identified, I doubt I'd have realised what it was, not because it's treated so as to be unrecognisable (though some processing appears to have taken place), but because the textures sound quite electronic in nature. 2012's other Corner archival finds – *Italian Air* on Ricerca Sonora and *Gong/Ear* on Roaratorio – have more composerly appeal. But there's something gratifying about this mischievous blast of a record.

Gregor Cürten & Anselm Rogmans
Planes
Entr'acte CD

By my count only the second reissue on Entr'acte, in a catalogue of almost 150 titles. The first was a Fluxus cassette; *Planes* was a private press LP recorded by Cürten and Rogmans in one take in Germany in May 1974. It's not quite Krautrock: while their contemporaries were aiming cosmic pulses into the bright sunset, Cürten and Rogmans directed blank synth drones nowhere in particular. The first side serves up dense, oscillating frequencies and wordless, moaning vocals, more failed motion than psychedelic transcendence. The more melodic second adds cyclical patterns of chiming guitar notes and electronic

arpeggios. The usual Entr'acte vacuum packaging supplies only the bare minimum of information. A shame in this instance, as there's surely plenty of context to be unpacked. Nonetheless, it's a pleasure to have this charming obscurity back in print.

Giuseppe Ielasi & Enrico Malatesta
Rudimenti
Entr'acte CD

Like much of Giuseppe Ielasi's recent work, *Rudimenti* focuses on the potential of rhythm through compositional techniques reminiscent of sampling but closer in style to musique concrète. Its principal sound source is recordings of percussionist Malatesta improvising, stitched together – by Ielasi, presumably – into a disorientating 26 minute patchwork. There are very few beats to be heard – the emphasis is on sustained clusters of small percussive sounds, along with varieties of rubbing, bowing and scraping. Ielasi juxtaposes them adeptly, creating polyrhythmic contrasts which would have been impossible for Malatesta to achieve naturally, but which are never showy and always true to the style of his playing.

Tomasz Krakowiak
Moulins
Bocian CD

An album which links two infrequently connected forms: solo percussion and field recordings. Its titles mostly allude to locations in Canada, leading one to expect the latter. But what Krakowiak is evidently doing is using percussion to convey or recreate the locations' sound environments, or at least his memories or impressions of them – the rather coy sleevenotes don't clarify whether he actually visited them or not. The connection is sometimes quite literal: "February, Stream In High Park" summons rushing water with layered rhythmic density; "Approaching Miller's Creek" (in a speedboat?) is a cacophonous blast. Elsewhere, less so: "Never Ending Wait For Train To Pass, Six Nations Reserve, Ontario" offers quiet rattling and a fait metallic drone. The locations Krakowiak references give the album some metaphorical ballast, and his playing – equal parts high energy and extended technique – is impressive, conjuring polyrhythmic barrages or delicate micro-patterns as the situation requires.

Joke Lanz & Shelley Hirsch
Berlin + Brooklyn
Rossbin CD

The first release on Rossbin in a few years. It's unlikely to be remembered as one of their stronger titles. Vocalist Shelley Hirsch certainly has plenty of range. Her stream of narrative snatches draws on banal overheard conversations and the detritus of popular culture. Lanz, whose contributions are largely electronic rather than vocal, isn't known as an improvisor, but acquits himself moderately well. The problems are

a lack of variation in register and lack of contrast in playing styles. For all Hirsch's outlandishness, much of the album is simple call-and-respond Improv, the two mimicking each other with bursts of activity and rapid cutaways. That said, the Berlin recording is the better of the two, Lanz broadening his palette to provide a bit more dimension.

Ergo Phizmiz
Eleven Songs
Care In The Community CD/DL/LP

Renaissance man Ergo Phizmiz's weighty back catalogue covers a range of styles, including radio plays, collages and film soundtracks. From time to time he indulges himself with a cleverly and lovingly constructed pastiche of late 60s psych-pop. The last was 2010's *Things To Do And Make*. Now comes *Eleven Songs*, whose clearest precedents are Harvest-era Kevin Ayers and the less droopy tracks on Syd Barrett's two albums, with the odd nod to Robert Wyatt. The songs are played relatively straight, albeit with plenty of attention to detail. The lyrics imbue the album with much of its character, gently spinning quirky fables and absurdist scenarios.

Billy Roisz
Walking The Monkey
Editions Mego LP

Billy Roisz has been operating at the fringes of post-Mego Viennese electronics and electroacoustic Improv since the late 90s, with very little to show for her efforts in the way of documentation. She's primarily known as a video artist, her most notable musical projects being her Skylla duo with Sylvia Fässler and the AVVA collaboration with Toshimaru Nakamura, who released a synapse-melting DVD on Erstwhile a few years back. *Walking The Monkey* is her solo debut, and is a sharp piece of work. Its six tracks keep themselves busy with chunky frequencies and noisy slabs of sound, into which Roisz mixes granular static, clipped pulses and stuttering rhythms. They're all carefully balanced, their ostensibly loose, roaming motion belying a smart compositional sensibility. □

Jan Stradtmann

Size Matters
By **Byron Coley**

BRB>Voicecoil
These Are Not Our Borders
alt.vinyl 8"
Manipulated field recordings, made throughout England by Newcastle's Kevin Wilkinson (aka BRB) over a couple of years. The first side makes me think of trying to sleep under a highway overpass. The flip reminds me of waking up in a kitchen's laundry cabinet with a bad hangover.

Cheap Time
Other Stories
Sweet Rot 7"
Nashville trio who continue to pump out charmingly classicist 1970s glam pop readymades.

Dharma Dogs
Drown
Kitschy Manitou 7"
Nice debut slice of Grunge revisionism from this Madison, Wisconsin trio. It's nice that they grab for the noisier (as opposed to the poppier or Zeppier) elements of the style from which to do their exercises. I'm betting they're fine and extremely loud live.

Egg Eggs
Zygotic Crack
No Basement Is Deep Enough MC
Nice new tape by this Western Massachussetts ensemble, held in one of the typically arty/opaque packaging jobs for which this Serbian cassette label is known. Hard to figure how many Eggs there are on it. I can make out Ed Lee and Dave Russell, but other members may as well be imaginary. The two side-long pieces are as chaotic as expected – lots of manipulated concrète soundscapes with chipmunk-like vocals, plus portions that sound more like deep space thought control experiments than anything else.

Tom Fazzini
Castle On Wheels
Loophammystery 7"
Another great solo single by the creator of *Neck To Neck*. The guitars are a mix of electric and acoustic this time, and other voices are heard, so it lacks some of the creepiness of the last one. But it's still a bizarre, unique and utterly mesmeric piece of otherworld volk.

Go Genre Everything
Domestic Dreams & Robots
Vacant Valley 7"
This single, near as I can figure, is related to the documentation of a stage extravaganza recently presented at the Melbourne Fringe Festival. And while my weak imagination may have prefered the plebeian contours of GGE's earlier recordings, there is something quite majestic about what they're up to here. Try to picture a collaboration between David Byrne, Meatloaf, Robert Forster and The B-52s. It's like that, but good.

Gooch Palms
R U 4 Sirius
Anti Fade 7"
This Australian duo from Newcastle, New South Wales (north of Sydney) often draw comparisons to The Ramones, but their leaky organ tones make me think more of certain West Coast US groups of the 1970s wave era, and the songs' structures are as likely to be Crampsian as Ramonesy. Still, the sound is basic "shit-pop" (their own description) and should appeal to any Rezillos fan still alive.

Kitchen's Floor
Bitter Defeat
Negative Guest List 7"
Since their excellent US tour last year, this Brisbane trio has made a big line-up shift, but not a huge form-leap. Matt Kennedy is still in charge and sounds as drunkenly bummed as a Guinea hen with its pants full of fire-poop. I sense a few more overt South Island New Zealand moves here, but then I often feel that way.

Mordecai
Drag Down
Wantage 7"
Boseman, Montana is not country I'm much familiar with, but the fact it can produce such an interesting avant punk trio is testament to something. The sound here is a mix of classic Cleveland 1970s weirdness, no-fi shit-rock à la Mike Rep or Bruce Cole, and various other 'once lost, now found' threads of goodness. Quite lovely.

My Carapace Is Leaking/Astral Social Club
Split
Tor Press MC
Dastardly listening here. MCIL is the solo bass project of Joincey from Inca Eyeball (among a million other places), but has sonics that belie its origins. The sound is very machiney and far higher in pitch than you'd expect. The notes say it was recorded live to one track, but the sensation you get

Astral Social Club

is of a wind tunnel throbbing. The side by Astral Social Club (Neil Campbell's berserk solo plus guest project) is a relentless battle of rising tones, gloops, twizzles and mid-air dithers, that provide a shocking cavalcade of pleasures.

The No Real Need
Nonlocal Motives
Do Your Block MC
Cassette reissue of the second CD by this Melbourne quartet, led by Guided By Voices fanatic Steve Hewitt. You can hear the GBV influence quite clearly at times, but when it's really cooking this seems not an imitation so much as an exploration of similar styles. 1960s Brit freakpop readymades, the kind of post-core hecticity the early Replacements did so well, some tactics from the Paisleys, all wrapped up in a lo-fi bow. Extremely hook-laden, but not offensively so.

Cian Nugent
Grass Above My Head
VHF 7"
The Irish acoustic guitarist returns with a melodic, wandering orginal and a cover of Black Flag's "My War" worthy of Jack Rose. Can't say I ever heard some of these blues resolutions in Ginn's original, but maybe I was just listening wrong.

The Plums
Nixon's Mess
Prison Art MC
Excellent DC area free rock unit with *The Wire*'s own Marc Masters in the mix. These guys jammed for ten years before their first album, and now it only took 'em a year to do the second. Which is good for us. Depending on what you want to listen for, you'll be able to interpret this tape in a variety of ways. Could be in the tradition of New Zealand free rock. Might be in the outsider tracks of *Daily Dance* or *Nuts Music As Free As The Squirrels*. Or is that a whiff of the Japanese trio Friction? Or the French quartet Mahogany Brain? They're all there, in one way or another. A very solid release.

Rambutan
Surrounded
Obsolete Units MC

Rambutan/Fossils From The Sun
Split
House Of Alchemy MC
Rambutan is the solo project of Albany, NY's Eric Hardiman (also of Burnt Hills and Century Plants). In this guise, Eric creates thick, lardy waves of guitar/amp psychedelia in a direction not unlike Dead C or Gate, although certain sequences have some of the leavening of UK folks like Dreams Of Tall Buildings. Anyway, good stuff, all of it. Fossils From The Sun is the solo handle of Ray Hare, Hardiman's compadre in both Hills and Plants. And Ray's approach is parallel to Eric's, but on his side of the split he starts off with quieter acoustic guitar

figures, before moving into deep electric riff raunch and reverbed screams. Quite cool.

Rejections
Clone EP
alt.vinyl MC
A solo project of Teesside's Michael Hann, this material seems to get classified as Techno, but it's fairly beat-free and filled with waves of echoing reverb and delay that seem to get everything swept up like some big-ass tsunami of pure coiled metal. Fetching.

Bruce Russell
1968
Imminent Frequencies MC
Although Wayne Kramer (and his lovely American flag shirt) may dapple the front cover of this cassette, there's precious little rock-qua-rock aktion at work here. A compilation of four solo guitar tracks by Russell (Dead C, A Handful Of Dust), *1968* was recorded between 1995 and 2011, although his technique does not seem to evolve linearly enough to be able to identify which tracks are from when. The way Russell attacks his guitar is muscular and abstract in a way I always find quite psychedelic – full of long mutating tones and clusters of feedback. And the side-long track is as whacked as anything by Keiji Haino, although (of course) headed in a different direction.

The Sensibles
Dino
Reverb Nation 7"
Yow. Italian power pop in the classic NYC style. Makes me almost remember either Nervous Rex or Regina Richards!

Mike Shiflet
Forgotten Somewhere
Obsolete Units MC
Columbus, Ohio's tireless Mike Shiflet appears with another great two-sided abstracter. The first piece is an aggressively abstract slab of clanging, upper middle range static manipulation, seemingly made up of countless smaller sources. Very dense and interesting (although my dogs didn't much care for it). The second piece sounds as though the basics were more amp-derived than not, and while it has a lower tone centre and a quieter, ratchety feel, there's a weirdly flabby telegraph-key kind of sound laid over it that makes me keep thinking of guys with large moustaches in great distress. Odd.

Southern Comfort
Silver And Gold
Black Petal 7"
Devolved from Circle Pit and Ratsak, both from Melbourne, Australia, this zoney duo forsake scummery for a sort of Azalia Snail-like psych folk wooze. The Neil Young cover strains against the pillow covering its face, but eventually surrenders. Poof! □

Sébastien Agnetti

The Inner Sleeve

Artwork selected by **Alasdair Roberts**

Pan-Ra
Music From Atlantis
Pan-Ra 1978
Design by Emmanuelle Hélène

A brown furrowed field; massed tongues of flame; a shoal of silver fish in the brine; geese soaring amid clouds. Four castles, red, yellow, green and white. The heads of four deities from some unknown pantheon hover at the cardinal points of the compass alongside 12 naïvely rendered zodiacal pictograms. In the centre floats a cross-section of planet Earth, each geological layer revealed, out of which sprout four trees, one for each season. On the back cover, two gaunt faces peer through unkempt hair and straggly beards. 'Chobo' Csaba Koncz (we'll call him Pan) is the older of the two, and has the cold, commanding gaze of a cult leader. The younger man is Michel Poiteau (aka Ra), whose haunted eyes reveal the look of an awestruck disciple. Their horoscopes are listed, and we discover that, on six of the tracks, Pan plays two flutes simultaneously in addition to crumhorn, darbouka and singing. His adept is consigned to open-tuned guitar (and bass on one track). This is Pan-Ra – not Sun Ra, although there is clearly a similar preoccupation with eccentric astrology and a highly personalised cosmology. They play the music of Atlantis, however, not of outer space, and the tracks include such

antediluvian favourites as "Centaure", "Sabbat", "Tehuti" and "Isis".

Closer inspection reveals that Pan and Ra are not really Atlantean, but Hungarian and French respectively. How they came to channel the sound of that fabled lost continent is unclear, but who am I to doubt their authority? They certainly *look* the part. Let's drop the needle. There's a droning, open-tuned guitar with a Mixolydian feel followed by some tinkling tambourine and pounding tom-tom; these pave the way for Pan's masterful double flute playing. Each track continues in a not dissimilar fashion. The music of Atlantis seems to be quite typical of a lot of New Age-y, mildly psychedelic, vaguely freaked-out music being produced at the time in Europe and elsewhere, and is doubtless still being produced whenever sensitive (male) humanities students in their early twenties with easy access to psilocybin and a library full of the writings of Carl Kerényi and Joseph Campbell get their hands on an armoury of antiquated and exotic acoustic instruments.

Circa 1986, as an eight year old kid in a small town in central Scotland, I found this LP disturbing to look at, so much so that I was afraid to play it. My musical tastes at that time were based around what was on Radio Clyde and *Top Of The Pops*, and the work of artists such as The Communards, Erasure, The Pet Shop Boys and Boy George

still resonates with me profoundly when I hear it. In the corner of the living room of the family home, however, lurked an older, stranger musical legacy – my parents' record collection from the 1970s, amassed while running a booking agency (The Flying Scotsman) in Germany. My German mother Annegret and Scottish father Alan booked mainly Irish and Scottish folk acts – The Tannahill Weavers, Silly Wizard, The Battlefield Band and The Bothy Band – whose music I grew up with, and whose LPs I still revisit from time to time. There are many other interesting LPs I inherited, including highly regionalised folk rock from Swabia, Frisia, Hungary and Normandy from the likes of Linnenzworch, Perelaar, Kolinda and La Bamboche, but Pan-Ra's Atlantean prog-folk is certainly the quaintest of the lot.

I have a naive theory that the huge popularity of das keltische Musik in Germany in the 70s can be accounted for by the unwillingness of Germans to celebrate their own musical/cultural heritage, in light of the country's then-recent history. Irish and Scottish music presented a more innocent, less problematic alternative. I have a recent edition of the German magazine *Folker*, with Woody Guthrie on the cover, which suggests that the phenomenon persists: the gig listings reveal that outfits such as Bardic ("acoustic Music and Celtic Folk"), Celtic Cowboys ("Greengrass meets Bluegrass") and Connemara Stone Company

("Celtic Folk Rock") enjoy healthy German touring schedules.

Any readers who are familiar with my own music will probably be aware that there is a strong desire to interrogate the notion of tradition: increasingly, as it develops into the future (and, necessarily paradoxically, into the past), I see my work engaging creatively and innovatively with the song and music cultures of the country in which I live, Scotland, in all their beauty and variety. This is not born out of any nationalistic feeling – it simply makes sense to me for an artist to make use of the raw materials closest to hand. At times, of course, I want to destroy the past and forge something entirely new. But I know that, for better or worse, I will always be to some extent under the spell of the ancestral voices which move me so – the kinds of Scottish voices which can be heard online now through the School of Scottish Studies's Kist O' Riches website. In some ways, I see in myself (and surely many other Scottish musicians of my generation) an embodiment of what the late, great Hugh MacDiarmid would have called 'the Caledonian Antisyzygy'. Likewise, I am sure Chobo and Michel, in their way, embody the Atlantean Antisyzygy. If you want an explanation for it in my own case, you need look no further than that inherited 70s record collection. □ Alasdair Roberts & Friends' *A Wonder Working Stone* is out this month on Drag City. kistoriches.com

Print Run

New music books: devoured and dissected

Reggae Going International 1967–1976: The Bunny 'Striker' Lee Story
Noel Hawks & Jah Floyd
Jamaican Recordings Hbk 200pp

Edward O'Sullivan 'Bunny' Lee is one of the greatest of Jamaican reggae producers. Born in 1941 and raised in the West Kingston neighbourhood of Greenwich Town, Lee belongs to a sub-generation of producers who emerged in the 1960s. He will likely be most remembered for his hand in developing dub music via his friendship and partnership with King Tubby, but Lee's contributions to Jamaican music are much broader than dub, spanning the years from Jamaican R&B and ska in the early 60s, rocksteady in the late 60s, the roots breakthroughs of the 70s, and onto the dancehall style of the early 80s. Given the enormous amount of music he released during these years, there have occasionally been quality control issues (especially since he hit his creative peak at the same time as versioning became a core practice in Jamaica). But the heights of Lee's output holds a place among the greatest Jamaican music ever produced.

Essentially self-published on the same Jamaican Recordings imprint that has been Lee's main reissue label since the 1990s, this book is not organised as a formal autobiography. Rather, it reads as a loose transcript of casual conversations with ghostwriters Jah Floyd and longtime reggae historian Noel Hawks. The presentation here does not necessarily seem befitting of a man who has created so much important music. But the anecdotal history Lee weaves here remains an organic account of a crucial era of music, and gives an impression of authenticity that can only come from a person who has spent a lot of time around musicians, and who considers them his comrades. Virtually every significant figure in Jamaican music passes through these pages at one time or another. Some receive intimate portraits, while even those mentioned in passing lend colour, personality and texture to the story. This is an account with all the attendant facts, eccentricities and mythologies that only an insider could offer. Who, for example, would have thought that one of the iconic riddims of the roots era (George Faith's "I Forgot to Be Your Lover") is considered cursed, since virtually everyone who sang upon it has since passed away? That Santa Davis's popular flyers (flying cymbal) drum pattern was so-named not because of the soaring filtering effect that it often received courtesy of King Tubby, but because Lee coined the term while eating his favourite dish of chicken wings? Or that the canonical one drop drumming pattern was initially known locally as the cow shit splash, since the musicians thought it sounded similar to the sound of dung hitting the hot pavement after dropping from the behinds of cows that were plentiful in the streets of Kingston at that time?

The Jamaican producers of Lee's generation were similar to multitasking entrepreneurs at the birth of the recording industry everywhere – they essentially operated within a lawless, Wild West business environment in which it was a given that only the strong and cunning prospered. Perched at the top of a highly volatile heap of often cutthroat competitors, producers like Coxsone Dodd and Duke Reid were notorious tough guys with the scars to prove it. Lee had to be equally tough, but he makes a different impression in these pages than the gun-toting Reid or the taciturn Coxsone. Known for his genial grin and ever present sailor's cap, Lee comes across as likeable, mischievous and fun-loving through all the moments of transcendent camaraderie and despicable skullduggery one would expect in such a story. At different times in his career before becoming a producer, he worked as a dancer and a plugger for studios, labels and sound systems. These experiences endowed him with an eye for the latest scam or prank that would get his artist heard, with an ear for catchy riddims, melodies, hooks, and with an instinct for spotting musical mistakes that ended up forming the basis of new styles or sub-styles.

The history of this music took an unexpected and radically transformative turn in the 1970s, once Bob Marley transformed reggae from just another Caribbean island style into a global mega-phenomenon. Lee largely avoids the dark side of the business here, but it was as a result of the destabilising influx of money, crime and politics that he decided to ease himself out of the industry as a frontline producer, and to concentrate instead on recycling his sizeable back catalogue. The world probably lost out on a lot more great music, but in avoiding the madness and politics of the era, Lee has survived to tell his story. With the exception of David Katz's exhaustive biography of Lee Perry (who exists in a category of his own), this is the only biography of a major Jamaican producer and it brings a welcome dose of clarity to the history of one of the world's most influential and profusely creative music cultures.
Michael E Veal

Word Events: Perspectives On Verbal Notation
John Lely & James Saunders (Editors)
Continuum Pbk 488pp

As an anthology of hundreds of important text based scores, or verbal notations, as the book's editors John Lely and James Saunders call them, *Word Events* is a noble achievement. Gathered within its pages are the documents of both widely acclaimed and rarely seen scores, spanning generations of avant garde composition from Erik Satie to Seth Kim-Cohen. For each of the 50 pieces that have been handpicked for closer examination in the book, there are commentaries from the composers, critical examinations by the editors, and historical ephemera from occasions when the texts were realised as performances.

The question of how to exactly define a verbal notation takes up the first large segment of the book. In their introduction, Lely and Saunders state that verbal notation is "an approach to scoring that uses the written word as opposed to symbols, to convey information to whoever chooses to interpret it… it makes associations with other writing genres, such as poetry, rule books, instructions, recipes and koans." For anyone with even a passing knowledge of the postwar history of music or the visual arts, that would be enough of a refresher to be able to follow the kinds of works that make up the book.

Unfortunately, though, before getting to the scores themselves, there is a lengthy chapter that attempts to sift, sort and categorise the various pieces by their grammatical attributes. To say that it is an overly academic system would only partially locate the problem. But grammar! If any quality were to bridge all of the disparate compositions in *Word Events*, it would be a sense of humour. Grammar may be the antithesis of humour. To have 70 pages devoted to picking apart texts by their declarative versus imperative clauses, tense choices, or relational processes seems to truly miss the spirit of playfulness contained in these pieces. Why not parse the scores in another way? Perhaps by whether they feature a drawn circle (Tony Conrad's *1961 Compositions* or Malcolm Goldstein's *wood stone metal skin, with voice*); whether they involve food (Bengt af Klintberg's *Twenty Five Orange Events* or Alison Knowles's *Proposition* (the full score: "Make a salad."); or whether they play with mapping (Takehisa Kosugi's *South No 3* or Mieko Shiomi's wonderful *Spatial Poem No 2*), as some potential would-be categories.

What that long and somewhat pedantic first chapter misses is how strange and clever many of the compiled scores are, regardless of their approach to grammar. For example, from Gavin Bryars's *Far Away And Dimly Pealing*: "Cause sounds to occur at least one mile from the performer. Do not use explosives and do not allow someone else to make the sound for you." Or Ken Friedman's *Mandatory Happening*: "A card printed: 'You will decide to read this score or not to read it.' When you have made your decision, the happening is over." Or any of Yoko Ono's early scores, like *Disappearing Piece*: "Boil water."

The spectre of Fluxus looms large over all this. Nearly a quarter of the featured composers were either foundational members of the group or tangentially related to their joyfully irreverent activities. One could even claim, despite the inclusion of precursors like Satie and Cage in the volume, that word scores are inherently and forever linked to the history of Fluxus. Bearing that in mind, it seems somewhat fitting that, through the book's alphabetical order, La Monte Young gets the final word on the subject with his essay "Why I Withdrew From Fluxus". Responding to why he gave up writing his earlier word pieces, Young claims that music "is an infinitely more complex language with infinitely more elements than languages comprised of words".
Matthew Erickson

Perpetual Frontier: The Properties Of Free Music
Joe Morris
Riti Pbk 179pp

Coming barely a year after Eddie Prévost's book *The First Concert: An Adaptive Appraisal Of A Meta Music*, Joe Morris's *Perpetual Frontier: The Properties Of Free Music* offers another perspective on improvisation and its nature and practice in music – to invoke the title of another great improvisor's primer on his art. It would be easy to presume that these two books are rooted in common concerns. No commercial publisher is likely to show any interest in a volume about free improvisation; no surprise then that both tomes are published as imprints of their authors' own in-house record labels. Being the considered thoughts of musicians most right thinking people would agree have made generous, game-changing contributions to improvised music, both carry natural weight and authority. But beyond agreeing that Wynton Marsalis, and everything about the scene he sustains, is highly questionable, and that he's a bit of a shit, their ways of addressing the subject and the conclusions readers are invited to take away from their books could hardly be more distinct.

Which, frankly, is a good thing. It would have been somewhat disheartening if it transpired that a founder member of AMM, born 1942 in London, a onetime colleague of Cornelius Cardew and Keith Rowe, had cooked up the same recipe for 'good' improvisation as a 50-something American guitarist (and latter day bass player) who has worked with David S Ware, Anthony Braxton, William Parker and Sunny Murray.

And it's not just that Morris equals free jazz, and Prévost is free improv: Morris has collaborated with John Butcher, Barry Guy, Simon H Fell et al, while Prévost regularly plays time alongside his AMM gigs. No, their differences travel to the core of their existence as musicians, telling us something fundamental about the nature of improvised music. At times their vocabularies might fall into uncanny alignment – Morris terms his approach a meta-methodology – but you can't escape the fact that Morris is a schooled musician and proud of it, while Prévost is just as proud to be an autodidact who doesn't read music and is quite happy to discuss whether music is actually the right word for his practice. Morris's goal is to leave his readers with practical guidelines about how to play free music; he wants to lead by example. Prévost's book contains not one word that could be misconstrued as an improvisor's user manual; here are my ideas, he says, ponder them – then what you do with them is up to you.

It wasn't my intention to go on so much about Prévost. *Perpetual Frontier* is a fantastic book that deserves to be assessed on its own terms. But I can't unread *The First Concert*. Better two books than one, especially if their subtle contradictions spell out a wider truth. Morris complains that too much writing about free music quickly collapses into well-meaning soundbites about spirituality; that there's an abundance of writing about why, where and when, but not enough about how free music operates. In his definition, free music grows from his idea that "jazz hails its innovators of the past while it suppresses its innovators in the present". Jazz, he argues, has become a creatively restrictive and meaningless label. "Instead of forcing (a new definition) to fit within the now-restrictive confines of jazz, it is better to give it a new name that clarifies its uniqueness… This book proposes that it be called free music."

One myth is scotched from the get-go. Freedom does not equate to playing without intention (on the contrary, Morris states, music that draws on non-intention has to do so intentionally). Moreover, he continues, "free music is not music that is free of deliberate content or structure". On that premise he pulls apart the parameters of free playing. Chapters heading up approach, platform, melodic structure, pulse, interaction and form begin, at first, to look worryingly like a conservatoire textbook. But Morris tells it as he sees it. "Attempting to perform a random improvisation is in fact a formal technique. It is always done with a degree of preparation. And the history… is detailed enough to show consistency in the methods used." You can only be truly free through understanding the history and technical nuts and bolts of these methodologies; then you can construct your music from whatever materials feel appropriate. Morris tests these theories against Cecil Taylor's Unit Structures (as technique rather than album title), Ornette Coleman's Harmolodics, Anthony Braxton's Tri-Axiom Theory; and it is refreshing to read about these cornerstones refracted through a musician's mind.

If Prévost's buzz words for how improvisation's great learning works are dialogical and heuristic, Morris prefers synthesis, interpretation and invention. As an extended coda, Morris asks 15 improvisors including Alex Ward, Mary Halvorson, William Parker, Joe McPhee, Matthew Shipp and Ken Vandermark, to assess their own work against the methodologies he outlines. And he gets back 15 radically different perspectives on those whys and hows, like Ward telling us "Spiritually – I do not personally have an understanding of this concept", while William Parker implies that music is his hotline to God. Saxophonist Jack Wright prefers not to list any musicians who inspired him ("I constructed my own discipline and put myself to work with a heavy practice schedule," he says), as opposed to pianist Jamie Saft, who lists all points between Dylan and Nono. The more books that try to nail free Improv, the more questions are generated. That sounds about right: freedom's perpetual frontier. □

Brad Harris

Nothing is free: Joe Morris

A how-to handbook for free music by guitarist **Joe Morris** offers radical questions rather than easy answers. By **Philip Clark**

The Wire bookshop

An online store dealing in selected specialist music and art books. Many of the books stocked in the shop have been signed by the authors (many of whom are regular contributors to *The Wire*). All subscribers to the magazine get special discounts on all titles in the shop

For details of prices, signed copies and how to order, go to thewire.co.uk/shop

Erewhon Calling: Experimental Sound In New Zealand
Bruce Russell (Ed)
Audio Foundation/CMR Pbk 192pp

Berlin Sampler: From Cabaret To Techno: 1904–2012
Théo Lessour
Ollendorff Verlag Berlin Pbk 365pp

Dan Graham: Rock My Religion
Kodwo Eshun
Afterall Books, Pbk 112pp

Electric Eden: Unearthing Britain's Visionary Music
Rob Young
Faber and Faber 664pp

No Regrets: Writings On Scott Walker
Rob Young (Ed)
Orion Hbk 278pp

Source: Music Of The Avant-Garde, 1966–1973
Larry Austin & Douglas Kahn (Eds)
University of California Press Pbk 384pp

Sonic Warfare: Sound, Affect And The Ecology Of Fear
Steve Goodman
MIT Press Pbk 270pp

Trip Or Squeek's Big Amplifier
Savage Pencil
Strange Attractor Press Pbk 272pp + set of four Trip Or Squeek postcards

The Wire Primers: A Guide To Modern Music
Rob Young (Ed)
Verso Pbk 198pp

Luigi Russolo, Futurist: Noise, Visual Arts And The Occult
Luciano Chessa
University of California Press Pbk 288pp

Sounds From Dangerous Places
Peter Cusack
ReR Megacorp/DAAD Hbk 80pp + 2CD

Special Sound: The Creation And Legacy Of The BBC Radiophonic Workshop
Louis Niebur
OUP Pbk 260pp

On Screen

Films & DVDs

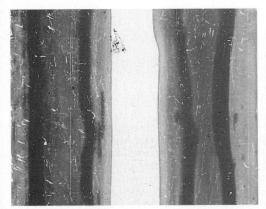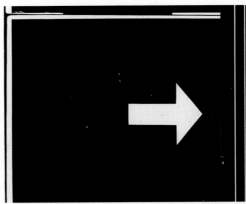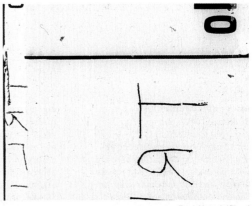

From *Materialfilme I*

W+B Hein
Materialfilme
Edition Filmmuseum DVD 2012, 130 mins

Wilhelm and Birgit Hein's creative partnership began in 1966 and lasted for 22 years, the first 11 of which they spent working exclusively in film. *Materialfilme* rescues five key works from the more than 30 they created in this period, when their output was as prolific as it was explosive. The Heins were very active in this era, operating as curators, projectionists and installation artists, but four decades on, their films are very rarely screened and almost forgotten outside their native Germany. As this typically meticulous Edition Filmmuseum retrospective makes clear, their films are just as strong as those of their peers in Europe and the US, many of whom enjoy a superior profile and critical reputation.

In his lucid and perceptive booklet essay, Marc Siegel outlines the Heins' formal concerns and their encounters with mid-60s avant garde film, in particular the then dominant strain of structuralism, which proceeded from the idea that a film's form was just as important as the images it contained. Structuralist films analysed their own means of production in an attempt to disrupt the dominant narratives and ideologies of industrialised commercial cinema. Hence Malcolm Le Grice's *Little Dog For Roger* (1967), whose content was comparable to Owen Land's accurately titled *Film In Which There Appear Edge Lettering, Sprocket Holes, Dirt Particles, Etc* (1965–66).

Like the structuralists, the Heins were fascinated with the physical and material qualities of film – which explains their notion of material film, not to be confused with materialist film, as theorised by Peter Gidal. They combined this with a visceral intensity and a confrontational stance inherited from Austrian film makers Peter Kubelka, Ernst Schmidt Jr, Hans Scheugl, and particularly the landmark early 60s works of Kurt Kren, with whom they maintained a long friendship. Along with their use of sound and their emphasis on duration, these are the characteristics which set them apart from their contemporaries.

Rohfilm (1968) is an extraordinary retina-assaulting barrage which runs for a draining 20 minutes. Its method of construction illustrates the Heins' interest in the process of reproduction – how our perception of imagery is altered when it is filmed, photographed or projected – and their desire to complicate it. Image fragments, perforated tape, dirt, hair, ashes and sprocket holes were glued on to clear film, which was then repeatedly projected and rephotographed, disintegrating further throughout the process. The soundtrack, by Birgit's brother Christian Michelis, was intended to be asynchronous with the images, but its electronic cut-ups and swingeing noise frequencies suit it well. Certain images recur occasionally, but the film's structure remains pointedly random, with any possibility of narrative strictly denied.

The 28 minute *Reproductions* (1968) makes a similar point more gently. Images from holidays abroad were cut into strips, hand-manipulated and projected on a Movieola, then filmed. Interpretation is repeatedly thwarted as fragments of photos flash by, blur, cut to black or jump in and out of focus and view. The soundtrack offers prickly, trebly static. *625* (1969) is pure abstraction, a film of television footage shot with a 16 mm Bolex camera. The two devices' different scanning frequencies produce a roll bar, which the Heins modulated further by varying shooting speed and processing the film in negative. The result is blizzard-like textures of visual static, oscillating in random, high-speed rhythms. Its 34 minute duration is deliberately overlong, a none too subtle challenge to their audience's patience.

Materialfilme I and *II* (both 1976) comprise header and footer offcuts from commercial films, collected by the Heins during their projectionist stints. The first is a delirious, mesmeric collage; the second is slower moving, with more static vertical banding and colour washes. They predate Morgan Fisher's better known *Standard Gauge*, made using the same technique, by several years. Edition Filmmuseum have commissioned new soundtracks for both, an unnecessary move given that Michelis's are perfectly good. The selected artists add little, if anything: Starving Weirdos predictably turn in dopey communal dirges and drones; Tim & John Blue's contributions are tastefully dull; Roel Meelkop's efforts are either too literally related to or too disconnected from the images they accompany; and while Sister Iodine's fizzing distortion and feedback capture the films' starkness, they bypass their playfulness and humour altogether.
Nick Cain

Searching For Sugar Man
Malik Bendjelloul (Director)
Studio Canal DVD 2012, 85 mins

The unexpected rise to world fame of cult late 1960s Mexican-American singer-songwriter Sixto Diaz Rodriguez (aka Rodriguez) was surely one of 2012's most endearing comeback stories. With an ongoing UK tour and everybody from Jools Holland to political pundit Andrew Marr eager to have him as a guest on their weekly television slots, the Rodriguez phenomenon shows no signs of slowing down just yet.

If you have yet to experience the man and his music, Swiss director Malik Bendjelloul's documentary *Searching For Sugar Man* is the perfect primer. It successfully tells Rodriguez's story through those who were initially attracted to his soulful songs and their socio-political messages. This melodic protest song approach formed the core of the material he recorded for his albums *Cold Fact* (1970) and *Coming From Reality* (1971), which were originally released (and swiftly deleted) by independent label Sussex Records. To make matters worse, his musical career was terminated after a rumour that Rodriguez had committed suicide by setting himself on fire on stage. In reality, however, it seems he had simply decided to walk away from the music business and concentrate on bringing up his family, settling in Detroit, Michigan – where he lives to this day.

Rodriguez's resurrection came about when he was finally tracked down by two South African fans who had discovered his music via a bootleg that had found its way into their country. Over the next two decades, this recording caused a cultural and political sensation, with the right wing apartheid government of the time desperately trying to suppress certain songs from broadcast. The dividing line between state censorship and fan worship are tellingly recounted, with footage showing a deliberately scratched-out radio station copy of *Cold Fact* and, further along, a tattoo of the cover image on the arm of a devoted Rodriguez admirer. Eventually both albums were released on CD in South Africa and the singer was persuaded to tour in 1998, when he was met with the kind of enthusiasm usually reserved for rock legends. This story of the rediscovery of a seemingly lost musician invites echoes of John Fahey and Al Wilson's search for blues legend Skip James, while Rodriguez's eventual landing in the country that adopted him and his music has flashes of the European exodus that American free jazz musicians made in the early 70s and the similar welcome reception they received.

Watching Rodriguez perform after decades of isolation, one is also reminded of Jandek's first live performances, where an otherwise secretive, unattainable cult figure was suddenly invoked to appear onstage in front of an enthralled live audience who couldn't believe what they were witnessing. Bendjelloul's joyful film is brimming with such moments of excitement and renewed hope, and gently reminds us about the powerful, enduring and universally healing force of music that connects.
Edwin Pouncey

On Site

Exhibitions, performance art, installations, etc

Mark Peter Wright
30 Minutes Of Listening
IMT Gallery, London, UK

Mark Peter Wright's installation at London's IMT Gallery is composed around field recordings of South Gare, an area of reclaimed land and breakwater along England's north east coast. This manmade jetty offers a safe harbour from the sea, and is used to transport materials to and from a nearby steelworks. Its historical and ecological distinctiveness lends a fascinating location to Wright's phonographic project, which also looks back to Land Art.

In the main gallery space, a video recording of South Gare circles round and round, compressing a dusk to dawn cycle into a 30 minute loop. The curved gallery wall echoes the circling motion of the projection, and a small round mirror at the back, with words engraved on it, completes the loop. These words – "Herring Gull", "Seaweed", "Swallow", "Boat", "Engine", etc – reflect the movement of the image, and the objects they signify can be heard on the soundtrack.

In another room, a split-screen video shows Wright's torso, filmed both on site in South Gare and in the gallery space, hitting together two slag stones taken from the jetty. The same stones sit silently on a little white shelf. This sounds out not only the stones as objects, but also their dual presence at IMT and at South Gare.

The focus here is not so much on the authenticity of the sounds' source, but on emphasising Wright's commitment to observation and recording as acts in themselves. It is this committed listening which merges his composition of South Gare with the contingent soundscape here on Cambridge Heath Road. Wright challenges listeners to think about the distinctiveness of South Gare from the specificity of their own location: not only, as in Land Art, to contemplate the actual site – its historical, geological and economic reality – but

to generate this aesthetic and political consequence in the gallery: uprooting the work from the landscape by highlighting the place of its encounter.

Every detail of Wright's work is sincere; there is a fervent desire to persuade us of its worth – not its value as a piece of art but as an endeavour, a thing to do and know the world by. This impression is confirmed in the back room of the gallery, where, on an A4 sheet of paper, he gives us instructions on how to do a 30 minute listening to our own surroundings. It is a call to a kind of musica practica of field recording, an invitation to share in Wright's sincerity.

Salomé Voegelin

There's no place like *The Zone*: still from People Like Us's latest video work

People Like Us
The Zone
The Arnolfini, Bristol, UK

The Zone is Vicki Bennett's (aka People Like Us) first feature-length video collage work. Tonight is its premiere in the Arnolfini's Auditorium, a theatre-cum-installation space with a small rack of seating. The idea behind *The Zone* is simple: a split-screen work where Tarkovsky's *Stalker* and *The Wizard Of Oz* are played side by side from start to finish. Both pivot around a moment in each film when the action turns from black and white into colour, and Bennett hooks them together at this moment (upon entering the psychically disturbed Zone in *Stalker*, and the Land of Oz in *The Wizard Of Oz*), editing outwards from this point.

At moments, one narrative absorbs the other. Stalker (the guide who takes the characters of the Writer and the Professor into the Zone to visit the wish-granting Room) is sleeping with his family, three to a bed, as Dorothy's first rendition of "Over The Rainbow" plays out. The two sequences merge into one story, and Dorothy becomes their dream – a far cry from Stalker's dank room and threadbare sheets.

At times the syncs are so potent it's as if one film has suddenly become aware of the other's presence. As a parade of Oz drones troop into the Emerald City, Stalker says: "Oh God, what people... They've got empty eyes." While the Oz gang are being spruced up to meet the wizard, the Writer asks direct to camera: "Are they ready for it?"

The sound of both films is played in tandem too, at the same volume. Far from being cacophonous, the ominous silences and hollow clunks in *Stalker* impose themselves on the relentless chirruping singalongs in *The Wizard Of Oz*, dulling their sparkle to something bearable.

From the two films emerges a third narrative. Nobody has any evidence for the existence or nature of either the Room or the wizard. In both, our characters must make a Kierkegaardian blind leap to faith: to believe without rationale or reason. In *Stalker*, the characters decide not to enter the Room – they cannot make the leap. In Oz, the blind faith of Dorothy, the Lion, Tin Man and the Scarecrow means all their wishes come true. As *The Zone* progresses,

Dorothy's and Stalker's paths cross: they share their darkest moment weeping, but at the point where Stalker loses all hope, Dorothy is restored.

The Zone relies on a simple idea which it transcends to become more than the sum of its parts. At the close of the film, Stalker's wife's monologue runs together with the saccharine strings of "Over The Rainbow". She says: "It is better to have bitter happiness, than a grey dull life." But Dorothy has just accepted the opposite, that "there's no place like home" – home being life in black and white. We're asked a direct question by Bennett's editing here: when the credits roll, who's better off?

Jennifer Lucy Allan

On Location

Live and kicking: festivals, concerts, events in the flesh

Hair metal: Stian Westerhus

Living space: Body/Head's stage set-up

Supersonic

Custard Factory, Birmingham, UK

Without typecasting Capsule's Supersonic festival, this year celebrating its tenth birthday, it's reasonable to point out that scuzz, grind, boom, bleed and whine are its dominant aural properties. Fortunately, the abandoned warehouse scene in Birmingham's industrial zone of Digbeth allows an unselfconscious devotion to volume abuse. But Supersonic's finer points lie in its dynamics: the passages of low activity that often frame or shape the coming eruptions. As well as this, the weekend's multiple sonic orgies are made possible by expert punctuality, creating wild abandonment within a strong organisational framework.

Friday night belongs to local Birmingham evergreens Modified Toy Orchestra, followed by Justin Broadrick's incarnation as JK Flesh, which gives equal rights to guitar and laptop. The climax of the evening arrives with local drum 'n' bass duo PCM, who ram home the low end in a way that feels absolutely undiluted, no digressions or distractions allowed. In contrast, The Bug's set the following night is too teasing. The speed-ragga eruptions are frequently subjected to rewinds, repeatedly interrupting the bass momentum in favour of digressions from MCs Daddy Freddy, Miss Red and Flow Dan.

The adjoining solo guitar sets by Stian Westerhus and Sir Richard Bishop at the start of Saturday afternoon are similarly oppositional. The Norwegian Westerhus emphasises a one-toned sludge density, avoiding the beyond-guitar transparency and bowed textures of his recorded work. Immediately afterwards, Bishop plays as if it's his final appearance, enthralling the silenced gathering with flaring Arabic-tinged blues arpeggios, shot out in compact spirals. There's some canny capitalising on the day's players, as Bishop joins Rangda, whose drummer Chris Corsano also plays in a duo with Michael Flower. Rangda's other member, Ben Chasny, then leads his own Six Organs Of Admittance.

It's the Japanese contingent who ultimately make the deepest cuts during the weekend. On Saturday, Merzbow immolates the Boxxed stage with an unremitting onslaught of laptop processed guitar (occasionally bowed), with the help of Oxbow's Eugene Robinson and Niko Wenner. Later, KK Null and Tatsuya Yoshida appear as Zeni Geva, then separately solo on Sunday. Together, they make no concession to space. Their sound has a hard density, their gruff vocals grinding together and bass-flooded guitar riffs and scattershot drums interlocking intimately .

When Yoshida plays as Ruins Alone, he's drumming and singing, triggering keyboard stutters, and in the process delivers the most intricate, consistently surprising music of the weekend. Your reviewer customarily shuns earplugs, and Yoshida's vocals provide the festival's sole instance of overly trebly eardrum-rattling distortion as he shoots his perfectly timed lines.

KK Null's solo set reveals his feel for environmental electronics. He paints layers of rough, granular wind tunnel sound, which steadily amasses into total coverage. This eventually gives way to the second phase of his set: a collaboration with Birmingham tuba duo Ore. Null powers down, then rears up again out of Sam Underwood and Stuart Estell's sustained interchange of drone tones. Clifford Torus are one of the few non-Japanese acts to deliver precision heaviness. A Norwegian trio featuring members of MoHa! and Noxagt, they are less concerned with sonic strafing and more attached to complex and angular riffs.

Hype Williams typically obscure themselves with floods of dry ice and pulsing strobes, sidestepping stage presence in favour of a nameless sonic impact, although tonight they are joined on stage by the silhouetted figure of a woman on a motorcycle, who remains almost static throughout the set. They might have stolen the visual thunder from the next day's Lash Frenzy performance, which uses even more extreme mist/strobe effects, but the latter is such a powerful spectacle that the similarity doesn't matter. Lash Frenzy, led by artist Andrew Moscardo-Parker, are virtually invisible onstage, but my corner of the room has its own explosive drummer, hinting at similarly placed players across the other side of the space. A string section is devoted to the common drone. Spotlights are manually hoisted. A topless woman emerges from the clouds and the tumult roars higher and louder.

The Oxbow Orchestra are doubtless intended as Supersonic's climax, but their core songs don't have sufficient substance to warrant the elaborate surrounding arrangements. The real peak arrives just before Oxbow's set, with Body/Head, a pairing of Kim Gordon and Bill Nace. The latter is very much an accompanying guitarist, in terms of both his much lower volume and his generally subtle colourations. It's mostly Gordon's display, and she gives a performance of anguished intensity, her cranked-up, fragmentedly emphatic guitar matching her possessed vocals, as she stalks the stage, flailing her axe, then lies supine on the amplifier stack.

Martin Longley

Tusk

Star & Shadow Cinema, Newcastle upon Tyne, UK

As Newcastle's Tusk Festival opens for its final day, the appearance of a Javanese gamelan set on the stage of the Star & Shadow is exotic, but not exactly incongruous, even if the gleaming bells and gongs almost dwarf the amplifier stacks in the small, volunteer-run space. This highly formal East Asian music became raw material for Western experimentalists throughout the 20th century, inspiring John Cage's prepared piano pieces and John Fahey's sound collages. Today's performance by members of Pelt and Part Wild Horses Mane On Both Sides recalls 1970s and 80s collectives like the New York based Gamelan Son Of Lion or the more anarchic Bow Gamelan, bashing homemade instruments on a tributary of the Thames, who saw in gamelan ensembles a model of democratic music making. Pelt and Part Wild Horses approach improvisation with a non-idiomatic, almost ritualistic attitude, drawing on ethnic musics, Noise and, in Pelt's case, American Primitivism. It's easy to see how both groups are drawn to the sonic and social aspects of gamelan, and thus how these ornate instruments have found their way into a three-day festival that also takes in Noise, drones, psychedelic folk, mutant Acid, Sacred Harp singing, instrument building and contrasting takes on avant rock.

The brightly lit lunchtime set is hypnotic to watch as well as listen to. The musicians work their way around the stage with quiet deliberation, tapping and stroking as if carrying out research on the singing bowls, bar percussion and huge gongs of almost a metre in diameter. It is as if we are discovering the instruments' properties at the same time as the ensemble, although this charmed spontaneity is also a prosaic result of their having had minimal time to explore the gear. This kind of live workshopping doesn't feel odd at Tusk, an experimental festival in the sense that you can try things out here and people will listen. Part Wild Horses take advantage of this in their early Friday evening slot with a set full of charged silences amid bursts of noise from Pascal Nichols's drums and flautist Kelly Jones's basic electronics set-up, from which sampled voices clamour. The duo end their set at the side of the stage, moulding bowls out of clay. The audience's response to this silent coda is benignly curious, an openness that continues into the next set by guitarist/synth player Stian Skagen as a disruption in the crowd – a dancer with a suitcase unpacking masks, maps and a protective paper suit – turns out to be his collaborator, performance artist Erikk McKenzie.

Pelt's Patrick Best starts on the floor too, pounding on a battered upright piano before switching to harmonium. Best, Nathan Bowles (on banjo) and violinist Mike Gangloff attack instruments associated with ragas and folk with the white-hot, gritty zeal that has always made Pelt's recordings far more than blissed-out drone escapism, and live, the intensity wrested from their acoustic sources seems to warm the small room, as does the presence of Gangloff's young son on sruti box. Their set, like many of the

weekend, builds slowly – unusually for a festival, no one seems hurried, despite a packed bill with little time between shows.

On the Friday and Sunday, this makes for evenings full of gradual developments and intense, often surprising denouements. After a long instrumental build, Desert Heat guitarist Steve Gunn pulls out an ecstatic cover of The Velvet Underground's "Oh! Sweet Nothing"; Hild-Sofie Tafjord's horn and laptop set grows from polite electroacoustics into an overpowering mist of breath and synthesis; and Hieroglyphic Being's meandering, sub-aqueous House brings Friday night to a slow close, winding down rather than igniting a dancefloor.

Saturday's harder, noisier line-up makes this intensity claustrophobic at times, not least because all acts are confined to one packed 200-capacity room that also contains a bar. After Pain Jerk's ear-splitting amplified and processed spring reverb and Kouhei Matsunaga's brutally upbeat loops, it is hard to sink into Michael Morley's drifting guitar feedback, not least because it sounds as if Matsunaga has blown out one side of the PA. It's a relief to trek over the motorway bridge into the city centre for Hieroglyphic Being's disco-inflected DJ set, which takes place in an office building repurposed as art studios.

The Star & Shadow's cinema room screens music films every day, including a rare 1995 Dead C live video and Harry Smith's animations accompanied live by Rhodri Davies. On Sunday afternoon, I skip the films in favour of a Sacred Harp singing workshop above a nearby pub, which goes so well that leaders Phil Tyler and Vicky Langan present us as impromptu openers for local acid rock group Lobster Priest. Although this direct hit of participatory performance is unusual, most musicians are seen happily mingling with the audience throughout the weekend. But Keiji Haino and his group Fushitsusha have been glimpsed only rarely, and anticipation for their headline set builds through one of the day's clear highlights, a quietly confrontational exposition of how to do live DIY musique concrète by Graham Lambkin and Jason Lescalleet in which it feels as if every surface in the room is amplified and resonant, *Stone Tape*-style.

I find a relatively calm spot to the side of Haino's Hi-Watts, initially distracted by the guitarist's roadies, two young men who attempt to impose a photography ban in between changing strings and adjusting Haino's mic. But the set's first searing half hour, before it slows into sludgier long-form workouts, quashes any cynicism. Haino's choreographed un-riffs and anti-grooves do not let up, settle down, or allow for easy immersion, while bassist Futoshi Kamekawa and drummer Ryosuke Kiyasu invert group logic as they follow his rhythmic lead. The audience surges with the sound as if blissfully breaking through multiple pain barriers, and it becomes clear that this chaos is many people's organising principle, its untogether togetherness offering a communality as deeply felt as that offered by gamelan playing or Sacred Harp singing or Hieroglyphic Being's after-party.
Frances Morgan

Monkeying around: Stian Skagen (left) and Erikk McKenzie

Drone zone: Pelt's Tycho Gangloff (left) and Patrick Best

Alex Woodward

Lee Gamble + Hieroglyphic Being
Shacklewell Arms, London, UK

With his new 12" for Pan, *Diversions 1994–96*, Lee Gamble has stepped away from the mangled electroacoustic compositions of previous releases into a blurry and collapsed sound suggestive of slow decay. Sourced entirely from Jungle cassette mixtapes from that period, its largely beatless murk evokes both the sensory immediacy of the dancefloor and its swift fading from memory into a series of vague impressions.

His rather brief performance this evening matches those themes well: it flickers abruptly between energy levels, each shift quickly erasing that which came before. As a result, the set arrives as an ongoing stream of heightened moments, each grasping for full attention. It opens in a beatless quagmire, with rave synth stabs casting backwards through UK dance music in much the same way as the dilapidated gloom of V/VM's *The Death Of Rave*. Heartbeats eventually begin to throb through the mix, ruffling its placid surfaces, before coalescing into a sustained four-to-the-floor pulse. Similar patterns repeat several times during the set, before each time being abruptly shredded by some form of interference: salvoes of bleeps that percolate loudly upward through the mix, destabilising the overriding rhythm, or sudden cuts to extremely tense periods of near-silence.

Jamal Moss, aka Hieroglyphic Being, who follows Gamble's set, might ostensibly sound very different and reflect a separate lineage, but the two are linked by a common use of space and noise to hack away at club music's edges. Early in his set, Moss plays two copies of what appears to be the same record – an Acidic jack track that crunches roughly from the speakers – simultaneously. Flicking from deck to deck, he increases the tempo of each in turn, producing a stepwise escalation that weaves in and out of phase with itself, ratcheting up the intensity to a screaming crescendo. Blisteringly raw House tracks collide with analogue electronic scree suggesting collapsing architecture. Disco tracks cut in abruptly at a tempo several bpm lower or higher than the common pulse of the mix, repeatedly shaking a shrinking number of dancers out of their attempts to fall into reverie. The attitude – DJing as a means of shocking the nervous system into confronting what it's experiencing – isn't far at all from Gamble's, whether in the spiky contours of his performance tonight, the abrasive fizz of earlier records like 2009's *Join Extensions*, or the more smoothly defined curves of his current Pan output.
Rory Gibb

Death Grips
Electric Ballroom, London, UK

This London appearance by Death Grips comes with a whiff of good old fashioned rock 'n' roll swindle. Following their freely distributed 2011 mixtape *Exmilitary*, the Sacramento hiphop trio signed a deal with Epic Records and released *The Money Store*, the first of two major label releases scheduled for 2012. But when Epic decided to push the follow-up *No Love Deep Web* back to 2013, Death Grips leaked the completed album for free on Soundcloud and torrent sites last October, with a cover image depicting the album title sharpied on an erect penis. Then, to add insult to injury, they posted the label's cease-and-desist letters on their Facebook page.

It's almost enough to make you feel sorry for major labels, although Epic must have suspected they were little more than a prick to kick against. A spirit of nonconformity runs like wiring through Death Grips' music, paranoia and violence deployed reflexively, like coping mechanisms. In the best song of the night, "I've Seen Footage" – a brutal détournement of 1980s party rap such as Salt N Pepa's "Push It", retooled with squealing sirens and distorted synths – the group's lone rapper, Stefan 'MC Ride' Burnett, articulates his psychosis: "*I stay noided, stimulation overload account for it/Desensitised by the mass amounts of shit*".

Glutted on culture Death Grips may be, but there's plainly care in the way they assemble it. Memphis Slim's raw, carnal "Grinder Man Blues" plays over the PA as a quixotic stage set-up is constructed, a mix of the jerry-rigged and the ultramodern: Zach Hill's drum kit is honed down to kick drum and twin snare, while visuals appear on a pair of large iMac monitors secured on their side. Hill and Burnett strip to the waist as they take to the stage, and the rapper writhes his muscular, tattooed torso in snakelike fashion as "Come Up And Get Me" commences with waves of undulating, saturated low end. The screens flash up images: flames, a boxing match, bare male buttocks. The group's third member, producer Andy Morin, aka Flatlander, is either parked out of view or, more likely, absent altogether.

Sonically, too, it's an assault: a seldom relenting barrage of strobe-speed rhythms, bass throbs, the gunfire rattle of Hill's live drums. Ride's vocal flips between hoarse raps and the staccato bark of a red-faced drill sergeant. There are antecedents to Death Grips' sound towards the weirder end of Def Jux's catalogue, and in the hyperspeed rhythms of trap rap or Footwork, although another touchstone is the testosterone-fired rock/rap fusions of Nu Metal (no giant leap: while best known for his role in math rockers Hella, drummer Zach Hill has also served time in Deftones frontman Chino Moreno's Team Sleep project). "No Love", in particular, feels paced to kick off a circle pit, Ride threatening to show "the proper meaning of a beatdown" over sick-sounding drones.

For those attracted to hiphop by dexterity of flow or a cleverly-spun sample, Death Grips' sustained battery may have a deadening effect. In places, they're not even playing their trump cards well. Hill's hyper-complex drumming seldom leads the rhythm, instead sitting inside a framework of stiff electronic beats; he's not quite redundant, but the group as a whole would benefit from giving him a more leading role. The machismo, meanwhile, can leave a sour taste. Towards the end of the set, Miss Red, MC for Death Grips' support act The Bug, shimmies out from the wings, only for Burnett to shove her back to the side of the stage. But for all about them that jars, something in Death Grips' frenetic perseverance remains compelling. They're sensation junkies, always searching for the next, biggest hit. If authenticity means anything these days, we could say it's the state of truly living one's condition; and in that respect, Death Grips appear to be really *really* real.
Louis Pattison

Rip it up: Death Grips' Stefan Burnett

Kemar Reid

Specialist music, radio-art and sonic experimentation on Resonance104.4fm

Monday, 5pm: Artrocker, with Paul Cox
Monday, 10pm: Luscombe's Choice, with Will Luscombe
Monday, 11pm: Soundsoup, with Joel Cahen
Tuesday, 1pm: The Nest Collective Hour, with Sam Lee
Tuesday, 3pm: Isotopica, with Simon Tyszko
Tuesday, 5.30pm: A Colder Consciousness, with Flora Pitrolo
Tuesday, 9.30pm: Wolf Fifth, with Luuk de Weert
Tuesday, 11.00pm: Abject Block, with Tim Goldie & John Wild
Tuesday, midnight: Is Black Music, with Art Terry
Wednesday, 2pm: Late Lunch with Out To Lunch, with Ben Watson
Wednesday, 4pm: Bonanza & Son, with Martyn Myers
Wednesday, 6.30pm: World City Live, with Cultural Co-Operation
Wednesday, 10pm: The Cafe Oto Show, with Clair Urbahn
Wednesday, 11pm: 50/50 Sound System
Thursday, noon: Counter Culture Radio, with Rough Trade Shops
Thursday, 2pm: The Traditional Music Hour, with Reg Hall
& Kevin Sheils
Thursday, 4pm: The Opera Hour, with Richard Scott
Thursday, 5pm: Pull The Plug, with Johnny Seven
Thursday, 9pm: Adventures in Sound & Music, with The Wire
Thursday, 11pm: Bermuda Triangle Test Transmissions

Friday, 2pm: Sound Out, with Carole Finer
Friday, 3pm: Wavelength, with William English
Friday, 5.30pm: The Sound Projector, with Ed Pinsent
Friday, 9pm: The Exotic Pylon, with Johnny Mugwump
Friday, 10.30pm: (...) Such a Nice Radio Show,
with Band of Holy Joy
Friday at 1.30pm: Flomotion, with Nick Luscombe
Saturday, 6.30pm: This Music Wins, with Peter Lanceley
Saturday at 8.30pm: Sound Check, with James Hodder
Saturday 9pm: Sine of the Times, with Rita Maia
Saturday, 11pm: Free Lab Radio, with Fari Bradley
Saturday, midnight: Sicknotes, with Arthur Bently, Michael
Colvill & Veronica Zubic-Nahvi.
Sunday, 12noon: House Rent Boogie, with Nikki Brooks
Sunday, 1pm: Latin Waves, with Javier Chandia
Sunday, 10pm: Drones of Hell, with Ray Kirby
Sunday, 11pm: framework, with Patrick McGinley
Visit http://resonancefm.com/schedule

Registered charity 290236
(London Musician's Collective Ltd)
With thanks to all our Friends
and individual donors

WIRE
thewire.co.uk

ARTS COUNCIL
ENGLAND

Contact us:
Resonance104.4fm
144 Borough High Street
London SE1 1LB, U.K.
info@resonancefm.com

ADELAIDE ◆ FESTIVAL

1–17 March 2013

DEERHOOF
SEVERED HEADS
DOVEMAN LUSTMORD
BUKE AND GASE ACTRESS
VAN DYKE PARKS WITH
GUESTS INC. DANIEL JOHNS
BRYCE DESSNER (THE NATIONAL)
THIS IS THE KIT JHEREK BISCHOFF
NEIL FINN PAUL KELLY
GLEN HANSARD ARCHIE ROACH
LAURIE ANDERSON & KRONOS QUARTET

JG THIRLWELL'S MANOREXIA ATOM™
CLOGS (FEAT. PADMA NEWSOME) GORAN BREGOVIĆ DEMDIKE STARE
SOLARIS (BEN FROST WITH VISUALS BY BRIAN ENO) ROBIN FOX POLE
TIM HECKER & DANIEL LOPATIN (AKA ONEOHTRIX POINT NEVER) BEN FROST
TRINITY (BIOSPHERE, LUSTMORD & MFO) THE CARETAKER/V/VM

ADELAIDEFESTIVAL.COM.AU

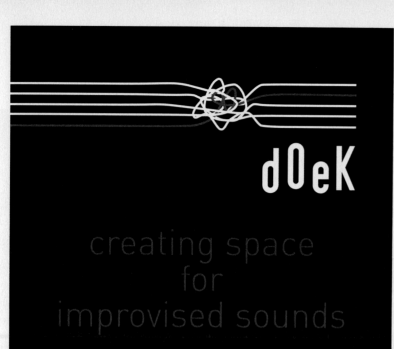

dOeK

creating space
for
improvised sounds

Catch them at dOeK Festival #11
1 - 5 May 2013 • Amsterdam

www.doek.org

ANIMAL COLLECTIVE
BAT FOR LASHES
CHARLIE BOYER
& THE VOYEURS
CHVRCHES
DAPHNI
DAUGHTER
DISCLOSURE
DO MAKE SAY THINK
EMERALDS
EVERYTHING EVERYTHING
FOUR TET
FRANCOIS & THE
ATLAS MOUNTAINS
FUCKED UP
GINGER BAKER
JAZZ CONFUSION
HESSLE AUDIO DJS:
BEN UFO
PANGAEA
PEARSON SOUND
HOW TO DRESS WELL
JACQUES GREENE
JAMES YORKSTON
JULIO BASHMORE
KARENN
MULATU ASTATKE
(ETHIOPIQUES)
THOMAS MAPFUMO
TIM BURGESS
TNGHT
VIRALS
VONDELPARK

25-05-13
VICTORIA PARK
LONDON E3

fielddayfestivals.com
 fielddaylondon   ticketweb.co.uk
 @fielddaylondon   seetickets.com

FIELD DAY

entertainist.net

LATEST DOCUMENTARIES:
**Field Day / James Holden / Kieran Hebden / Pond /
Alexander Robotnick / Magic Waves / The Hacker / Legowelt /
Richard Sen (Padded Cell)**
London's only indie flyer pack.
Delivering top quality service to the venues, independent record labels, festivals
and promoters. Most on it detailed music and club events listings. Exclusive DJ
mixes and video interviews.

EAT YOUR OWN EARS PRESENTS

STEALING SHEEP
SPECIAL GUESTS
BUSH HALL
Monday 10 December

VERITY SUSMAN
SPECIAL GUESTS
ELECTROWERKZ
Thursday 24 January

ROCKET NUMBER NINE
SPECIAL GUESTS
ELECTROWERKZ
Wednesday 20 February

SAVAGES
SPECIAL GUESTS
ELECTRIC BALLROOM
Thursday 21 February

ESBEN & THE WITCH
PLANNINGTOROCK
THE SCALA
Tuesday 26 February

FOUR TET
SPECIAL GUESTS
HEAVEN
Thursday 28 February — SOLD OUT

EGYPTIAN HIP HOP
SPECIAL GUESTS
XOYO Monday 04 March

THE SEA AND CAKE
SPECIAL GUESTS
THE SCALA Wednesday 6 March

SEAMS
SPECIAL GUESTS
ELECTROWERKZ
Thursday 21 March

seetickets.com ticketweb.co.uk eatyourownears.com   lost.fm

THE GOLDEN AGE

CTM.13

FESTIVAL FOR ADVENTUROUS MUSIC & ART
28.1.–3.2.2013 BERLIN

MATMOS → DIAMOND VERSION & ATSUHIRO ITO → MYRNINEREST → ꝏ UZ ꝏ → SKREAM FEAT. SGT POKES
SIMIAN MOBILE DISCO → FLORIAN HECKER → KEITH FULLERTON WHITMAN → EMPTYSET & JOANIE LEMERCIER
TERRE THAEMLITZ → D'EON → ATOM™ → DEMDIKE STARE → MARK FELL → PETE SWANSON → GATEKEEPER
ERNSTALBRECHT STIEBLER → EAN → FOREST SWORDS → HEATSICK → ICEAGE → LEE GAMBLE
NECRO DEATHMORT → ONEIROGEN → SAMUEL KERRIDGE → JAR MOFF → WIFE → AND MANY MORE

WWW.CTM-FESTIVAL.DE

A project by DISK CTM | Funded by HAUPT STADT KULTUR FONDS | Culture Programme | in cooperation with UT toueremediale ⬛ KULTUR PROJEKTE BERLIN | norden | Media partner WIRE thewire.co.uk

Bard's unique summer-based MFA in Music/Sound seeks students pursuing advanced work in contemporary and electroacoustic music, performance, installation, and experimental sonic forms. In this interdisciplinary program, anchored in the theory and diverse practices of contemporary art, students work with a distinguished faculty of composers and sound artists, and are in close dialogue with faculty and students in Film/Video, Painting, Photography, Sculpture, and Writing.

Music/Sound faculty include:

David Behrman   Marina Rosenfeld
Bob Bielecki   Marcus Schmickler
Anthony Coleman   Laetitia Sonami
Bill Dietz   Richard Teitelbaum
Miya Masaoka   Terre Thaemlitz

Photography: Peter Mauney '93, MFA '00

mfa@bard.edu
845.758.7481
bard.edu/mfa

BardMFA
MILTON AVERY GRADUATE SCHOOL OF THE ARTS

KRAAK FESTIVAL 2013
2nd MARCH
NETWERK (Aalst, be)
WWW.KRAAK.NET

Electric Spring | 2013
Five days of sonic exploration

Franck VIGROUX (FR)
John WALL (UK)
Francis DHOMONT (FR)
Nicolas BERNIER (QC)
Bensios BARN (BE)
RUST: Benjamin THIGPEN (FR)
+ Jean-François LAPORTE (QC)
Eryck ABECASSIS (FR)
  MSP Poweruser Symposium
  & more!

February 20-24, 2013
University Of Huddersfield, UK

www.electricspring.co.uk

University of HUDDERSFIELD

hyponik.com
No.1 for the latest in Bass & Electronic club music

JEAN-YVES BOSSEUR / TAKUMI FUKUSHIMA / ANNE PESCE / JOHN CAGE PROJECT PAR LE CABARET CONTEMPORAIN AVEC ETIENNE JAUMET / SUBSPECIES / JULIEN BLAINE / ERIKM & NATACHA MUSLERA (EN COLLABORATION AVEC ALPHABETVILLE) / ALEX GRILLO / OHNE TITEL (LIVE) AVEC ALEXANDER SCHELLOW & JEAN-MARC MONTERA / ZA! / LA TERRE TREMBLE!!! / BERNARD BLOCH / SÉVERINE BALLON / FREDDY EICHELBERGER / TALWEG / GHOTUL / MARSEILLE-MANHATTAN / SARA HAEFELI / CHRISTIAN WOLFF / GASTON SYLVESTRE / BRIGITTE SYLVESTRE / ALEXANDRE RÉGIS / PAUL ELWOOD / LUCIE ROCHE / CHRISTOPHE MODICA...

Sans titre, 12 x 21 x 12 x 2012, techniques Mixtes

GRIM PRESENTS
NUIT D'HIVER FESTIVAL
MARSEILLE (FRANCE)
12 - 21 DECEMBER 2012
GRIM-MARSEILLE.COM

Out There

This month's selected festivals, live events and clubs

UK Festivals

Evan Parker's Might I Suggest UK
The Instant Composers Pool collective take up a residency in Dalston with Evan Parker, to celebrate the release of a box set covering their 45 years in operation. London Vortex, 29 January–2 February, £20–£15, icporchestra.com

OxJaMS UK
The Oxford Jazz Masters trio of George Haslam/Steve Kershaw/Richard Leigh Harris launch a new season of concerts, with Steve Beresford (4 January) and Alan Tomlinson (5). Oxford Burton Taylor Studio, oxfordplayhouse.com

The Rest Is Noise UK
Year long series of concerts, talks, films, performances and more inspired by Alex Ross's book of the same name, surveying 20th century classical and contemporary music through the historic and cultural contexts that shaped them. More details to be announced. London Southbank Centre, 19 January–December 2013, southbankcentre.co.uk

International Festivals

Around Hong Kong
Sound art festival followed by a two day retreat (Kadoorie Farm & Botanic Gardens, 2–3 February), with presentations by sound artists Salomé Voegelin and Carlo Fossati, installations by Viv Corringham, Tetsuya Umeda and Akio Suzuki, plus field recording projects by Mike Cooper, Alessandro Carboni and more. Hong Kong various venues, 26 January–3 February, soundpocket.org.hk

CTM: The Golden Age Germany
The 13th edition of Berlin's CTM festival, this time themed The Golden Age, will feature Matmos presenting their album *The Marriage Of True Minds*, plus Emptyset, David Tibet's Myrninerest, Diamond Version, and a Pan label evening with Florian Hecker, Keith Fullerton Whitman, Lee Gamble and more. Berlin various venues, 28 January–3 February, ctm-festival.de

Mofo Australia
Tasmanian music festival featuring David Byrne and St Vincent, Dirty Projectors, Death Grips, Robin Fox, Susan Philipsz, Pretty Lights and more. Hobart Museum Of Old And New Art, 16–20 January, mofo.net.au

Norient Switzerland
Music focused film festival, with a programme that takes in hiphop in Morocco, the Egyptian belly-dancing industry, polyphonic chanting in Albania and more. Bern various venues, 10–13 January, norient.com

Présences Electroniques Genève Switzerland
Live music and DJ sets by Chris Watson, Moritz Von Oswald Trio, :zoviet*france:, Speedy J, Emika, Dieter Moebius, Anstam, Shed, plus an Acousmonium loudspeaker installation. Geneva various venues, 11–12 January, presenceselectroniques.ch

Special Events

Artists' Film Club: Mark Leckey UK
Screening of a selection of the London based artist's moving image works and short films, followed by a Q&A. London ICA, 9 January, 7pm, £5/free to ICA members, ica.org.uk

Acts Of Voicing: On The Poetics And Politics Of The Voice Germany
Group exhibition on the agency of the voice, with performances, lectures, workshops and works by Karl Holmqvist, Anri Sala, Gary Hill, Samuel Beckett, John Baldessari and more. Stuttgart Württembergischer Kunstverein, until 13 January, wkv-stuttgart.de

Better Books: Art Anarchy And Apostasy Germany
The exhibition celebrating the 1960s Better Books counterculture bookshop, moves from London's Flat Time House to Germany. Featuring Luke Fowler's *Pilgrimage From Scattered Points* film about Cornelius Cardew, a concert by Fowler and Richard Youngs and more. Karlsruhe ZKM Center For Art And Media, 3 November–6 January, on1.zkm.de

Delia Darlings UK
Touring event launched with a mini-symposium titled Delia Derbyshire Day, featuring a panel with Mark Ayres, David Butler and more discussing Derbyshire's work. The touring section comprises a screening of *The Delian Mode* documentary by Kara Blake, new commissions by Ailís Ní Ríain, Caro C and Naomi Kashiwagi and live visual accompaniment by Blake. Manchester Band On the Wall (12 January), Liverpool FACT (16), Sheffield Sensoria Film Festival (18), Newcastle Upon Tyne Star And Shadow (20), deliaderbyshireday.wordpress.com

Nayland Blake: Free! Love! Tool! Box! USA
Tribute exhibition to the 1980s San Francisco based performance artist, featuring an installation where the audience is invited to DJ, a video booth inspired by Wilhelm Reich's orgone accumulator, a cast recording of Richard Foreman's staging of *The Threepenny Opera*, *Ruins Of A Sensibility* and more. San Francisco Yerba Buena Center For The Arts, 12 October–27 January, ybca.org

ECM Germany
Major exhibition on Manfred Eicher's German jazz and New Music label, with audio, photography, film and commissions from contemporary artists, plus live performances, children's workshops, discussion panels and more. Munich Haus Der Kunst, until 10 February 2013, hausderkunst.de

Ernest Edmonds: Light Logic UK
First UK solo exhibition for a pioneer of computer generated art. Sheffield Site Gallery, until 2 February 2013, sitegallery.org

Jean-Claude Eloy Germany
Series of seminars on the work of the prodigious electroacoustic composer. Cologne University, until 1 February, every Wednesday, 5:45pm–7:15pm, klips.uni-koeln.de

Henry Flynt Germany
Retrospective exhibition with the artist, philosopher and composer developing new works on site specifically for the show, plus film and sound based performances. Düsseldorf Kunstverein, until 20 January, kunstverein-duesseldorf.de

From Tape To Typedef: Compositional Methods In Electroacoustic Music UK
Four day symposium on electroacoustic music and composition including talks by Pete Stollery, Andrew Lewis and Leigh Landy, plus workshops and performances. University Of Sheffield, 30 January–2 February, music.dept.shef.ac.uk

Beatrice Gibson: *The Tiger's Mind* UK
Solo show of the London based artist featuring *The Tiger's Mind*, an abstract thriller which takes its structure from a score by Cornelius Cardew. Plus a series of talks, screenings and events, including a live performance by AMM (John Tilbury and Eddie Prévost). London The Showroom, until 12 January, theshowroom.org

Gesture Sign Art Germany
Group exhibition exploring the relationship between hearing and non-hearing culture through artists working with sound, music, speech, sign language and written language. Featuring works by John Cage, Die Tödliche Doris, Christine Sun Kim, Flying Words Project, Valeska Gert, Wolfgang Müller, Magnús Pálsson, Roman Signer, Ming Wong and more. Berlin Kunstraum Kreuzberg, until 13 January, kunstraumkreuzberg.de

Improve 2.0 Serbia
Monthly Improv and sound art series, this month featuring Milana Zarić on harp and zither, Woo, Igor Stangliczky, Lukatoyboy and the sound art of Svetlana Maraš. Belgrade CZKD, 15 January, aboutme/i2.0

I Was Told There'd Be Champagne Belgium
Audiovisual event with performances by Francisco López, João Onofre's *Box-sized Die* featuring Serial Butcher and a talk with artist Mira Sanders. Christina Kubisch will also be looking for electromagnetic sounds in the exhibition space and Kasper Andreassen presents his latest book, *Writing Over*. Aalst Netwerk, 18 January, 8pm, netwerk-art.be

I Wish This Was A Song: Music In Contemporary Art Norway
Group exhibition on the use of music in the visual arts, featuring works by Libia Castro & Olafur Olafsson, Graham Dolphin, Goodiepal, Bruce Nauman, Dan Graham, Rodney Graham, Sophie Clements, Susan Philipsz, Her Noise Archive, Erkki Kurenniemi and more. Oslo Museum Of Contemporary Art, until 20 January, nasjonalmuseet.no

Kraftwerk Germany
The electronic music pioneers take 1 2 3 4 5 6 7 8 to their hometown of Düsseldorf, presenting each of their albums on the separate nights. The programme is as follows: *Autobahn* (11 January), *Radio-Aktivität* (12), *Trans-Europe Express* (13), *Die Mensch-Maschine* (16), *Computerwelt* (17), *Techno Pop* (18), *The Mix* (19), *Tour De France Soundtracks* (20). Düsseldorf Kunstsammlung Nordrhein-Westfalen Museum, kraftwerk.com

Material Studies: Plastic Edition UK
SoundFjord's monthly improvisation workshop led by Matthias Kispert, Blanca Regina and Andrew Riley, this time featuring Steve Beresford as special guest. London SoundFjord, 19 January, 2:30pm–6pm, £5/£4, soundfjord.com

Micro Lunch Concerts USA
Brutal Poodle perform one to five minute concerts to random passersby in a Los Angeles shop window. Los Angeles 4613 1/2 Valley Blvd, 8, 15, 22 and 29 January, 1pm, thefrontla.com

Jonas Mekas UK
Solo exhibition of the artist and film maker with new video and photographic work plus highlights from his career spanning over 60 years. London Serpentine Gallery, until 27 January, serpentinegallery.org

No One's Land: Sonic Cartography Mexico
Sound installation of recordings from deregulated and disorienting spaces by Concha Jerez and José Iges. Mexico Museo Universitario De Arte Contemporaneo, 3 October–6 January, muac.unam.mx

Number Six: Flaming Creatures Germany
Group exhibition adopting the title of Jack Smith's controversial film, featuring works by Bruce Nauman, Tony Oursler, Mike Kelley, Peaches, Ryan Trecartin, Ed Ruscha and more. Düsseldorf Julia Stoschek Collection, until spring 2013, julia-stoschek-collection.net

Recurrence Sweden
Exhibition exploring repetition in contemporary art, with works from EVOL, Tom Richards, Damien Roach, Peder Mannerfelt of Roll The Dice, Yoshi Sodeoka and more. Curated by Emptyset's Paul Purgas. Stockholm Färgfabriken, 6–13 January, fargfabriken.se

Screen Bandita & The One Ensemble UK
Archival Super 8 films and slides on the subject of road trips, accompanied by a live psych folk soundtrack by Daniel Padden's One Ensemble. Part of the London Short Film Festival. London The Roxy Bar And Screen, 6 January, screenbandita.org

Sonic Acts: The Dark Universe Netherlands
Introductory exhibition to the Sonic Acts music festival (Amsterdam various venues, 21–24 February), with sound art and installations by HC Gilje, Ivana Franke, Matthew Biederman, Semiconductor, Justin Bennett and more. The opening night (12 January) features performances by Pete Swanson and DJs. Amsterdam NASA, 13 January–24 February, midday–10pm, free, sonicacts.com

Sound Art. Sound As Medium Of Fine Art Germany
Major exhibition running throughout 2012 that attempts to chart the development of sound art in the 20th century including works by Maryanne Amacher, John Cage, Kaffe Matthews, La Monte Young & Marian Zazeela, Eliane Radigue, Ryoji Ikeda, Christian Marclay, Akio Suzuki, Carsten Nicolai, Iannis Xenakis, CM von Hausswolff and many more. Karlsruhe ZKM Media Museum, until 6 January, on1.zkm.de

Soundtrackcity Rotterdam Netherlands
Four soundwalks starting at Rotterdam's Lantaren Venster and ending in Wilhelminapier, with soundtracks created by Francisco López, Jeroen Stout, Jan-Bas Bollen, Katarina Zdjelar, Maziar Afrassiabi and Lee Patterson. Rotterdam Lantaren Venster (starting point), 26 January–4 February, 12:30pm–8pm, €11/€8.50/€5.50, soundtrackcity.nl

Speaking Tubes UK
Sound installation of steel air ducting tubes transmitting and transforming the music of composer Yannis Kyriakides. Halifax Dean Clough, until 31 January, ioutheatre.org

STEIM & Geluid van Nederland Workshop Series: Composing Audiotours With Arnoud Traa Netherlands
Sound artist Arnoud Traa will lead participants in the composition of audio tours, with the final works being added to the online field recording library of Het Geluid van Nederland. Amsterdam STEIM, 19–26 January, 10am–6pm, €35, steim.org

Sublime Transactions UK
15 artists have been invited to create works inspired by the Armitt Museum's collection, featuring contributions from David Toop, Ian Walton, Jon Wozencroft, John Ellis, Derek Horton, Russell Mills and more. Ambleside

The Armitt Museum and Library, until 22 March, armitt.com

Schwitters UK
The first major exhibition of the UK work of German dadaist Kurt Schwitters, exploring the impact of the art he made while in exile in the Isle of Man, the Lake District and elsewhere. London Tate Britain, 30 January–12 May, £10, tate.org.uk

Tokyo Art Meeting Japan
The third in a series of exhibitions, this time supervised by Ryuichi Sakamoto, looking at the way the senses can be fused together via works and music by John Cage, Tōru Takemitsu, Otomo Yoshihide, Carsten Nicolai, Stephen Vitiello and more. Tokyo Museum Of Contemporary Art Tokyo, until 3 February, mot-art-museum.jp

Watch That Sound Belgium
Sculptures, images and installations by Pierre-Laurent Cassière, Stefaan Dheedene, Mira Sanders, João Onofre and Sarah van Sonsbeeck on the subject of silence and quiet. Aalst Netwerk, until 10 March, netwerk-art.be

On Stage

3 Duos
Electroacoustic and improvised collaborations by three duos: Sebastian Lexer & Evan Parker, John Butcher & Seymour Wright, and David Toop & Daichi Yoshikawa. London Cafe Oto, 15 January, 8pm, £8/£7, cafeoto.co.uk

Collectress with Jo Thomas: Glitch
The 2012 Prix Ars Electronica winner presents her 21 minute multispeaker performance titled *Alpha Live*. London Kings Place, 28 January, 8pm, £12.50/£9.50, kingsplace.co.uk

Dinosaur Jr
Grunge axe grinders tour their latest album *I Bet On Sky*. Glasgow Arches (30 January), Leeds University Stylus (31), Manchester Ritz (1 February), Brighton Concorde (2), Bristol Fiddlers Club (3), dinosaurjr.com

Fourth Page + Gordon Dawes
Improv from acoustic quartet and percussion duo. London St Leonard's Church, 11 January, 8pm, 4thpagemusic.blogspot.co.uk

Gravenhurst + Ralfe Band
Singer and songwriter Nick Talbot with support from Ralfe Band. London Kings Place, 11 January, 7:30pm, £19.50/£14.50/£12.50, kingsplace.co.uk

Morgan Guberman/Gail Brand/John Edwards/Mark Sanders/Maggie Nichols/Alexander Hawkins
Improvised music with vocalists Morgan Guberman and Maggie Nichols, Alexander Hawkins on piano, Gail Brand on trombone, John Edwards on double bass and Mark Sanders on drums. London Cafe Oto, 21 January, 8pm, £8/£7, cafeoto.co.uk

Alexander Hawkins Trio
The pianist and composer in a trio with Neil Charles on double bass and Tom Skinner on drums. London Cafe Oto, 16 January, 8pm, £8/£7, cafeoto.co.uk

The Horse Improv Club
Regular improvised music night with Adam Bohman, Patrizia Paolini, Eddie Prévost, Jennifer Allum, Hutch Demouilpied, Sue Lynch, Jim Dvorak, Harrison Smith, Olly Blanchflower, Dave Fowler (8 January), Roger Redgate, Emmanuel Spinelli, Grundik Kasyansky, Ute Kanngiesser, Richard Sanderson and more (29). London The Horse Bar, 8pm, £6/£5, flavors.me/horseimprovclub

Ideologic Organ #3
Third instalment of Stephen O'Malley's event series, with Hyperion Ensemble performing works by Iancu Dumitrescu and Ana-Maria Avram joined by the Romanian spectralist composers themselves, plus Tim Hodgkinson, Chris Cutler, O'Malley and Mats Lindström. London Cafe Oto, 7 January, 8pm, £10/£8, cafeoto.co.uk

Dominic Lash/Alexander Hawkins/Javier Carmona/Ricardo Tejero
Improv quartet. London Vortex, 14 January, 8:30pm, £8, dominiclash.co.uk

Lemur
Free jazz and Noise from the Norwegian quartet of Bjørnar Habbestad on flutes, Hild Sofie Tafjord on horn, Lene Grenager on cello and Michael Duch on double bass. London Kings Place, 21 January, 8pm, £12.50/£9.50, kingsplace.co.uk

Lubomyr Melnyk
The pianist and composer presents his 'continuous music', a technique he created based on rapid note playing to create a tapestry of sound. London Cafe Oto, 24 January, 8pm, £10/£8, cafeoto.co.uk

Roscoe Mitchell/John Edwards/Tani Tabbal
Two day residency with saxophonist Roscoe Mitchell, joined by John Edwards on double bass and Tani Tabbal on drums. London Cafe Oto, 29–30 January, 8pm, £27 (two day pass)/£18/£15, cafeoto.co.uk

The Music Of Making Strange: Works By Alex Hills
Lucy Railton, Aisha Orazbayeva, Serge Vuile, Severine Ballon, Roderick Chadwick and soprano Natalie Raybould perform chamber music by composer Alex Hills. London Cafe Oto, 14 January, 8pm, £7/£5, cafeoto.co.uk

Cian Nugent & The Cosmos + The Family Elan
Suburban guitar blues by Dublin based Cian Nugent & The Cosmos plus support from The Family Elan's electrified bouzouki, electric bass and vocals. London Cafe Oto, 12 January, 8pm, £7/£6, cafeoto.co.uk

On The Edge
Regular improvised music night with

Heimweh & Alberto Popolla and Noel Taylor. Brighton Good Companions Pub, 30 January, 8pm, £6/£5, safehousebrighton.co.uk

Emile Parisien Quartet
Free jazz and Improv quartet led by Parisien on sax, Sylvain Darrifourcq on drums, Julien Touery on piano and Ivan Gélugne on double bass. London Vortex, 18 January, 8:30pm, £9, emileparisienquartet.com

Jim Perkins & Friends
Acoustic instruments and electronic experiments. London Vortex, 10 January, 8:30pm, £8, vortexjazz.co.uk

Orphy Robinson/Fumi Okiji/Noel Taylor/Nick Stephens + Heimveh
Jazz improvisation with vocalist Fumi Okiji, Orphy Robinson on vibraphone, Noel Taylor on clarinet and Nick Stephens on double bass. Plus support by Rome's Heimveh (Alberto Popolla/Alessandro Salerno/Francesco Lo Cascio/Mario Paliano). London Lumen URC, 31 January, 8pm, £7, orphyrobinson.co.uk

Roland Ramanan Tentet
The trumpeter and Peter Brötzmann collaborator launches his own ten piece ensemble which includes, among others, Ian Smith (trumpet), Adrian Northover (sax), Ricardo Tejero (tenor sax), Dominic Lash (bass) and Mark Sanders (drums). London Cafe Oto, 13 January, 8pm, £8/£7, cafeoto.co.uk

Martin Speake Trio
Improvised music by the saxophonist with Mike Outram and Jeff Williams. London Kings Place, 19 January, 8pm, £12.50/£9.50, kingsplace.co.uk

Streifenjunko + Memorize the Sky
Tenor sax and trumpet duo Streifenjunko, plus drones from trio Memorize The Sky, part of the Ny Musikk and Oto Projects series. London Cafe Oto, 23 January, 8pm, £10/£8, cafeoto.co.uk

Pete Swanson
Distorted electronics and Techno stomp from the former Yellow Swans member. Cambridge The Portland Arms, 15 January, 8pm, crushingdeath.com

Tropa Macaca + Helm
Electronic Noise from the Software signed Portugese duo, plus Luke Younger (aka Helm). London Sebright Arms, 23 January, 8pm, £6, upsettherhythm.co.uk

Mika Vainio + Lee Gamble + Will Guthrie
Abrasive electronics and improvised music by the former Pan Sonic member, Lee Gamble and Will Guthrie. London Cafe Oto, 11 January, 8pm, £10/£8, cafeoto.co.uk

Valerie And Her Week Of Wonders + Bird Radio + Phil Martin
Experimental folk and ethereal lullabies by Valerie And Her Week Of Wonders, with Television Personalities' Jowe Head, flautist Bird Radio and punk-folk by Phil Martin. London The Stag's Head, 5 January, thestagshead.tumblr.com

Guillaume Viltard/Eddie Prévost/Seymour Wright/Nat Catchpole
Improv set by Viltard on double bass, Prévost on percussion, Wright and Catchpole on saxes. London Cafe Oto, 22 January, 8pm, £7/£6, cafeoto.co.uk

Alan Wilkinson/Steve Noble/John Edwards
Improvised music by the trio. London Cafe Oto, 9 January, 8pm, £7/£6, cafeoto.co.uk

Alan Wilkinson's Freefall
Free improvisations by Wilkinson (sax), Pat Thomas (piano & electronics), Neil Charles (double bass) and Mark Sanders (drums). London Vortex, 22 January, 8:30pm, £8, vortezjazz.co.uk

Richard Youngs & Damon Krukowski + Damon & Naomi + Seaming
Guitar-based sets by Youngs and Damon & Naomi. London Cafe Oto, 26 January, 8pm, £10/£8.50, cafeoto.co.uk

John Zorn: A Portrait
Concert with the BBC Scottish Symphony Orchestra celebrating the 60th birthday of John Zorn, featuring the premiere of a newly commissioned work titled *Suppôts Et Suppliciations*, plus older works like wordless opera *La Machine De L'Être*, *Kol Nidre* and more. Glasgow City Halls, 12 January, 7:30pm, free, bbc.co.uk

Club Spaces

Boat-Ting
Improv and poetry club on a boat in the Thames with Steve Noble/John Edwards/Alex Ward, Matt Chilton/Sharon Gal/Anthony Donovan, Barrel (Alison Blunt/Hannah Marshall/Ivor Kallin), Dave Russell (7 January), Charles Hayward, Adrian Northover & Tasos Stamou, Ian Smith/Pete McPhail/Orphy Robinson/Pete Flood, Ronnie McGrath (21). London Bar & Co, first and third Mondays, 8pm, £6/£4, boat-ting.co.uk

Flimflam
Alan Wilkinson's regular Improv night with Julie Kjaer/John Edwards/Steve Noble (23 January), Pat Thomas & Ansuman Biswas and more (30). London Ryan's, 8:30pm, £6/£4, flimflam.org.uk

Hessle Audio
Release party for Ben UFO's *FabricLive* mix with label cohorts Pearson Sound, Pangaea, Optimo, MMM (live), Call Super, plus Peverelist, Illum Sphere and more in the other rooms. London Fabric, 11 January, fabriclondon.com

Mopomoso
Monthly Improv meet with Stefan Keune/Dominic Lash/Steve Noble, Hannah Marshall & Paul G Smyth, John Russell and others. London Vortex, 20 January, 8pm, £8/£6, mopomoso.com

Incoming

Adelaide Festival Australia
Performance arts festival taking in aspects of theatre, dance, music and visual art, and featuring performances from Laurie Anderson, Deerhoof, Clogs, Bryce Dessner & Kronos Quartet, Van Dyke Parks, Severed Heads, Atom TM, Daniel Lopatin & Tim Hecker, Robin Fox, V/Vm, Biosphere, Actress, MFO, Lustmord, Demdike Stare, Pole, plus Ben Frost & Daníel Bjarnason playing their reimagined soundtrack for *Solaris*, and more. Adelaide various venues, 1–17 March, adelaidefestival.com.au

Dancing Around Duchamp UK
Series of multidisciplinary events centred around Marcel Duchamp. Featuring performances by Laurie Anderson & Kronos Quartet, Bobby McFerrin, works by John Cage, Merce Cunningham, Robert Wilson and more. London Barbican, February–June 2013, barbican.org.uk

dOeK Festival Netherlands
Free improvisation festival with Marcus Schmickler/Jérôme Noetinger/Cor Fuhler, Monitor (Michael Moore/Tristan Honsinger/Cor Fuhler), Theo Loevendie & Arjan Gorter, Jon Dikeman/Klaus Kugel/Raoul Van Der Weide, Achim Kaufmann/Frank Gratkowski/Wilbert De Joode, Oscar Jan Hoogland & Han Bennink, Okkyung Lee, Richard Barrett, Tony Buck and more. Amsterdam various venues, 1–5 May, doek.org

Electric Spring UK
Noise, acousmatic and experimental music with live performances by Franck Vigroux, John Wall, Rust , Nicolas Bernier, plus public talks, a sound installation by Scott McLaughlin and more. University Of Huddersfield, 20–24 February, free, electricspring.co.uk

Field Day UK
East London one dayer with Animal Collective, Do Make Say Think, Emeralds, Four Tet, Ben UFO, Pangaea, Pearson Sound, How To Dress Well, Karenn, Mulatu Astatke, Bat For Lashes, Daphni, Julio Bashmore and more. London Victoria Park, 25 May, £45, fielddayfestivals.com

Focus Festival UK
Welsh music festival and conference, with guitarist Michael Rother presenting music from his former groups Neu! and Harmonia, plus his solo projects. More artists to be announced soon. Wrexham various venues, 25–27 April, focuswales.com

In Britten's Footsteps UK
New work by Chris Watson, commissioned by Faster Than Sound, retracing Britten's daily composing walks around Aldeburgh with sounds recorded on location and played on an ambisonic sound system. Snape Britten Studio, 1 February, 8pm, £10, aldeburgh.co.uk

Kraak Festival Belgium
Musique concrète, folk, psychedelia, noise, sound poetry and free jazz one dayer. More details to be announced. Aalst Netwerk, 2 March, €25/€20, kraak.net

The Master Musicians Of Joujouka Morocco
Sixth edition of the 50 capacity trip which takes the audience to the Sufi trance masters in a small Moroccan village. Joujouka various venues, 7–9 June, joujouka.org

Mutek.Es Barcelona
Spanish edition of the Canadian electronic music festival featuring workshops, Q&As and music by Jeff Mills, Monolake, Raime, Vessel, The Mole, DeWalta, Jon Hopkins and more. Barcelona various venues, 4–6 February, mutek.es

Sónar Reykjavík Iceland
Barcelona's electronic music festival travels to Iceland for two nights featuring James Blake, Squarepusher, Modeselektor, Alva Noto & Ryuichi Sakamoto, Ólafur Arnalds, GusGus and more. Reykjavík Harpa, 15–16 February, sonarreykjavik.com

SoundOut Australia
International festival of free improvisation, jazz and experimental music with the Abaetetuba collective, Barcode Quartet, Jon Rose, Tony Buck, Magda Mayas, James Waples and more. Canberra's Theatre 3, 2–3 February, soundout2013.blogspot.co.uk

Send listings to: *The Wire*, 23 Jack's Place, 6 Corbet Place, London E1 6NN, UK, fax +44 (0)20 7422 5011, email: listings@thewire.co.uk

---

Adventures In Sound And Music Resonance FM

The Wire's weekly show on the UK's community arts radio station is broadcast across Central London on 104.4 FM every Thursday between 9–10:30pm, with simultaneous streaming at resonancefm.com. All editions of the show are archived at thewire.co.uk

WIRE
Resonance104.4fm

Rewired NTS

The Wire's show on the UK net station is streamed online at ntslive.co.uk biweekly. This month's shows are broadcast on 3, 17 and 31 January between 6–8pm. All editions of the show are archived at ntslive.co.uk

NTS

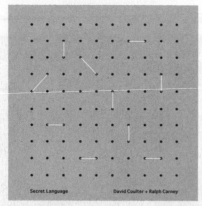

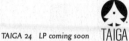

Subscriptions

Subscribe online at thewire.co.uk/subscribe, tel +44 (0)20 7422 5022 , mail subs@thewire.co.uk

Full subscription

| 12 issues of the print magazine | + | 1 year's access to every digital issue* |

*Since issue 270 August 2006

3 volumes of *The Wire Tapper*
on CD and as downloads

1 year's access to *Below The Radar* downloads
(see opposite)

Save money
Wherever you live, a subscription issue will cost you less than if you bought the print magazine from a news stand, record store or book shop.

Discounts
on back issues, books, T-shirts and other *Wire* merchandise

Prompt delivery
Direct to your door: UK 3-5 days, Europe/ USA/Rest of World by airmail 1-3 weeks

| £40 UK | £56 EU/US/Can | £66 Rest of World |

£56 = approx US$90/€69

Digital-only subscription

| 1 year's access to every digital issue* |

*Since issue 270 August 2006

Features include:
- Access to each new issue instantly on the day it is published
- High quality printable pdfs
- Fully searchable text
- Interactive contents and Index pages
- Hyperlinks from editorial and adverts
- Access via web, Android or iPhone/iPad

1 year's access to *Below The Radar* downloads
(see opposite)

3 volumes of *The Wire Tapper*
as downloads only

NB Digital-only subscribers don't get physical copies of *The Wire Tapper* or other free CDs, nor any additional offers and benefits that are available to full subscribers.

| £30 |

£30 = approx US$48/ €37

More extras for subscribers

All new subscribers get access to all volumes of *Below the Radar* – see opposite. The latest volume in the series features Roly Porter & Cynthia Millar, Anders Lauge Meldgaard, Magda Mayas & Tony Buck, TVO, Holly Herndon, Seaven Teares, Robin The Fog, Lotte Anker & Fred Lonberg-Holm, Thomas Bel, Sami Pekkola, Garry Bradbury & Dave Noyze, Meitheal, Pat Maher

Below The Radar

Below The Radar is a series of downloads compiled by *The Wire* and made available free and exclusively to all subscribers four times a year. The compilations are designed as showcases for just some of the underground, outsider and experimental sounds that have been featured in recent issues of the magazine.

New subscribers automatically get access to all volumes of *Below The Radar* and *Below The Radar Special Editions*

Go to thewire.co.uk/subscribe for details

BTR Vol 1 Issue 307 September 2009
A Broken Consort, Afternoon Brother, Jamie Coleman/ Grundik Kasyansky/Seymour Wright, Concern, Rhodri Davies/Michel Doneda/Louisa Martin/Phil Minton/Lee Patterson, Gareth Davis & Steven R Smith, James Ferraro, Dredd Foole & Ed Yazijian, Harappian Night Recordings, The Hunter Gracchus, LSD March, Jonathan McHugh & Mark Wastell, Brian Morant, Part Wild Horses Mane On Both Sides, Starving Weirdos, Sudden Infant, Ghédalia Tazartès, Uton

BTR Vol 2 Issue 311 January 2010
Blood Stereo, Carlos Giffoni, The Haxan Cloak, Mazen Kerbaj & Sharif Sehnaoui, Leyland Kirby, Leisure High (Blevin Blechdom & Eugene Robinson), Mattin, MV & EE with Willie Lane, Marina Rosenfeld, Skull Defekts & The Sons Of God, Ishmael Wadada Leo Smith, Gary War, Zavoloka vs Kotra

BTR Vol 3 Issue 315 May 2010
Jacques Beloeil, Borbetomagus, Burning Star Core, Alan Courtis, The Cray Twins, Demdike Stare,

Denseland, Filter Feeder, Graveyards, High Wolf, Hong Chulki, LA Vampires, Anthony Levin-Decanini, Oneohtrix Point Never, Sone Institute, Weasel Walter/Sheik Anorak/Mario Rechtern

BTR Vol 4 Issue 319 September 2010
Marc-Henri Arfeux, Tony Bevan/Dominic Lash/Phil Marks/Paul Obermayer, Rhodri Davies/Joe Williamson/ Stefano Tedesco, Failing Lights & Howard Stelzer, Giuseppe Ielasi, Grasslung, Group Inerane, K11 & Philippe Petit, Munma, Peeesseye, Renato Rinaldi, Pete Swanson, Nicholas Szczepanik, Twins

BTR Special Edition: Melting Pot – Free Improvised Music From Istanbul Issue 321 November 2010
Nilüfer Akbayoğlu, Şevket Akıncı, Korhan Argüden, Demirhan Baylan, David Brosset, Oguz Büyükberber, Umut Çağlar, Kevin Davis, Burçin Elmas, Turgut Erçetin, Korhan Erel, Giray Gürkal, Florent Merlet, Robert Reigle, Amy Salsgiver, Volkan Terzioğlu, Özün Usta

BTR Vol 5 Issue 322 January 2011
Borful Tang, The Dead C, eRikm & Norbert Möslang, Dylan Ettinger, Expressway Yo-Yo Dieting, Hammeriver, Hisato Higuchi, Suzanne Langille, LOUP, Stephan Mathieu, SAWS, Trawler Bycatch, Jennifer Walshe

BTR Vol 6 Issue 328 June 2011
AGF, Borngräber & Strüver, Mark Bradley, Chandeliers, Dalglish, Eleven Twenty-Nine , Mark Fell, Ga'an, Moon Wiring Club, Douglas Quin, Sleeps In Oysters, Jo Thomas, Trembling Bells, John Wall & Alex Rodgers, Wet Hair

BTR Special Edition: Telephone Music Issue 331 September 2011
Aphasiacs, Grains, KWJAZ, Todd Lerew, Macaw, Jon

Porras, George Pritzker, Rangers, Jeff Striker, Swanox

BTR Vol 7 Issue 332 October 2011
Ed Atkins, Meg Baird, Justin Bennett, Michael Chapman, Ectoplasm Girls, Heatsick, Helm, Hieroglyphic Being, Richard Pinhas & Merzbow, Sculpture, Torlesse Super Group

BTR Special Edition: ...A Quiet Position: Edition Two Issue 335 January 2012
Jez riley French, Anne Guthrie, Julia Holter, Sarah Hughes, Jason Kahn, David Lacey & Patrick Farmer, Signe Liden, Kiyoshi Mizutani, Embla Quickbeam, Dawn Scarfe, Stefan Thut, Peter Toll, Els Viaene, Anne Wellmer, Alexander Wendt, Manfred Werder

BTR Vol 8 Issue 337 March 2012
The Automatics Group, BD1982 and A Taut Line, Carlos Casas, Decimus, Emptyset, Peter Evans, The Julie Mittens, Mazen Kerbaj/Charbel Haber/Sharif Sehnaoui, Eli Kezsler, Ian Nagoski, Ashley Paul, Maja S. K. Ratkje/ Paal Nilssen-Love/Lasse Marhaug, Jason Urick

BTR Vol 9 Issue 340 June 2012
Damir Avdić, Bass Clef, Ilia Belorukov, Cream Juice, Patrick Farmer, Head-Boggle, House Of Low Culture, Kuupuu, Lucy, Israel Martínez, Polysick, Shiggajon

BTR Vol 10 Issue 343 September 2012
Joshua Bonnetta, Austin Cesear, Hem, Anna Homler & Sylvia Hallett, Kaba Blon, King Felix, Mdou Moctar, Dieter Moebius, Duane Pitre, Frank Rosaly, Sauce & Cop, The Celebrate Music Synthesizer Group, The Sonic Catering Band, Simon Whetham

The Wire Tapper

The Wire Tapper is a special series of CDs that archive a broad spectrum of underground music. The CDs are given away to all readers three times a year with copies of the magazine. Copies of previous volumes are available when ordering the relevant back issue. Go to thewire.co.uk/shop for details

The Wire Tapper 1 Issue 170 April 1998
17 tracks incl: Vega/Vanio/Vaisanen, Mixmaster Mike, Roedelius, Kreidler, Arto Lindsay, Porter Ricks

The Wire Tapper 2 Issue 177 November 1998
15 tracks incl: Rhys Chatham, DAF, Tom Ze, Jad Fair & Yo La Tengo, The Pastels, Labradford

The Wire Tapper 3 Issue 182 April 1999
16 tracks incl: Rothko, We, Gas, To Rococo Rot, Paul Panhuysen, Robert Ashley, Sheila Chandra

The Wire Tapper 5 Issue 193 March 2000
17 tracks incl: Wire, John Wall, Fennesz/O'Rourke/ Rehberg, Arne Nordheim, Vert, Fushitsusha

The Wire Tapper 7 Issue 207 May 2001
15 tracks incl: Four Tet, Daniel Figgis, Bigg Jus, Mice Parade, Illusion Of Safety, Eardrum, Lasse Marhaug

The Wire Tapper 8 Issue 215 January 2002
17 tracks incl: 23 Skidoo, Jah Wobble, Fog, Chas Smith, Murcof, Electrelane, No-Neck Blues Band, Noxagt

The Wire Tapper 10 Issue 236 October 2003
30 tracks (2 CDs) incl: Animal Collective, Loren Connors & David Grubbs, Faust & Dälek, David Sylvian, Laibach

The Wire Tapper 11 Issue 244 June 2004
16 tracks incl: To Rococo Rot, Albert Ayler, Matthew Dear, Arthur Russell, poire_z & Phil Minton

The Wire Tapper 13 Issue 256 June 2005
20 tracks incl: Alexander Hacke, Matt Elliott, Juana Molina, Kid606, Ariel Pink, John Surman, Fovea Hex

The Wire Tapper 14 Issue 262 December 2005
16 tracks incl: Oren Marshall, Kieran Hebden & Steve Reid, Cobra Killer, This Heat

The Wire Tapper 15 Issue 268 June 2006
20 tracks incl: Leafcutter John, Machinefabriek, Giuseppe Ielasi, Gerritt & John Wiese

The Wire Tapper 16 Issue 274 December 2006
21 tracks incl: Alan Vega, Carter Tutti, Pansonic, Derek Bailey, Califone, White Magic, The Slits

The Wire Tapper 17 Issue 279 May 2007
20 tracks incl: A Hawk And A Hacksaw, Kammerflimmer Kollektief, Von Südenfed, Throbbing Gristle, Fridge

The Wire Tapper 18 Issue 284 October 2007
19 tracks incl: Cath & Phil Tyler, The Ex & Getatchew Mekuria, Damon & Naomi, Goodiepal, Mordant Music

The Wire Tapper 19 Issue 290 April 2008
20 tracks incl: GF Fitz-Gerald & Lol Coxhill, Daniel Figgis via Somadrone, Illusion Of Safety, Phog Masheen

The Wire Tapper 20 Issue 296 October 2008
19 tracks incl: Mike Osborne, Grails, Pantaleimon, MoHa!, Paavoharju, Zavoloka

The Wire Tapper 21 Issue 302 April 2009
21 tracks incl: Sweet Billy Pilgrim, Jim McAuley (with Nels Cline), Barbara Morgenstern, Felix Kubin

The Wire Tapper 22 Issue 308 October 2009
20 tracks incl: STEARICA feat Dälek, Elodie Lauten, Clang Sayne, Franck Vigroux, Pink Mountain, Plaetner

The Wire Tapper 23 Issue 314 April 2010
20 tracks incl: Nico Teen, Soom T, The A Band, Raymond Dijkstra, Han Bennink Trio, Rolf Julius

The Wire Tapper 24 Issue 320 October 2010
20 tracks incl: Ninni Morgia & William Parker, Dawn Of Midi, Nicholas Szczepanik & Jenks Miller

The Wire Tapper 25 Issue 326 April 2011
20 tracks incl: My Cat Is An Alien, Philippe Petit, Tchicai/Hurley/Sanders/Coxon, Obsil, Melmac, Hana

The Wire Tapper 26 Issue 330 August 2011
20 tracks incl: Anne James Chaton & Andy Moor, Joe Morris Wildlife, Kikuchi Yukinori, Enablers

The Wire Tapper 27 Issue 333 November 2011
20 tracks incl: Ekoplekz, Dalglish, Phog Masheen, Gary Smith/Silvia Kastel/Ninni Morgia

The Wire Tapper 28 Issue 337 April 2012
20 tracks incl: Bader Motor, JLIAT, Big Nils, Mark harris, Teho Teardo, Tonesucker, Ifmilk, To Blacken The Pages

The Wire Tapper 29 Issue 341 July 2012
20 tracks incl: Momus & John Henriksson, LOUP, Golden Disko Ship, Lushlife, The Fractal Skulls, L A N D

The Wire Tapper 30 Issue 344 October 2012
20 tracks incl: Rhodri Davies, Lind Bohm, Manuella Blackburn, Lasse-Marc Riek, Captain Miki, Merzouga

Epiphanies

Sonic youth: Charles Hayward aged 12 (left) with his brother Tony

Drummer **Charles Hayward** recalls how a series of childhood experiences introduced him to the sounds of the interzone

E·piph·a·ny (-pf-n): *a sudden manifestation of the essence or meaning of something. A comprehension or perception of reality by means of a sudden intuitive realisation.*

A lot seems to happen in childhood: time moves slower, space is wider, further. Slowed down, brief snatches of time engrave into memory, moments transform into deep neuronal totems, sustained on a scaffold of image, sound, story, smell. Engrams. A lot of mine centred around sound, and the immediate sensations are still with me and inform my everyday life. Accumulatively, they fold out into a network of experiences that make choice irrelevant, obsolete, a deception designed to distract me from a life that seemed to me to have no choice – a luxurious situation.

Year 1 at school we had music lessons; everyone got given an instrument. The first week I was handed a beautiful little wooden snare drum, with a strap worn round the neck and a pair of short sticks. The teacher praised my playing. The following week I got a triangle.

"But last week you said I played the drum well."

"Yes, but everyone has to have a chance to play the different instruments."

But the other kid didn't mean it like I did, wasn't concentrating hard enough, didn't hear when it was working and when it wasn't, so forget fairness. Sound like sullen granite. Flecks of scratched blotches, stretched skin.

August 1958, a family summer holiday in Blankenberge, Belgium, extremely early morning, no real breakfast, on a coach to Brussels Expo 58. Lightly spaced feeling all day, out of sync, slightly hungry. I'd already been learning piano for a couple of years, loved the diversity of musical instruments and their sounds, loved the way they related to different aspects of physics, the smell, the process of it all.

In one of the pavilions displaying an array of Africana, spears, jewellery, animal hides, photographs of intrepid European colonialists in amicable discourse with African chiefs, I heard a gentle ripple of sound – not the dark drums I had expected, but silver, water, thinking back probably a kora or an mbira, and which reminded me of the beautiful Bach studies I had been playing for a while. Meanwhile, with the Atomium brooding above and through the trees like a hybrid of sci-fi and René Magritte, it was just a question of stepping out onto the terraced space between to time-travel across to the Philips Pavilion, where electronic sound moved through space, across the strangely arced ceiling, kinetic. I was suddenly confronted by an additional parameter, movement, with sound fleet and transient, glimpsed in the corner of the ear, flickering like starlight. And science and engineering were vital ingredients. For a seven year old sound/music-obsessed child, this was a fantastic experience, a beautiful collision, and the sense of moving *between* remains at the centre of this experience for me: music of the interzone, between fixed points, hovering at a slight remove from social time, in several places at the same time, breathing.

For one reason or another, family holidays invariably included a few weeks in Blankenberge, a seaside town with a name so ambiguous it seemed to contain the possibilities found in a Ballard novel or the cult TV series *The Prisoner*: beaches out of Tanguy, big-sky seascapes and a postwar American influence that vaguely implied *Pet Sounds*. The coast was paralleled with dunes, tramlines, electricity lines, telegraph wires, roads, fences. One tram journey, sun hot and bright through the pane, I half-slept as we waited for the delayed oncoming service, held by the sound of the high-voltage cable overhead: a celestial choir, imperturbable, a sound with so much, but so still you could practically walk around inside it. Is that minute flux in the sound really happening? Is that the interaction? Is that me making it happen? Straight lines.

I was obsessed with the phenomenon of hearing a sound change just by repeating it, hours spent with my ear pressed against wind-up alarm clocks, listening to the rhythm reassemble itself as I wandered around inside the sound, sometimes thinking it was the clock rejigging, sometimes thinking I was just focusing in different ways, sometimes controlling, sometimes being controlled. Slight shift of light through net curtain.

Playing piano in some sort of spontaneous duet with a thunderstorm. Getting an electric shock, loose wiring and a little white dot on the fingertip where I had touched the mains, fading like the TV switching off; six months later, another faulty appliance or a cracked Bakelite plug, the same again. I like it, not afraid, even though, or perhaps because, the body jolt is out of my control. Do it again! Electric itch. Do it again! Feedback violence.

Dentist gas, opiated cough medicine dreams. Loose timber in the back of an open van in the middle of the night, the Dover Road through Camberwell, London.

One half-term I saw *The Ipcress File* at the Camberwell Odeon. I heavily identified with Harry Palmer, Michael Caine's character in the adaptation of the Len Deighton novel; in class-conscious 1960s Britain, my weirdly privileged, grant-assisted education at an old-style public school had a strangely dislocating outsider effect on me, which even now explains a lot. Palmer was a secret agent at odds with his environment – all the other blokes seemed to be wearing bowler hats. The John Barry score was impeccable, with its gorgeous hammered dulcimer theme, but it was the tape that intrigued me: the Ipcress Noise that was the secret at the heart of the story, that resisted decoding. The idea that magnetic tape made to store sound could also contain number or text was amazing enough; but the real shock was the narrative twist that it resisted code-crack because there was no code. Sound organised simply as itself, with direct connection to the central nervous system, used as a weapon for mind control. Now that's what I call music... ☐

Charles Hayward's *Trademark Ground* is out now on Otoacoustic